Isn't it just so wonderful when y[...] your heart and makes you fall in [...] is called, Not by my Wings Alone an inspiring Memoir by Carolyn P. Henry. In this compassionate and inspirational story, Carolyn despite her odds, being in foster care, a group home, and dealing with her own personal tragedies along the way, manages to finish high school with honors and gets accepted to Howard University. This book is a true testimony that anything in life is possible as long as you have positive influences in your inner circle and always persevere no matter what life throws at you! In my endeavors as a former therapeutic foster parent and now a licensed school social worker this is truly a triumph of her spirit! A terrific book.

Katrina Lawson-Bates, MSW, CSSW, LMSW
Social Worker-Durham,NC

With true candor, Carolyn P. Henry has produced a memoir, *Not By My Wings Alone*, that offers an honest look into the life of a young black female who, despite the hand she has been dealt in life, rises to the occasion achieving more than many (even herself) could have imagined. Her story speaks to a life of disadvantages, hopes, neglect, dreams, setbacks, goals, and accomplishments in the face of numerous challenges. Many will connect with skinny little "Pippa" growing up in New York during the early 1960's, as she transforms into a consummate young woman equipped with tools given to her by positive key players in her life. Henry's first book is a coming-of-age story that reveals her as an awesome storyteller. *Not By My Wings Alone* is sure to encourage and inspire all!

Review by Dr. Jacquelyn Jones, PhD Educational Leadership (Capella Univ.)
30 years in education with Dekalb County School district,GA
2016-2017 Teacher of the Year
8 years as elementary classroom teacher
22 years as media specialist
Also a product of Dekalb County School District

Thanks for purchasing my book. Please go to the website www.subscribepage.com/carolynphenry to get your FREE Discussion Questions, Bonus Questions and Digital Bookmark

Not by my Wings Alone

A MEMOIR

FROM HARLEM TO HOWARD
UNIVERSITY, A JOURNEY OF *COURAGE,
RESILIENCE* AND *HOPE*

CAROLYN P. HENRY

In loving memory of the Paige sisters
Ruth, Lillian, Stella and Liz

"A lot of people have gone further than they thought they
could because someone else thought they could"
Zig Ziglar

"You have not because you ask not"
James 4:2

Contents

PART THREE: HOPE

Acknowledgments

To my husband Andre - thank you for your unwavering love, quiet strength and consistent support.

To my sons Anthony and Andre Jr. – thank you for encouraging me to write my story and stay true to my authentic self.

To Dr. Jacquelyn Jones, Lisa Fields, Faye Jones, Stephanie Hunt and Donya Jones – thank you for your wisdom, support and motivation during this journey.

To my many friends, extended family, teachers and students who inspired me along the way - thank you all from the bottom of my heart, for being there every time I needed you.

To my Leake and Watts family especially Mr. and Mrs. Walter Brown, Mrs. LaFredia Davis, Mrs. Dorothy Wesson and Mr. Wiley Hammond – thank you for guiding me, believing in me, nurturing me and pushing me out of my comfort zone and into my amazing, continuing life's journey.

To my editor Mr. Joel Pierson – thank you for your expertise and answering all my questions.

And most of all I give thanks to God for blessing me with the courage and strength to share my story with you, my readers.

PART ONE

Home

1

I was by myself but not alone. My earliest memories were warm and comforting. I must have been around two and a half or three. Lying in the top of a wooden bunk bed set, I could see the ceiling and figured if I stood up, I could touch it. A bare, clear light bulb burned brightly in the middle of the ceiling. I wanted to reach out and touch that too, but somehow knew it was beyond the grasp of my chubby arms.

I had on a T-shirt that was dirty, probably stained with old milk from my bottle or maybe dried vomit from earlier in the day. On my bottom was a cloth diaper, fastened with metal safety pins, and over that some hard, stiff plastic panties, I guess to keep me from getting everything around me wet and stinky. I had a Coke bottle in my hands that had a rubber nipple on it. I remember sucking chocolate milk from my glass bottle, slurping and tugging on it, tilting it upward in my mouth until I got the last delicious drop out. That was heaven to me. But when I finished, they never brought me more, and I certainly wanted more.

Lying on my back, sucking on my Coke bottle and chewing on the rubber nipple, I was content. Vaguely aware that I was alone in that room, but not totally alone. I could hear voices nearby, but I couldn't see anyone. I could make out music playing and loud, raucous laughter from several people. I didn't know who they were, what they were doing, and frankly didn't care, but I knew I was not alone. I was not scared, up there in my little area.

I tossed and turned, playing among the tussled bedsheets. Kicking up my legs, rolling around, and making incoherent noises as toddlers are supposed to do. I rolled around, banged on the wall, and tugged on the wooden railing that kept me from tumbling out onto the floor below. I don't remember anybody coming in to check on me, but I guess that was all right. Finally, tired and worn out, I drifted off to sleep, nestled in my rumpled sheets.

My ma's name was Ruth Paige. How did I know? I heard people constantly calling her that— "Hey, Ruth" or "Hi, Ms. Paige." There always seemed to be an endless flow of folks coming in and out, talking and laughing in loud, rowdy voices and wanting something. I guess you could say that she was popular and had a lot of friends. Ma had caramel-colored skin, dark-brown eyes, thin lips, and a wide nose. She was medium height and skinny. Her short-pressed hair was kept in curls, going back off her forehead. She usually wore short-sleeved print blouses, with collars that buttoned down the front, and always had on dark-colored pants. Ma normally had a lit cigarette in one hand, with ashes falling wherever they landed. When she didn't have me or one of my four older brothers in her other hand, she had a can or bottle of some drink. Much later, I would find out that it was Ballentine beer, a liquid that I couldn't stand the smell of and hated the taste even more.

As I said, my ma had a lot of friends. They came and went at random times. We lived in a tiny row house apartment in the middle of Harlem, and our home was a hubbub of activity. Ma let folks come to wash their clothes in the large kitchen sink or take a bath in our overused bathroom. There was a constant flow of people coming in to get spaghetti or fried chicken plates. Others came in to ask what the number was for the day or to take money from her so she could play herself. I didn't have a clue what that was or how the game was played. But I knew it was important to Ma. So important that I remember there were days when we didn't have food or milk in the house, but Ma played her numbers.

Another thing that Ma loved was giving what I thought were house parties, but I later learned they were card games that she hosted. I think they were called "poker, bid whist, and spade parties." You could say that she was in charge, sold and served food and drinks, and got a cut of the house. I didn't quite know what that meant, but I frequently heard her loudly arguing about her "damn cut of the house." Whatever that was, she was gonna make sure she got it, or there would be hell to pay.

A variety of men and women would come to our apartment and crowd around folding tables that Ma had set up in the living room and kitchen. Swirls of cigarette smoke mingled in the air and blended with the aroma of frying chicken and fish. Beer cans and paper plates were littered everywhere. Music of the times was blaring from an invisible radio. Was it Sam Cook, Chubby Checker, or Frankie Lymon singing their 1950s songs? I don't know, but the crowd was into the card game and the soulful music. It was a lively atmosphere. Ma was racing from folks at the card tables to the stove, piling plates with food, to the icebox getting beer. Everybody seem to be in good spirits, happy or drunk.

I remember these scenes happened frequently in our house. Periodically I would hear someone say, "Ruth, that child looks just like you," or "Girl, Pippa is getting so big." Pippa was the nickname my family gave me, so everyone called me that.

Life was fine with me and my older brothers. We would race through the kitchen when we wanted something, then run out and continue playing and living our lives.

Four years passed, and Ma added a couple more babies to her hips. By this time, there were seven of us. I had the four older brothers and two younger. I was the only girl, a mini-Ruth. Soft, brown skin, dark-brown eyes, nappy hair, a gap in my front teeth, and a wide nose.

My young world centered around keeping up with the boys. Whatever they did, I wanted to be a part of. I was vocal and just as loud as they were. I was nimble and fast and could fall, skin my knees, jump up, and continue the race. As far as I was concerned, I was one of them. We did everything together; they were my world.

I slept with the four youngest brothers in the bunk beds. James, who we called Googie, was a year younger than me. Gardiner, who was frequently referred to as Sloppy Joe, was the baby and was four years younger. Kevin was one year older than me. Ronald was four years older; Anthony was five years older; I believe but was never quite sure. Michael was the oldest and had seven years on me. He was born when my ma was twenty years old. Ma must have been extremely fertile because the babies just kept rolling out.

They were my six protectors. Many times, throughout my young life I heard people referring to me as "Paige's sister" or "You better leave her alone; her brothers are the Paige boys." "Isn't that Pippa, Ruth's girl? You know she got six brothers."

At some point in my young life, I began to notice that there were some differences between me and my brothers, except Michael. My five brothers were light skinned and had jet-black, soft curly hair. I remember thinking to myself that they could pass for something else, maybe Indian, or white people with suntans. I used to wonder why when their hair got wet from the bathtub, all they had to do was dry it with a towel. It would look just fine. But when my hair got wet from the bathtub, rain, playing outside in water from the fire hydrant, or a visit to the beach, I had hell to pay. Ma would yell out, "Come in here, Pippa, and let me take care of those peas and carrots."

Ma had to pull and tug on my hair with a hard plastic comb. It felt like she was pulling my brains out of my head, as she tried to untangle the "naps" to part and braid my hair. I would hunch my shoulders, make all kinds of faces, and whine. But none of that stopped the onslaught from her comb. This whole scene was a ridiculous ordeal, and I had no idea why I had to endure it and my brothers didn't.

When money was plentiful in our house from card games, playing the numbers, or the men in Ma's life, I suffered through another hair-processing ordeal. Ma would call over Jitter, a longtime family friend to "do" my hair. Jitter was an attractive, thick, light-skinned woman who was known in the neighborhood for pressing and curling hair. When you looked at Jitter's hair, it spoke volumes. Her hair was midnight black, with a tiny part on top and the rest going straight back off her forehead. She wore it in what Ma referred to as a French twist or ponytail in the back. I never, ever saw a strand of Jitter's hair out of place. Regardless of the weather outside, her head of hair was her crowning glory.

Apparently, Jitter's skills were in high demand, because I vaguely remember them going back and forth on a specific time to "do Pippa's hair." Before the appointed day and time, Ma washed my hair in the kitchen sink. What an ordeal! I had to stand on my tippy toes, while grasping the sides of our white porcelain sink for balance. Ma gave me a wash rag to cover my eyes as she commenced to push my head down in the sink and pour water over my hair. Using some strange brand of brown soap, she'd begin scrubbing like she was doing laundry in a tub. This was not a gentle head massage. This was "let me get the sand, dirt, dandruff, and old grease out of this child's hair." The soap got into my eyes and stung like someone had poured hot sauce in them. I squirmed, complained, and hollered loudly, but to no avail.

"Ma! My eyes are burning. Can't we stop now?" I think that made her scrub harder.

"Hush, Pippa, you know Jitter is coming to do your hair."

Lather, scrub, rinse, whine, cry, and repeat. As I'm suffering through this torment, I can hear my brothers running past, playing, and not having a care in the world. Life was not fair. Why didn't they have to get their hair washed like mine?

At the appointed time, Jitter would appear at our apartment door. She and Ma would make small chit-chat about things that didn't concern me—what the day's number was and how much money they had put down on it, what each had recently cooked, or how the rest of the family was doing. Ma would pull up a chair for me next to the stove, as Jitter set out her equipment on the counter. She'd get a stool that was in the corner of our kitchen for Jitter to perch her behind on. Then Ma would scream out my name, "Pippa!"

If I was in the next room playing with my pink plastic dolls, in the hallway, or outside, it didn't matter. Ma interrupted my life like clockwork so that another round of torture could begin on my head, but this time from a different tormentor.

"Sit down, Pip. It's time for me to work on these peas and carrots," Jitter would announce matter-of-fact-like.

Ma busied herself nearby or just sat at the table and watched, with a lit cigarette in one hand and a can of beer to sip on.

Reluctantly I'd appear, angry that my play was interrupted but also very anxious about the impending next hour. Being just five years old, I remember never concerning myself or even being aware of the appearance of my hair at that time of my life. But apparently it was a big deal to Ma.

Whatever section of my head Jitter worked on was in for a war. I'd start to wince, hunch my shoulders, make faces, and bend my head to the opposite side of where she was working.

"Ruth, this girl is so tender headed. I'm not even pulling hard. Sit still, Pippa, so I can work on these kinkerbobs!"

What in the name of child torture was going on? I had to endure the stench of my hair burning and the sizzling sounds from the hot hair grease that caused small clouds of rancid smoke to rise from my head.

This entire situation was a mess, but there were two occurrences that made me jump out of the chair whenever they happened. One was when Jitter would tell me to hold the top of my ear so she could get close with the hot comb, but she would burn me any-darn-way. Or when she was so distracted in laughter and chatter with Ma that she would burn the back of my neck with the hot comb!

I thought this whole process was utterly useless and a waste of my playtime. Even though my hair looked cute for the moment with little, shiny curls all over my head, I can tell you, they only lasted until my next bath, when the steam and water reverted my hair back to its natural state. I truly wished in my mind that my hair could look like Jitter's or my brothers', but not at the expense of being physically tormented and emotionally drained.

I also noticed that my skin looked cracked and ashy when water dried on me or when it was cold or windy outside. My feet, legs, knees, arms, elbows, hands, and the area around my mouth appeared light gray and parched. If my brothers' bodies suffered the same torment, you couldn't tell because of the lighter hue of their skin. Then here comes Ma yelling, "Pippa, put some Vaseline on those knees and elbows."

If I didn't move fast enough, Ma would snatch me as I attempted to run past her. She trapped me between her legs as she plastered grease on my face, arms, and knees. What in the world was going on here? Lathered my brothers with that greasy mess too!

For some reason, it seemed that my brothers required less personal care and attention than me. Was it because I was the only girl, to be spoiled, pampered, and treated like a little princess? Or was it because

I was notably different in my appearances than the brothers who were directly older and younger than me? At five years old, I certainly didn't have the answers to those questions. And the only time they popped into my head was when Ma or Jitter held me hostage.

My life continued, and as a five-and-a-half-year-old kid I thought it was good. My days were spent running around our two-bedroom, first-floor apartment. My brothers would throw open the front door and race through the kitchen into an open area that served as a living room. These were the areas where Ma had her parties. We'd push and run into each other as we made our way down the hall to the bedrooms. Our room was tiny and cramped, with a set of bunk beds and a chest of drawers. Ma's room had a bed that was larger, a dresser with a mirror attached to it, and a chair. Both rooms had tiny windows that I could look out, see the city streetlights, stars in the sky, and rain or snow coming down.

The only thing I remember about our bathroom was that it was small, and someone always seemed to be in it. We had to take turns using the toilet, brushing our teeth, and taking a bath. There was no such thing as privacy. What was that? There was no use in closing a bedroom or bathroom door when you had numerous brothers barging in all the time.

Days were spent outside playing on the sidewalks or in the streets. Neighborhood kids, along with my cousins, would gather from mid-morning until the evening darkness forced us back inside. The girls drew blocks and squares on the pavement with colored chalk and played hop-scotch with soda bottle caps. We would move to a game of pick-up-jacks with the little metal stars and a tiny red ball. The older girls jumped rope and were doing all kinds of magical things with their feet as they played double-dutch. I was only invited to jump when they were using a single rope. Everyone lined up and jumped in as the other girls sang rhymes and songs, to the beat of our feet hitting the ground.

Games that my brothers and male cousins joined in included Simon says or red light-green light 1, 2, 3. When we got bored with those games and wanted something more physical, we moved on to dodgeball. The boys were always overzealous as they threw the large rubber ball at our legs, chest, or head. They believed one of them would be the last man standing and win the game. They were usually right.

When we wanted to do something more daring and individual, we would roller skate on the sidewalks. We attached the skates to our sneakers by using a skate key to turn the metal grips that slowly closed and circled over the top of each sneaker. The skate key was a rare and prized possession. They were easily lost or misplaced. Whoever owned one usually wore it attached to a shoelace around their neck. When you wanted to skate, you had to find the person with the key, so you could tighten your skates. We would race each other up and down the sidewalks, yelling, laughing, and pushing each other out of the way. We had to be careful to navigate the uneven cracks on the ground. Skating around them or jumping over them was an art. If you didn't pay attention and your skate met one of these unfriendly raised grooves in the street, you would wind up sprawled out, face down on the pavement. Our knees, arms, and sometimes hands were scraped and bloody. After a quick trip inside for a Band-Aid, we'd be back outside to pick up where we left off.

As the sun began to go down each day and the darkness settled over the city, we would play one last game of hide-and-go-seek. During this time, you could hear adults calling for their kids to come inside for the night. We were never ready to go in but knew the consequence if we didn't.

My cousins Dino, Doran, Tyrone, and Lionel were so much fun. They were a few years younger than me and Googie. They would try to keep up with my brothers, had no fear in them, and were always up for a challenge. I remember all the boys used to climb up on a hallway radiator and try to jump onto the ceiling pipes. The younger cousins would not make it, so they would just climb the radiators and jump on the floor. My brothers Kevin and Ronald would swing from one pipe to the next, up and down the hallway. Not to be outdone by my cousins and brothers I would do the same. I was just as strong, physical, and agile as they were. I had no fear of heights or danger. I could take a dare right along with the rest of them. No test or obstacle would stop me from hanging with them. No situation was too far-fetched for me to participate in, if it involved them. When they teased me, I'd shrug it off. That only made my resolve stronger to prove to them that I could hang.

When we got tired of playing in the hallway, my cousins disappeared. Tyrone and Lionel went home to Aunt Stella, mom's younger sister. Dino and Doran who were with us for the summer, would follow my brothers into the apartment. True to form, my brothers and cousins would bust through our front door and into the kitchen. I remember eating lots of spaghetti and meatballs or fried chicken and potatoes. Those were usually complemented with some bread smeared with butter. Ma would busy herself fixing plates and handing them out in assembly-line format.

"Here Anthony, Ronald, here Kevin, Pippa, here Googie, Doran, and Dino."

Plates of food, along with a cup of Kool-Aid, that was our dinner.

Jitter and her older sister Dot sometimes joined our clan for meals. Dot did not look like Jitter. She was a tall, huge, dark-skinned lady with short, kinky hair. She looked intimidating, like she could whip any man's behind. But Dot had a big smile and loud laugh. I could tell Ma liked to be around them.

Periodically, Dot's teenage son, Penny, would appear. Penny was a skinny version of his mother. They always gave him a job to do. He would run to the corner store for cigarettes and beer or find out what the latest number was. When he returned, Dot usually gave him some money, and he would disappear. The ladies would continue their gossip, while we gobbled down our food and ran to the back room for hours of late-night TV time.

2

It was during this time in my life that I became aware of Mike. Mike was a white man who was my mother's man, boyfriend, head of the house. I'm not sure what I thought his title was back then. He was tall and had a head full of dark hair. He always seemed to be well dressed, or better dressed than the Black men who lived in the neighborhood or came to Ma's parties. The other thing that stood out to me, besides Mike being white, was that he did not walk like the rest of us. He used a cane, and at other times I remember seeing him in a wheelchair. I never knew why he couldn't walk, and no one ever discussed it.

I don't know how or when it became clear in my little head that this white man was "our father." Was it because he looked like my brothers? Was it something that Ma said, or maybe some comment that Jitter or Dot made? Or was it because Ma seemed to change when he came around? She was quieter, less animated. I couldn't figure it out, but there was a distinct change in her demeanor.

Mike would appear unannounced. I never remember him knocking on the door, so maybe he had a key. He seemed to command Ma's undivided attention. She was attentive to him, taking his cane, then his hat and coat before he sat down in a kitchen chair. I guess my Ma would cater to him, doing whatever he wanted. Did he eat, did he drink? I can't remember. I never saw him smoke a cigarette or drink a beer. He sat there looking around, taking in his surroundings, as he and Ma talked. He would reach in his pocket, take out a wad of money, peel off some bills, and give them to her. She would stuff the money down the front of her blouse.

Mike's visits were never lengthy. I don't remember him ever spending the night, and Ma never had other adults in the house when he came by. I never saw any touching, hugging, or acts of affection between them. I don't remember any laughing or joking. Sometimes I did hear Mike raise his voice at Ma. "Ruth, what the hell did you do with the money I gave you last week?"

Some explanation by Ma would follow, money given out, and then Mike would leave.

Five of my brothers looked like Mike. They had his skin color and his dark, thick head of hair. My brothers didn't pay him too much attention, or he them. However, he did seem to take an interest in me. He'd ask Ma about my hair, clothes, and if I needed anything. Was it because I was the only girl and he wanted to spoil me? Was it because I was different looking and needed more care, more maintenance? I don't know. I could sense that this white man cared for me. Maybe it was the way his face lit up and he smiled when I came in the room. Or because I would lay my head on his shoulder or climb up on his lap. Maybe it was because I was an affectionate kid and would unashamedly play in his hair or make him play hand-clap games with me.

We were all aware when he was around. Things seemed a little more bountiful. There was more food in the icebox and glass bottles of white and chocolate milk to drink. I got my hair pressed by Jitter on a regular basis. Ma dressed me in cute, frilly, colorful dresses on the weekends. I had a pink piggy bank that Mike would always put change in.

"Pippa, go get your piggy bank," he'd say, reaching into his pants pockets.

I knew I would have a pile of pennies to put in it. My brothers had toys, balls, water guns, and skates. I had a tiny piano, stuffed animals, tea sets, dolls, and dollhouses. In my little head, I thought life was good.

Sometimes when Mike came by, he would be in his wheelchair. He had a huge brown-and-black German shepherd dog that he kept on a leash. I don't remember the dog's name, but I liked him and used to pet and rub his head. The dog obeyed Mike's every command.

"Go, stop, sit," Mike would command, but I never tried telling the dog what to do. He seemed to know that he was there for Mike and that Mike was in charge.

When the weather was nice, Mike and I would leave the apartment to go for a walk. The dog pulled Mike in his wheelchair. I'd happily walk or skip beside him, talking and laughing the whole time. As we made our way down the sidewalk, people would sometimes call out, "Hey, Mike."

At other times, a man or two would walk with us for a few minutes. They usually had brief conversations with Mike before crossing the street or hurrying ahead of us. I never bothered to pay them any attention after they said, "Hi, Pip."

I was busy watching the big dog strain against the leash to pull Mike. Or I would take in the busy Harlem sights. People sitting on the stoops in front of their apartments, couples carrying on conversations, folks driving by in their cars, and kids playing in the streets like I often did. Sometimes we'd pass a man with his silver-colored cart, selling Italian ices to youngsters. I always had Mike buy me a cherry- or rainbow-flavored one. At other times, we'd see a man with a hot dog stand. If my hands weren't already holding an Icee, I'd ask Mike if I could have a hot dog with mustard. The one thing I noticed was that Mike never told me no. Was this the beginning of me being spoiled? I don't know, but what I do know is that I was happy when I had Mike's undivided attention. This was when Ma or my brothers weren't around.

Often Mike and I would walk to the corner of 125th Street and Park Avenue. The walk wasn't long, just a few city blocks from where we were living. There were elevated train tracks sitting on top of a mountain of arched steel beams. As we approached the intersection, I could sometimes hear the trains rumbling and screeching to a stop above us. We would wait for the light to change, then Mike in his wheelchair being pulled by his dog, and I would cross the many lanes of traffic.

There was a corner restaurant that he would take me to. Mike maneuvered his wheelchair as I held the door open and the dog pulled him in. We would go to his favorite table by the window, where we could look out at the bustling city, as we ate our food. All the people in the restaurant knew him; I guess he was a regular customer. They knew what Mike wanted to eat and drink, and I usually got a cheeseburger, fries, and a soda. Once I finished this, I'd walk toward the back of the restaurant and look at all the desserts in the glass case. Mike let me get whatever delicious treat I wanted. While we ate, a steady stream of different men would come in and speak to Mike. They never sat down. I used to think they were afraid of the big German shepherd. A few minutes would pass, and each guy exited the restaurant and disappeared into the hubbub of city life.

Once we finished our meal, we'd make our way back outside onto the New York City sidewalks. Mike maneuvered his way to the corner of 127th Street and Madison Avenue toward Sam's Barber Shop. Before I speak about Sam and his barber shop, I do recall an incident along the way that has remained with me all these years.

It was a hot, sunny afternoon. I had on shorts and a light-colored top. We had just left the restaurant, and my stomach was full. The dog was pulling Mike in his wheelchair and I was behind it, holding on to the arms, pretending I was pushing and guiding. Mike would periodically use his hands to grab the outer steel hand wheels on each side and push and turn them. I guess he was helping the dog, who was straining and panting. We were making our way steadily along the uneven sidewalk, when I noticed a group of people gathered about half a block ahead of us. I also noticed that one of the fire hydrants must have been opened, because I could see a stream of water spraying in the air above the people's heads. The cars going and coming in both directions were driving by unusually slow.

As we approached, people were instinctively moving out of our way along the sidewalk. I think more out of fear of the huge, panting dog that was coming toward them and not out of deference to the man in the wheelchair. As we got closer, I could see the group was made up of men and women, young and old, Black and Hispanic. They were looking down at something on the sidewalk or street.

The closer we got, the more I could feel the mist of spray from the open fire hydrant on my skin. The group slowly parted as we made our way toward them. Some backed up to the apartment building steps or storefronts. Others stepped out into the wet street. They were all talking quietly, looking, and pointing. No one was laughing or smiling, so I knew it was something bad. I could imagine in my young mind that someone's dog had been hit by a car. I felt a tug of sadness in my heart.

Now the cars were not only driving slower, but they were making a wide arc away from the side of the street we were on. As we approached, the crowd parted to let Mike pass. I let go of the wheelchair handles, made my way to the curb, and squeezed in between a few grownups who were standing there.

I looked down, and the hair on the back of my neck stood up. There, lying face down, halfway on the sidewalk and halfway in the street, was a man. His head was turned so that his face was right next to the curb. I couldn't see any of his facial features. His black hair and clothes were soaking wet. One arm and leg were twisted and sprawled out on the sidewalk. The man had on a short-sleeve shirt so I could see his skin coloring. He was much lighter than me, more like my brothers. I don't know maybe white like Mike with a tan, or maybe Hispanic like a few of the people who were in the group.

I looked up at the crowd of people and wondered why on earth no one was trying to help this man. What happened to him and what could he have done to wind up like that? Face down, drenched, with dirty water trickling down the street, washing over the outlines of his head, body, and clothes. Why wasn't anyone lending a hand to get him up out of the water? Where was his family? Where was the police and the ambulance? Didn't anyone care about this man? My throat got thick, and my eyes began to water. Then, from up ahead, past the crowd and the man lying still in the heat of the New York City street, I heard Mike yell out, "Come on, Pippa."

Shocked, unnerved, scared, and confused, I didn't know what to think. I didn't know what to say to Mike as I caught up with him. I retreated into a quiet shell, tightly gripping the wheelchair handlebars as we made our way up the street to Sam's Barber Shop. Mike and the dog worked to get the wheels over the holes, cracks, and raised areas in the sidewalk. Me? I was in a stupor, a trance, trying to understand what I had just seen. Mike wasn't paying me any attention. He was busy pushing and guiding the wheels as the dog pulled the wheelchair. He was dutifully saying hi and nodding to people as he navigated the streets.

As we pulled up to the corner where Sam's Barber Shop was located, there were lots of people coming and going, crossing the streets, and milling around chatting. Some were leaning against the building wall laughing, drinking beer, or smoking cigarettes. Others were throwing dice on the sidewalk. Everyone seemed to be in good spirits but me. Mike didn't seem to notice. Once inside the barber shop, people were coming up to him laughing, joking, or asking about the day's number. Mike and his dog settled in a corner of the shop. The dog lay down next to the wheelchair, putting his chin over his front paws, while keeping an alert eye on anyone who approached Mike.

"Hey, Pip! Hey, little girl, how you doing?" Sam called out to me.

I liked Sam. He was a friendly man who loved to talk. I used to skip alongside Mike's wheelchair and sing, "Sam, Sam, the barber shop man," over and over again. I looked up to Sam because I knew the shop was his, he owned it, he was the boss, he was in charge, and couldn't nobody take it from him.

"Say, Mike, did you hear about the guy who got shot up the street a little while ago? Dead right there in the gutter, they say."

Mike nodded.

"Deal musta went dead wrong," Sam casually remarked.

I had perched myself in one of the empty barber chairs and was spinning around in circles when I heard this. I stopped the chair and looked at Mike, then at Sam. Everyone had a strange expression on their faces, like someone had said a bad word that I wasn't supposed to hear. Sam stopped cutting the hair of the man he had been working on. Mike looked at me and asked, "Pippa, you hungry?" I nodded because I wasn't going to turn down an opportunity to get some food.

Sam stopped clipping his customer's head and turned to Mike. "I'll call Mattie down to get her."

Mike nodded in agreement. Something was wrong, but I couldn't quite figure it out. What was dead, what did that mean? Was it the same as being asleep, or knocked out with stars going around your head like in the cartoons I'd seen on TV? Whatever dead was, it wasn't good. The atmosphere in Sam's usually loud barbershop got quiet, except for the baseball game sounds coming from a small black-and-white TV nearby.

Sam went back to cutting the man's hair, and Mike continued writing things on little slips of paper.

Mattie was Sam's wife. They lived in an upstairs apartment nearby. I don't know if someone called her on the street payphone right outside the barber shop or if someone ran up to their house. Mattie appeared a few minutes later. She was a friendly, attractive woman. Everyone coming in and out of the shop liked her, including me.

Mattie and Sam were what I thought of as a perfect Ozzie and Harriet couple, except they were Black like me and not like the white folks on TV. They smiled and laughed with each other. They kissed and touched, and when we were about to leave, Sam swatted her on her behind. She giggled like a little girl and said, "All right, Sam, you gonna get in trouble."

She grabbed me by the hand. "Come on, Pippa, I got something good on the stove."

I remember spending a good amount of time in Sam and Mattie's apartment. I was comfortable and felt safe there. Mattie let me eat as much as I wanted of her home-cooked food. She set me up in her tiny living room in front of their TV. I ate my food on a thin, metal TV tray and enjoyed whatever show happened to be on. I don't know, maybe it was *The Lone Ranger*, *I Love Lucy*, or *The Honeymooners*. All I know is that I always had a great time at their house, just me and Mattie, good food and TV.

3

Life in the Paige household continued. For me it was a busy, fun-filled time living in New York City, *Harlem*, as it was referred to. I don't remember having a set time to wake up or go to bed. Whenever my brothers got up, so would I. We'd make our way to the kitchen still in our T-shirts and drawers, for a bowl of cereal with milk from the icebox. Or sometimes we would have cheese toast. One of the brothers would get the huge block of cheese out of the fridge, slice uneven chunks, and place them on slices of bread. Another brother would turn on the oven and carefully slide the scrumptious meal inside. You had to keep a close eye on it, otherwise the cheese would burn to a black crisp. Nobody wanted the black charred cheese toast, but if we were short on bread, one of us would eat it rather than go hungry. During this time, Ma never made us breakfast. It was every kid for himself. But since I was the only girl, my brothers Kevin and Ronald usually made sure I got a little something.

One Sunday morning, we were all still asleep in our bunk beds when I heard pounding on the apartment door. The knocking didn't stop, and no one in the house moved to answer it. I pushed my brother Sloppy Joe over so that I could climb out of the bottom bunk that we were sharing. Sloppy Joe was the baby and still in diapers. Why he slept with me and Googie, I'll never know. Anyway, I threw my legs over the railing and carefully stepped out onto the cold, linoleum floor. My three other brothers were crowded together in the top bunk. Arms, legs, and tangled sheets were everywhere.

I padded my way sleepy-eyed and barefoot across to the hallway, toward the door. I had on a pair of panties and an oversized T-shirt. My hair was a nappy mess from playing in the water from the fire hydrants the day before. Jitter probably was coming soon to "do" it anyway.

The incessant knocking continued.

"Here I come," I yelled out, irritated.

Who in the world could be banging on the door this early in the morning? Everybody else in my house was still sound asleep. When I got to the door, I had to unlock two locks, slide the gold-color chain lock off, then move the long, skinny metal security bar from a notch in the door and lean it against the wall.

"Who is it?" I asked in an angry tone.

A young girl's voice came from the other side of the door, "It's me. Open the door, Pippa."

I opened the door and standing there was one of my little girl-friends from up the street. She was cute, with her hair pressed in curls with bright ribbons to match her yellow dress. She had on shiny, black patent-leather shoes and dainty white socks folded over with little ruffles going around her ankles. She was so damn pretty. And there I was in my panties and dirty, gray-white T-shirt.

Neither one of us said anything for a couple of seconds. I guess we were sizing each other up. She, looking me up and down. Me, looking at her. Finally, I opened my mouth. "Hey."

"I just came by to see if you wanted to go to church," she said.

"Naw, plus my ma is still sleeping," I managed to get out.

Suddenly she scrunched up her face, grabbed her nose, and snapped her head back.

"What's that smell? Something stinks," she said, her voice rising.

"I don't know, it's not me." I was indignant.

"It smells like doo-doo!" she shrieked as she backed away from the door. I put one hand on my hip and stated, "Well I don't know who it could be. I just got out of the bed."

"It's not me, my momma just got me ready for church. Bye."

With her hand still covering her nose, she disappeared back into the hallway as I closed the door and uttered, "Bye then."

I stepped away from the door. "Humph, the nerve of her. Waking me up early in the morning, just to tell me that something stank."

I made my way to the bathroom to use the toilet. I looked in the mirror and saw that I was a mess. My hair was a knotty sight. But wait, something else was going on. I leaned closer over the sink, my face inches from the mirror. There was something that looked like green paste or mashed green peas from Sloppy Joe's baby food jar in my hair. I put my hand up and with my fingers tried to get the glob out. As I brought my hand down in front of my nose, I got a whiff. I looked at my fingers with the green glob smeared on them and screamed!

"Ma, Ma, Sloppy Joe doo-dooed in my hair!"

Horrified, I ran into her room with my right feces-filled fingers outstretched, as if the hand didn't belong to me.

"Ma, Ma wake up. I got doo-doo all in my hair!"

I pushed and tugged at her with my one good hand. By this time, I was crying huge sobs. I was going to be the laughingstock of the neighborhood when this gets out. Pippa had shit in her nappy hair on a Sunday morning. Or Pippa pooped on herself and it got in her hair. I was mortified.

"Maaaa," I wailed.

"Girl, go in the bathroom and wash your hands. I'll be in there in a minute."

Heaving and sobbing, I made my way back to the bathroom. By this time, all the ruckus I'd made had woken up Ronald, Googie, and Kevin. They came into the bathroom, uninvited of course, crowding on either side of me to see what the matter was. Maybe they thought I had cut myself and was washing the blood off. It only took a second for them to size the situation up and recoil first in horror, then in uncontrollable laughter.

"Pippa got doo-doo in her hair!"

They ran from the bathroom to the kitchen to Ma's room, falling on the floor, slapping their knees, and bouncing into the walls. Well, it must have been the funniest thing they'd ever witnessed, and the louder they laughed, the louder I cried.

Ma took her sweet time about getting to the bathroom to help me. She put on her short-sleeved bathrobe and made her way not to me, but to the bedroom where we slept. She came back with Sloppy Joe in her arms and his diaper hanging off one of his chubby legs. Green doo-doo was smeared all over him. We both stank. Apparently, his diaper had come loose during the night. He moved around all night long, as babies do, including over my head. Ma pushed me out of the way with her free hand and put Sloppy Joe in the sink.

"Pippa, I gotta clean this baby up first. Go grab those nasty sheets off your bed."

What? I had to walk back past my brothers with doo-doo still in my hair. Ma didn't get to me for at least fifteen minutes. This was the one time in my life that I wanted her and Jitter to go ahead and torture me with the eye-burning shampoo and the scorching-hot combs.

Life continued with me being the little rough-and-tumble tomboy trying to keep up with my brothers. Some days when the weather was nice, Penny and my brothers would go to Mount Morris Park, and I would tag along with them. During this time, we lived on Park Avenue, about four or five blocks from the park. Since we played hard every day, outside running, skating, and jumping, this little walk was nothing to us. I don't know if we ever had Ma or Dot's permission to go. That thought never entered my mind. We were carefree, happy-go-lucky, and unworried.

We went down Park Avenue for three blocks, then made a right turn on East 124th Street and walked for another block to the entrance of the park. Now, I really couldn't tell you the street numbers, addresses, or directions. I navigated by memorizing landmarks like the liquor store where the bums hung out, the candy store where I got my favorite Bazooka bubble gum, or the pizza shop with the extra-large slices.

When we got to the park, there were huge trees brimming with canopies of green leaves. Different types of bushes were everywhere. Beautiful flowers in a variety of colors were blooming. There was thick grass as far as the eye could see on both sides of the winding pathway. Couples were strolling along, holding hands. Mothers pushing their babies in huge, dark-colored strollers were here and there. Kids were running and racing, playing with balls, and flying kites. It was a wonderland to me. So different from the stark concrete jungle where I lived a few blocks away.

We took the same streets and turns each time we came. The boys didn't deviate from the path; that was how I memorized my way to the park. It was an adventure to me. We would make our way following the twists and turns into what I thought was a fairy-tale forest. As we walked, the path would go higher and higher. Sometimes it was so steep, we had to climb uneven, rocky steps. Up we would go until finally we arrived at our destination, our journey's end.

At the highest point in the park was a huge, black metal bell, surrounded by an iron fence. I had never seen anything like it. I often wondered how it got there, how long it had been there, and who carried it all the way up this mountain in the middle of the park. What was it used for, and did anybody ever hit it to make it ring? Why was there an iron fence around it? As my mind pondered over these profound questions in my head, we would race around the bell a few times before making our journey back down the path.

Each time we did this, it felt like a triumph, something we had mastered or conquered. It felt like we had passed a huge, insurmountable test, the boys and me.

What about just me? Could I do it by myself? I thought. *Yes, if they could do it, I could do it too.* I was just as strong and brave as they were, and I knew the way.

So, one day as we were playing out on the sidewalks like we usually did, I decided to break away from the group. I wanted to have my own adventure by myself. I wanted to prove to my brothers that I could do anything they could do. The girls were busy jumping rope, and the boys were playing stickball in the middle of the street. I saw that no one was paying attention to me, so I turned and started on my quest. My mission was to make it to the park and climb the mountain of steps up to the bell.

I navigated the city streets just like a pro. I dodged past people, making my way along each familiar block to its corner. I'd wait for the light to turn green, then run across to the other side. No one bothered me, questioned me, or stopped me. Why would they? I looked like a little girl on a mission, like I had somewhere important to go. Six-year-old me, confidently trekking my way alone to Mount Morris Park. I didn't have a care in the world as I walked what was probably twenty minutes to the entrance of the park, past my liquor store and pizza shop.

I made my one right turn and knew I didn't have far to go, just one more block. When I saw the tall trees and the entrance to the park, I got excited all over again. My mission was half-accomplished. *I'll show my brothers I can do what they do, and all by myself!* Crossing the last street, I ran into the park and along the familiar pathway. As usual, I passed kids playing, moms with their babies, couples holding hands, and people sprawled out sleeping on the benches.

Head held high, I marched on. I believed in myself and knew my sturdy little legs wouldn't fail me. Fifteen more minutes, ten more, five more, and finally, almost out of breath, I could see the huge, black bell before me. I bent over with my hands on my knees, trying to catch my breath. Beads of sweat were running down my face. I wanted to sit down, but there wasn't a bench nearby. So, I ran around the bell just like I did with my brothers, with my hands up in the air, yelling, "I did it. I did it, y'all. I did it all by myself!"

There was no one up there with me, no one to share my victory lap with. With hands on my hips, I was basking in my accomplishment when I noticed something. Flying through the air were little lightning bugs, with their tails emitting soft glows of light. I looked around, and to my horror, the sun had gone down, and darkness was beginning to settle over the park. What time was it? How long had I been gone? I instantly became anxious as I looked for the steps and path that would take me back down. Once I found it, I began running. Down twists and turns I made my way. Things did not look as familiar in the dark as they do in the bright light of day.

There were no children playing, no mothers with their babies, just a few men here and there, sprawled out on the benches. One or two had woken up, and others were drinking something out of bottles in brown paper bags. They looked at me curiously as I sped by, but never said a word. The closer I got to the park's entrance, the darker it got, and the more lightning bugs I saw. It was then that I thought about Ma. Was she looking for me? Did she even know I was gone from the block? Had my brothers noticed? With each step, I became more nervous, more apprehensive. The closer I got to the entrance of the park, the trees thinned out, and the sky didn't look as dark. I felt a little better.

At the corner, I waited for the light to change, then sprinted across the street. I'd run a little, then slow down into a fast walk. As I passed each familiar landmark, I relaxed some because I knew I was getting closer to home. Maybe I could make it back to my block, in front of the house, without anyone noticing. My plan was to blend in like I never left. I'd join whatever game the rest of the kids were playing.

I was about two blocks from home when a man smoking a cigarette by a storefront called out, "Yo, Pip! Your momma looking for you."

Oh shucks, she knew I was gone. That familiar feeling of dread began to creep in again. I was walking at a brisk pace, but this time I had a different mission in mind. I had to make it home and hope that Ma was in a good mood. Maybe she would be distracted by my brothers or some of her friends. Maybe she would have hit the number and was looking for me, to buy me something.

All sorts of thoughts were racing through my head as my feet pounded the pavement. It was slowly getting darker as I dodged and weaved, to keep from colliding with the people on the street. No one was in a hurry but me. A small group of pedestrians were coming toward me. Of course, I had to move to the right and go around them. When I did, I could see up ahead, about a half block in front of me. There was Ma, marching toward me. She didn't see me at first, because her head was whipping to the right, then to the left. She was clearly looking for something or someone. My paced slowed dramatically. Ma was speed walking like she was on a mission. Just like I was earlier, as I made my way alone to the park.

A moment later, she spotted me, and our eyes locked. I swear I thought her stride slowed. But she only halted for a second, when she must have gotten a second wind. I stood still in my tracks, in the middle of the sidewalk. I couldn't move; my feet felt like they had become glued to the concrete. She closed the distance between us in an instant. The look on her face told me she was not happy. Her eyes were like two huge saucers about to pop out of her head. Beads of sweat were glistening on her forehead. When she got within a few yards of me, she started yelling.

"Pippa! Pippa where the hell have you been? I been looking all over for you." By this time, she was standing in front of me. "I said where have you been? Where did you go?"

Ma looked a mess—hair standing up on her head, clothes rumpled, and the print blouse half in and half out of her pants. I opened my mouth to tell her how brave I had been and what I had accomplished, but after seeing the crazed, contorted look on her face, all I could get out was, "I went to the park."

"The park?" She screamed in horror. "By yourself? What the hell?"

She was like a deranged woman, and I couldn't understand why. All I wanted to do was to prove that I was brave enough to go to the park by myself.

"I wanted to see the big, black bell."

Ma looked at me in utter disbelief. "The bell? The bell! I'll show you some damn bell!"

At this point, she grabbed my left arm and held it above my head. She yanked me in front of her and from behind me, her right hand started smacking the mess out of my rear end. Ma marched home, holding and whipping me. With every word that she yelled, her free hand landed on my behind.

"Didn't I tell you to stay in front of the house?"

Each word was executed with a firm smack. Ma's ferocious hits landed on my butt repeatedly. I twisted and tried to turn my body so that her hand couldn't find its target. But to no avail. I cried so hard, tears and snot ran down my face. I yelled, "Ma, I won't do it no more!"

People were looking; some were clearly amused.

"That child getting her ass whipped!"

"Oh, I bet you won't do it no damn more! Had me and every damn body out here looking for your ass, and you all the way down here by yourself, looking for some damn bell!"

Lord, please let her arm get tired. Lord, please go ahead and break her hand, I thought, still crying the whole time.

"I'll be good, Ma, I promise. I won't do it no more," I pleaded. But my pleas fell on deaf ears.

"Some damn man coulda snatched your ass, and you out here alone, and it's getting dark."

More smacks, and my bottom was on fire. Ma was not getting tired, and no one on the streets was intervening on my behalf. Ma whipped my rear end for a solid block and a half, yelling, screaming, and cursing the whole way. When we got to the front of our apartment building, someone from an upstairs, open window called out, "Ruth, where was she?"

"At the damn park by herself, all the way up by the bell."

"What? Somebody coulda snatched that child!" the person yelled back.

With this, Ma pushed me toward the front door.

"Get your little ass in there and go to bed. And I better not hear shit outta you."

I ran to the door, busted inside, and dived on the bottom bunk bed. I was totally exhausted, drained, and cried out. All I could do was curl up in a tight ball and shake and heave. I heard somebody snicker, "Pippa got her butt whipped. Ha."

I don't know which brother it was, and I didn't care. I wanted the stinging sensation on my behind to stop. I wanted to be left alone so I could go to sleep, and that's just what I did.

That was the first and only butt whipping I ever got from Ma. Now I don't want you to think that I never did anything else wrong in those days. I did. Sometimes I got caught, sometimes I didn't. It wasn't until many years later that I understood why Ma was so upset and distraught about me going to the park alone, and why she acted like a complete fool out there in the streets, beating me mercilessly.

Yes, I learned my lesson that day. I could be brave, but I better not go to Mount Morris Park by myself. In fact, I better not go anywhere by myself. A good, steady stream of butt whipping by an upset momma is a strong deterrent.

4

Harlem was a hub of incessant activity and city life twenty-four hours a day. Something was always going on. The streets bustled with crowds of people and noisy traffic. I didn't know anyone with a car at that time. Folks got around by walking, taking cabs, the subway or train, and city buses. I remember seeing the old city buses coming and going, stopping at specific stops to let people on or off. I knew they weren't free but had no idea how much one cost to ride. Why would I? Every place my brothers and I needed to go was within walking distance. Clothes shopping on 125th Street, Mount Morris Park, Sam's Barber Shop, candy stores, the movie theater, pizza shop, and my school. We didn't need to take a bus for anything, or so I thought.

One afternoon, Kevin and Ronald came up with the bright idea of jumping on the back of a city bus and riding it to the next stop. I'm sure it probably started out as a dare, but who could resist? If they were brave enough to do it, so was I. We walked to a corner bus stop and waited. Anticipation was building. I was going to do something that I had never done before. It was exciting.

Ronald volunteered. "I'll go first since I'm the oldest."

That was fine with me, because I wanted to see exactly how he planned on doing it. A big yellow-and-green bus pulled up in front of us and ground to a stop. It looked like a huge, dirty metal caterpillar to me. We walked toward the back of the bus. While people got on and off in the front of the bus, Ronald hopped on the back. Kevin and I waited on the sidewalk, watching. No one seemed to be paying any attention to us.

Ronald's feet were on the back-silver metal bus bumper. His right arm and hand straddled the side of the bus. His left hand clung to the frame of the back bus windows. He looked at us and laughed. "Here I go."

As the bus pulled off into the street traffic, Kevin and I jogged along the sidewalk, trying to keep up. At the next corner, the bus screeched to a stop, and Ronald hopped off.

"Yeah, man, I told you I could do it," Ronald pounded his chest.

"So what, I can do it too," Kevin countered as he jumped on the back-left side of the bus.

"Me too," I chimed in and hopped on the right side.

My little arm could barely reach from the back to the side of the bus. My feet were perched on the rear bumper, and my right hand pressed against the bus, as my left fingers tried to grip the rubber surrounding the back window.

The bus pulled off. Kevin yelled out, "Hold on, Pip, here we go."

Ronald sprinted along the sidewalk, weaving in and out of people, trying to keep up with the bus. I hung on for dear life. Cars and cabs were passing us on the left side where Kevin was. His head whipped to the left, then to the right, taking in the sights as the bus plowed along.

"Yeah, this is fun. Look, Ron!"

Kevin looked back at Ron, trying to keep up with the bus. People on the sidewalk gawked at us in disbelief. Someone yelled out, "Look at those crazy, damn kids. Y'all gonna get hurt. Get off that bus!"

This had to be insane, dangerous, and against the law. But I was keeping up with my brothers. I wasn't no little punk. I was the Paige boys' little sister.

After about half a block, I felt my fingers cramping from gripping the bottom of the bus window frame so hard. My right arm was getting weak because I really didn't have anything to latch onto on the side of the bus. My legs were getting jostled from the up-and-down motion of the bus going over uneven areas and manholes in the streets.

"Kevin, I can't hold on." My fingers were starting to cramp even more.

"Yes you can, Pip. We're almost there."

I turned my head and looked behind me. There were no cars coming toward us.

"I gotta get off."

And with that, I let loose and jumped off the moving New York City bus. I hit the ground hard, landing on my feet, but immediately stumbled forward, falling, arms flailing, knees and hands angrily scraping the city street.

Ronald saw what was happening and ran to help me up.

"You all right, Pip?"

I gingerly stood up on shaky legs and limped over to the sidewalk. My left ankle hurt, and both my knees were skinned and bleeding. The palms of my hands had long scrapes on them and were bloody, with tiny pieces of street tar mixed with blood.

By this time, the bus had stopped up ahead, and Kevin jumped off and was heading back toward us.

"Man, that was fun!" He held his two fists up triumphantly.

"Yeah, Kip, let's get Pippa home and cleaned up before Ma sees her."

Ron pushed me in the direction of home. I couldn't agree with him more, because I didn't want Ma to find out what I did and give me another marathon butt whipping. I had successfully kept up with my older brothers and accomplished something I had never done before and haven't done since.

On another city adventure, my brothers decided to leave the block and explore an old, abandoned church. It wasn't far from the house and didn't take us long to get there. The building had windows broken out, splintered wooden doors, and cracked, broken bricks everywhere. We went around the side of the church, and Ronald pushed open a door. We ventured inside. It was dark; the only light was from the outside, streaming in through the dirty, busted windows. Thick dust floated through the air. Cobwebs were everywhere. Roaches and water bugs scattered as we approached. Broken pew seats were toppled over.

I stopped long enough to pick up a book. I couldn't read, so I didn't know whether it was a bible or hymnal. Torn pieces of paper littered the filthy floor. I picked up a piece of paper that used to be white, I guess. But it was dusty gray, faded and soiled. It had lines on it, with little squiggly things on and between the lines. I didn't know then that it was an old sheet of music. I quickly threw it down when I saw tiny spiders crawling over the paper and cobwebs sticking to my fingers.

"Ahh, bugs!" I shouted in disgust.

There was so much garbage and trash that I could not make out what color the floor was or what it was made of. We carefully made our way through the mess.

"Look at this."

Every few seconds Kevin or Ronald would call out, holding up a jagged piece of old stained glass or random section of rotting wood. We continued making our way through the dusty, musty church interior, zigzagging from one side to the other. Three explorers in a strange, new land.

Suddenly, a man's voice belted out from the side shadows, "What the hell y'all doing in here?"

It had been completely quiet except for the ruffle our feet made on the floor trash or an occasional peal of excitement from Kevin or Ronald. But the deep, slurred, booming voice scared the heck out of us.

"Let's get outta here. Come on, Pip," one of them yelled, and both bolted away from the voice.

Panic set in. My brothers ran; they didn't look back to see if I was behind them. Around broken, toppled pews they sprinted. I could barely see them ahead of me. Dust particles were getting in my eyes.

"Wait, wait for me!" I shrieked at the top of my voice.

"Get the hell outta here." I heard from behind me. I didn't stop or look back. I was scared to death.

Suddenly, I heard one of my brothers yell out in pain, then curse, "Ahh, shit!"

I could make out who I thought was Kevin in the distance ahead of me, climbing through a broken stained-glass window. I was afraid of being left behind in the dark church, with the bodyless voice. Sprinting like my life depended on it, I ran up to the broken window as Kevin was turning around, looking for me. He grabbed my hand as I stepped up onto the splintered window frame. I looked at the side of the window to find a spot that didn't have broken, jagged glass. Using my other hand to support my body, I hoisted myself up, then jumped out on the ground.

31

"Come on, we gotta get outta here," Ronald hissed.

We both turned to face him. He was grimacing in pain as he gripped his right arm. Blood was seeping through his clenched fingers, running down, and dripping onto the sidewalk.

"Let's go," he repeated in a commanding voice.

"Man, Ron, what happened?" Kevin looked at him, quite concerned.

"I cut my arm on a damn piece of glass sticking out the window."

With that, he was already several paces ahead of us. We walked quickly in silence. I had to almost jog to keep up with them. There was a sense of urgency. I was concerned but had enough smarts not to say or ask anything.

By the time we made it to the house, it was just beginning to get dark. Kids were still playing outside in the streets and hadn't been called in for supper. We were safe. Ma probably didn't even know we were gone. The three of us sprinted inside, and Ron went straight to the bathroom.

"Pippa, find me some Band-Aids and tape. Kip, go get me a long-sleeve shirt."

We did as we were told. When I got back to the bathroom, Ron had taken off his blood-spattered shirt and tossed it at me.

"Throw this in the garbage."

I did, then returned to the bathroom door. I didn't find any Band-Aids but came back with a roll of white gauze and tape. Kevin had brought back a long-sleeved plaid shirt, then disappeared. I guess he had had enough excitement for one day.

Ron's arm had a long, jagged gash. I could clearly see the pink skin peeled back as he ran cold water on his arm. Blood was trickling down the bathroom sink. He didn't flinch at the sight, so neither did I. He seemed to know what he was doing. With two fingers, he lifted the flap of skin and moved it back in place to cover the wound. Blood was still seeping from the edges, but not as much as before. He held the skin in place and said, "Pippa wind that stuff around my arm. Do it tight." I did as I was told, going around his arm again and again.

"Now get that tape and do the same thing."

I commenced with the clear tape, around and around, working quietly, methodically.

"Okay, good." He thought he had enough.

It was then that he finally looked up at my face and muttered, "You better not say anything to Ma about this."

"I won't," I whispered in a solemn voice.

He didn't need to tell me twice. If Ma knew what we had been doing, that would have been another butt whipping. Excuse me, three butt whippings, one for each of us, and I wasn't up for that.

Yup, it was another thrilling day with the boys, even though the ending had been a little scary. The one thing that amazed me about my brother Ron was how brave he was. He didn't cry from the pain or wince at the sight of all that blood. He didn't complain to us or run home whining to Ma. He took charge of the situation and did what needed to be done, and I hung in there every step of the way, like the super girl I thought I was.

My two oldest brothers, Michael and Anthony, didn't hang out with us too much. I guess they had friends of their own. I rarely saw Michael at all. He was seven years older than me. Tall, dark, and handsome with beautiful skin and black, shiny waves in his hair, he looked like me, nose and all. I remember him always dressing nice. His clothes were neat, clean, and pressed. He was quiet and kept to himself. I never heard him talk loud or raise his voice. He carried himself in a regal way, striding confidently, smoothly, with his head held high. Michael would appear one day and then disappear into thin air. I wouldn't see him again until several days later. When he did see me, his face would light up with a big grin.

"Hey, Pip." He'd give me a quick hug, then go about his business. I loved all my brothers, but I especially loved Michael. I guess he had friends and a life of his own.

When Anthony was around, which wasn't often, he would hang outside with us. He played stick ball or skully in the streets with the older boys. He was good at skully, tossing his bottle caps onto the numbered squares on the sidewalk. Other times, he would roller skate or ride in a makeshift go-cart. Even though he was busy, he kept an eye on us. He was in charge of rounding us up when it was time to go inside.

Ma always gave Anthony the money to buy us ice cream from the Mr. Softee truck. She would not give me the money, even when I saw the ice-cream truck first. Maybe it was because she didn't trust me, or maybe it was because I couldn't count yet. My brothers were so engrossed in whatever game they were playing, they never saw the white truck or heard the magical music coming from it. I didn't know why. I'm the one who usually screamed, "The ice-cream man is here!" Then everyone would scramble to find their parents to get change for the tasty treat. Anthony would get the money and the rest of us would have to tag along behind him and wait patiently.

One warm, lazy day we were all outside playing. Ma and some ladies were sitting on the steps, chatting, laughing, and smoking. My friend and I had been engaged in trying to get our hand-clap routine correct when Ma called me. "Pippa, run upstairs to Dot's house and get a dollar bill off her dresser in the bedroom."

I paused with my hand in midair and looked around for Penny, Dot's son. Why couldn't he get the money for his momma? But he was not with the group of boys playing in the street.

"Hurry up, you hear me talking to you?"

I sucked my teeth but didn't say anything as I moved toward the lounging ladies.

"Girl, I'm running out of cigarettes, only got three left in this pack," Ma said.

Dot then repeated the same directions Ma had already given me.

"Pippa, look on my bedroom dresser upstairs, and bring me a dollar. No, make it two dollars. Ruth, I'll buy you some Pall Malls for later," Dot offered.

"Thanks, Dot. I don't know when I'll see Mike again. You know how that goes."

I ran up the steps past them and into the dimly lit hallway of the apartment building. The brown wooden stairway was right in front of me. I bounded up the one flight of steps, then saw the open door to Dot's apartment. I made my way through the living room and toward the bedroom. It was ridiculously small, so the dresser with the large mirror was easy to spot. I walked up to it and looked for the dollar bills.

I did see them, but what caught my eyes was the large pile of pennies in the middle. I had never seen so much money in my life! My pink piggy bank at home didn't have this many pennies in it. Wow! I wondered if this was how Penny got his name. Did his mom love to collect pennies? I ran my hand across the pile, then spotted a few small brown paper bags near the edge of the dresser. *Dot wouldn't miss a few pennies*, I thought. My eyes darted from the paper bags to the pennies, then back again. Without giving it another thought, I snatched a bag, opened it and started scooping pennies toward the edge of the dresser into the bag. Suddenly, through the open bedroom window, I heard Dot's voice calling, "Pippa did you find it?"

"Yeah," I yelled back.

I was still sliding pennies in the bag when I thought to myself, *I'd better leave a good chunk of these here, or else Dot will know I took some of her pennies.* So, I pushed some of the coins back, rolled down the top of the paper bag, and stashed my newfound wealth in the front of my pants. I pulled my blouse over my pants, grabbed two bills off the dresser, and ran back down the steps.

"Here, Aunt Dot." I handed her the bills and continued past them onto the sidewalk.

"Ma, I gotta go to the bathroom," I pretended to whine while pressing my hand on the front of my stomach.

"Anthony! Take your sister home to use the bathroom."

Frustrated, Anthony uttered, "Come on, Ma. Pippa can go by herself."

Ma stood up and gave him the look. That *Boy, have you lost your damn mind?* look.

When we got to our apartment, Anthony threw open the door and then stood back.

"Hurry up, Pip." He was impatient.

I ran inside, pulled out the crumpled brown bag, and stuffed it under the bunk bed mattress.

"Come on, girl," he said.

"Here I come," I said, straightening up my shorts and blouse as I neared my brother. I had to make it look like I was coming from using the bathroom.

"Let's go, making me miss my turn," Anthony muttered under his breath.

We returned to Dot's stoop and rejoined our little friends to pick up where we had left off. I got engrossed in a game of pick-up-jacks. I wasn't as good as my friend, but I gave it my best shot. I was completely absorbed in the game, which I was losing when Ma yelled out, "Pippa, get your butt over here."

I glanced over my shoulder with my hand in midair clutching the little red rubber ball. Dot and my mom were both standing up on the steps. From the looks on their faces, they were no longer lounging and chatting.

"Get over here, I said." Ma had one hand on her hip and the other holding a lit cigarette near her mouth.

Dot had a blank look on her face. I got up from where I was sitting on the ground.

"Oh, oh Pip, looks like somebody's in trouble," my friend said, half-laughing. I wasn't, though.

I made my way over to the bottom of the steps and looked up at the two women. Something was wrong, and I think I knew what it was. Ma started undoing the belt around her waist.

"You got something you wanna say to Dot?"

I opened my mouth, but nothing came out. My mouth was moving, but the words just wouldn't come. Ma took one step down, closer to me. I felt my eyes begin to water.

"I-I," was all that came out.

By this time, the belt was off, and Ma had folded it in half. I thought I was going to collapse right there on the sidewalk.

"No, I-I nothing." Ma's voice was menacing. "I'm going to beat your little butt with this belt if you don't tell me something!"

By this time, tears were streaming down my cheeks. Dot had her arms folded across her chest and looked like she wanted to laugh. Ma smacked the belt in the palm of her hand. I winced. She took another step down, coming closer to me.

"You got something you wanna tell us?"

I swear Ma's eyes had gotten big as saucers again, with that crazy look she gets when she's mad. Whack! She slapped her hand again with the belt. I took a step back and opened my mouth again.

"Dammit. What did you do, Pippa?" she said, her voice getting louder.

I felt as if I was shrinking like that person in the movie, *The Incredible Shrinking Man*, that my brothers used to make me watch late at night.

"Leave her alone, Ruth. It was only pennies," Dot stated.

Oh, heck, I thought, *they really know. But how could they, there were so many pennies on the dresser.*

"Noooo, Dot." Ma dragged it out. "Imma beat her little butt from here to my house, if she don't open that mouth and say something."

I had an immediate flashback of Ma beating me from the park all the way home. I didn't want another repeat performance of that. Not here in front of my friends, my brothers, and all their friends. I knew Ma's arm would not get tired, and she had a belt!

"Aunt Dot, I'm, I'm sorry," I finally was able to get out.

"Sorry for what?" Ma roared.

"Lordy, Ruth, you gonna make that child pee on herself," Dot said, half-laughing.

I couldn't look either one of them in the eye. I felt so ashamed, so stupid. By this time, Ma had made it to the sidewalk and snatched me by the arm. She pushed me toward Dot. She held up her hand with the belt in it.

"What you wanna say? What you wanna tell Dot?" Ma's arm raised up over her head.

I looked up, from the belt to Dot. The belt was about to come down when I blurted out, "I won't do it no more Aunt Dot; I won't take your pennies no more, I promise!" By this time, I was a whimpering, shaking mess.

"Pippa, you shoulda known I could tell the change was missing." Dot took a puff on her cigarette. "All you had to do was ask me, and I would've given you some."

I guess that should have made me feel better, but it didn't. Not with Ma still gripping my arm and waving that belt above my head. She glared down at me and shook me again.

"I'm sorry, I won't do it again," I whispered.

"It's okay, Pippa, stop crying. Ruth, I think she learned her lesson," Dot said as she sat back down on the top step.

"I'm sorry, Dot," my mother mouthed, shaking her head. "This child, embarrassing me like that. We heading home. Come on, boys."

Ma turned me around and pushed me in front of her. I thought sure she was going to smack me with that belt, but she didn't.

Suffice it to say, I never stole from Dot again.

5

I hadn't started school yet. In fact, I don't think my neighborhood school, P.S. 24, offered kindergarten. This was of little concern to me, as I was busy living my life. In September, when my older brothers were in school, I would sleep late, then get up and hang out with Ma, Jitter, and Dot. Or my days would be spent sitting on the floor in front of our little TV for hours watching cartoons. Some of my favorites were Popeye, Yogi Bear, the Flintstones, and Sylvester and Tweety. The funny characters could entertain me all day. I would be lost in an animated world full of fun and laughter. Ketchup or mayonnaise sandwiches were my go-to snack. I had no trouble keeping myself entertained this way. Ma didn't bother me, and I loved it.

It was around this time that my oldest brother, Michael, had a girlfriend named Beverly. He would bring her to the house every now and then. I liked her. She was brown skinned, pretty, with a cute shape. Just like my brother Michael, Beverly was quiet, with a nice smile. She had a head full of hair that was always pressed and curled. They made an attractive couple, I always thought. Heads close together, holding hands, and having intimate conversations that only the two of them could hear. That is, until Beverly would throw her head up and bust out in laughter at something Michael was saying.

I also liked Beverly because usually when Michael brought her around, they were going to take me out with them. Not my other brothers, just me. Whether Michael asked Ma if he could take me, or whether he just told her, I didn't know and didn't care. When he came around and told me to get ready, that's all it took. Five minutes later, the three of us would be heading out the door.

They were the cutest pair, both dressed sharp as a tack! I remember all of us going to the movies on 125th Street. Michael had on sunglasses inside the darkened theater. I thought that was so cool. But I also wondered how he could see the movie screen with those dark glasses on. He would sit in the middle, me on one side of him and Beverly on the other. I probably spent as much time watching Michael out of the corner of my eye as I did watching the movie. I adored my big brother and was just so happy to be out with him, as I'm sure Beverly was.

Another time, Michael and Beverly took me to Jones Beach. It seemed like it took us forever to get there. We rode the subway and a bus. At this point in my life, I was not good with long directions, and I still couldn't read. But I can tell you this was a heck of a long ride. We walked to the subway station and got on a hot, crowded train with Beverly and me sitting, while Michael stood in front of us. Then we had to wait for a bus, which when it came was just as hot and crowded as the subway train. We were packed in there like the oily sardines in a can that Ma ate.

Black people, white people, Spanish people, everyone shoulder to shoulder touching, all trying to keep their balance while holding on to their beach bags and picnic baskets. I certainly didn't complain. No, not me, not a peep. I don't care how hot, how crowded, or how I hated that strange person's leg touching me as we sat on the subway or bus. I did not complain. I just concentrated on looking at Michael, Beverly, or out the nearest window at the city sights flashing by. Yup, I was in heaven. I was the lucky one, I thought. Out on a daylong trip with my big brother. I felt special.

When we finally arrived, we had to do some more walking to get to the beach area. The sun was high in the sky; it was blazing hot. Michael and Beverly had sunglasses on to protect their eyes, but I didn't have any. They carried our belongings and took turns holding my hand as we made our way through the masses. Throngs of people were everywhere. Some were couples, but most seemed to be families and small groups.

Beach chairs with colorful umbrellas dotted the long expanse of hot sand. Brightly decorated blankets were spread out everywhere. Little kids were digging in the sand with plastic buckets and shovels, building round mounds of sand. Older kids were playing catch with big beach balls and Frisbees or racing into the water. Adults organized food, drinks and all their containers and baskets on the blankets, while others were eating and drinking. I could see hundreds of bodies stretched out soaking up the sun. Folks walking leisurely in all directions. People of different sizes, shapes, and colors as far as my eyes could see.

I was so enthralled, captivated by everything I was seeing for the first time. Walking closely behind Michael and Beverly through the myriad of beachgoers, I tried to keep my balance in the sinking sand. Periodically one of them would turn around to make sure I was with them.

"Come on, Pip, keep up," Michael said.

When we came to a spot in the sand that was satisfying to the lovebirds, they stopped, and Michael spread out a blanket. Beverly told me to take off my shorts and top and put on my bathing cap, as she and Michael organized our few items. Once this was done to their liking, they took off their clothes. Beverly in her cute, colorful two-piece and matching cap and Michael in his bathing trunks showing all his toned, brown muscles.

We made our way down to the water's edge, my feet sinking deeper into the wet sand the closer we got. People were running past us, either coming out of the water or going into it. As they did, cold ocean water would spray us. I'd squeal out loud, "Awww that's cold," while gripping my arms.

We waded further in, Michael holding me with one hand and Beverly with the other. When we got to the point where the cold, gray water was about to my knees, I said, "Okay, Imma stop here, Michael." He let go of me, laughing.

"Stay right here. Beverly and I are going a little further."

They made their way out into the crowd of people frolicking and carousing in the water.

Sounds of chatter and laughter were all around me. The sun was beaming directly down on us. Huge waves of water washed up, almost knocking me down, then rolled out, causing my feet to sink even deeper in the ocean sand. I had to use my arms to keep my balance, as I shifted with the rolling waves. I couldn't see my feet, but I could feel the sand between my toes and the small rocks or shells underneath my heels.

Sometimes a piece of long, green seaweed would get wrapped around one of my legs, and after untangling it, I'd toss it as far out into the water as I could.

To get the rest of my body wet, I would slap the water with my hands or bend down in a squatting position, so the waves could wash over me, or take scoops of water in my pail and throw it on my shoulders or chest. Other times I'd bend down and let the waves wash over me. Holding my arms in the air, I would turn around fast in circles, often losing my balance and falling into the water. Jumping up, I'd try to wipe the stinging, salty water out of my eyes.

This was so much fun. I was having the time of my life, playing in the ocean water on a beautiful day, as I kept my eyes on the two people who made this wonderful experience possible. When Beverly and Michael had had their fill of ocean entertainment, they walked toward me, and the three of us made our way through the twisted crowd of sunbathers back to our blanket. We flopped down exhausted, as we tried to get some of the drying sand off our bodies. By this time, we were thirsty and hungry. Beverly opened the chicken they had bought, and Michael passed around sodas.

After eating, they got comfortable and stretched out on the blankets. I had taken off my cap, which did little good, as my hair was matted and wet. I sat Indian style near them and marveled at all the people around us. Some were lounging, walking, playing in the water, or setting up as we had earlier. Many were beet red as though they had gotten burnt; others were looking dry and ashy like me. There were a couple of kids nearby who were piling so much sand on a man that you couldn't see any of his body except for his cap-covered head.

Different-sized transistor radios could be heard all around, with a mix of Spanish and soul music playing. People were walking past us with a wide variety of food items from the beach vendors. I was amazed at all the happenings around me. I could literally watch these people all day and not get bored. We were different. We were the same. But the one thing we all seemed to have in common was that we were enjoying this day. This day on the beach with my big brother, that I will never forget. This was my first and only trip to the beach when I was little.

6

Every day in the Paige household was an adventure, but what about the nights? Things were sort of routine, if you could call it that. Whenever we came in from eating, we would take turns taking a bath and then retreat to our back room to watch TV. Sometimes Ma was home, and sometimes she wasn't. When she was, there was usually something hot to eat, but when she wasn't, my brothers would make sure we had cereal or a sandwich. It seemed fine with everybody. No one was complaining, so I thought that was the way it was supposed to be.

Sometimes in the late evenings, Ma would have Jitter and Dot over to smoke, drink, and chat while Ma got her hair done. On other nights, the apartment would fill up for Ma's house parties.

Nestled in our back room with the TV on, we didn't care much about what was going on in the other parts of the house. When I was in the bunk beds with two older brothers and two younger brothers, we had our own activity going on. I was never in control of the TV when Kevin and Ronald were around. They argued and fought each other over what to watch. Googie and I just went along, and Sloppy Joe was still a baby, so he didn't care one way or the other. Just give little man a bottle, and he was fine.

For some reason, my two big brothers loved scary TV shows that came on late at night. All these shows were in black and white. We used to hunch together at the end of the bed to look over the railing at the TV on the dresser. Pushing and shoving each other, we jockeyed for a good space to see the TV. Sometimes we would be on top of the rumpled sheets and covers; other times we would get underneath. Either way, I always had a swatch of sheet to cover my eyes when I got scared.

So now, here we are, five kids in two bunk beds, late at night, getting ready to watch TV. Scary TV shows with the lights out. Every night, my brothers turned to the horror movies. It was either the wolfman, the mummy, or Dracula. Some poor soul was always getting snatched, attacked, ripped apart, strangled, or bitten when he or she least expected it. Blood dripping, limbs hanging off or missing altogether, menacing fangs, and hair growing from body parts filled our nightly TV viewing.

The wolfman roamed around in wooded areas that looked like Mount Morris Park at night. Dracula, dressed in all black with blood-shot eyes, disappeared into the darkness. The mummy stumbled along with nasty, dirty bandages hanging off everywhere. The music was eerie and scary enough by itself to make me jump.

Because I wanted to be one of the boys, brave and unafraid like them, I never cried or said, "Change the channel." Instead, I cowered under the sheets and peeped out, jumping and shaking from the real and intense terror that I was feeling. People being maimed and killed, ripped apart, and being turned into unholy creatures of the night. Women throwing their hands up in the air and letting loose ear-splitting, blood-curdling screams as they were being savaged by monsters.

Night after night, week after week, and month after month, this was our nightly ritual. Was this age-appropriate viewing for a kid five or six years of old? The thought didn't cross my mind, and Ma or Mike never came in the bedroom to tell us that it wasn't.

Three interesting things I do know, and I am not sure if they can be traced back directly or indirectly to this incessant, reoccurring barrage of nightly terror.

One is that I became deathly afraid of the dark. But then, why wouldn't I? Many of the god-awful things I was seeing on TV were happening to those innocent, unsuspecting people at night, in the dark, in the shadows. I always wanted the hallway or bathroom light on. Also, if I was the last one to fall asleep, I'd make sure the curtains on the window were pushed back, so the light from the streetlamp could spread a soft glow over our room. We could not have any clothes hanging from the curtain rods, because to me, they looked like the vampire and other creatures of the night trying to come in.

Two, sudden loud noises, especially slamming doors, rattled my nerves immensely. Right before someone gets killed in the horror movies, the music is always slow and menacing. Then when the creature is about to strike, the person is cornered, and the sound on the TV reaches a sudden pitch or boom that makes the hair on your body stand on end. How many of these scenes take place behind doors that have been slammed shut and locked? Too many! Any door that slams, whether by the wind or a person, makes me cringe or jump.

And three, the most interesting thing I believe is that possibly because of this continuous onslaught of nightly violence, three of my brothers and I stuttered. Yup, that's right. Anthony, Kevin, Googie, and I all repeated and tripped over our words. We didn't tease each other about it, and no one outside our family did either. Who would want to get a beat-down from four or five Paige brothers?

It was a normal part of our communication growing up. When I tried to say something, everybody would either wait until I got it out or they would finish the sentence for me, and we would move right along. It was the same with the boys. We would either wait for them to finish or finish it for them or ignore the babble and get on with whatever we were doing. Of course, I never thought about teasing my two older brothers when I sounded just like them. And Googie, well, he was just learning to repeat what he was hearing all around him.

I guess a typical conversation among us would take twice as long as it would with other kids. But who cared? When we were young, nobody ever said, "Lord, that child is stuttering something fierce!"

No one offered to help us by saying, "Take your time, speak slowly, think about what you want to say." Nope. It was the bunch of us happily trying to talk over each other as we stumbled, messed up, and repeated the beginning sounds of every other word.

Ma didn't stutter, but she didn't try to help or correct us either. I guess when you have seven children to raise by yourself, you just try to survive. Life was hectic enough, hard enough for her without having to worry about correcting our speech. I know she never gave a second thought to what we were doing or watching back in our bedroom. But

I am sure that the onslaught of nightly terror had some kind of impact on us. I know it made a lasting impression on me.

Late one afternoon, I had the bedroom all to myself. This was the quiet, alone time when I could enjoy my ritual of cartoons and a mayonnaise sandwich. There was no one to argue with about what to watch. No one to bicker with about not having enough room on the bed and no one to share my food with or tell me what to do.

I figured watching from the top bunk would be a cool thing to try, since the older brothers usually claimed that space for themselves. Yeah, that's what I'll do, I'll climb up and look down from my mountaintop. The view that Anthony and Ronald usually had would finally be mine. Our little TV was on a long, old, wooden dresser about four feet from the end of the bunk bed. It had six drawers, each with a round knob to open and close them. That's where all of us kept our clothes and little toys. We each owned a drawer, and better not be caught going in somebody else's.

My outfit for the day was an oversized, faded, T-shirt with holes in it and a pair of pink-and-white panties. Dirty socks that I had worn maybe one day too many kept my feet warm on the linoleum floor. Returning from the kitchen with my snack, I turned the TV on to find the current Jetsons cartoon show.

Now it was time to climb up, settle down, and enjoy the good life. With my sandwich in my left hand, I grabbed the wooden ladder that was on the end of the bed. I had to gingerly hoist myself up on each rung while balancing my food in the other hand. I had never done this before but had seen the boys do it dozens of times. So of course, I thought I could do it too. In my mind, I could do anything they could. It didn't dawn on me that this may not be the case. The idea that this scenario may be a little precarious or slightly dangerous wasn't even a fleeting thought. There was no hesitation, no fear. Why would it be? I was only going five or six rungs up to the top bunk. I was in my own bedroom, where I slept every night.

"It's *The Jetsons*," the TV announcer said in a loud, animated voice.

Shucks, I only had a few seconds to get up and get settled before the fun started. I didn't want to miss a thing. Right arm stretching up for a high wooden rung, then leaning in, I pulled myself up on the first wooden bar. Now I had to try to wrap my sandwich-holding hand and arm around the side of the bunk bed for leverage.

"Whew." This was a little trickier than I thought and taking far more time than I anticipated.

"Dang." The cartoon was starting.

I noticed that my socks were slipping on the slick, wooden rungs.

"Hmmmm." I hadn't planned on that.

Having to balance myself yes, deal with slippery stuff no! I was the Paige boys' little sister. If I could hang on to the back of a moving bus, I could most certainly hang on to a bunk bed ladder. One more rung and I was almost able to reach far enough to place my delectable mayo sandwich on the top bunk sheet. As I made what was to be my last step to the top of the bunk bed, something terrible happened.

I didn't realize it, but my right foot got caught in one of the big holes in front of the oversized T-shirt. As I leaned in to hug the side of the bunk with my left arm, my slippery sock was now tangled in a ragged T-shirt hole. In a split second, I lost my balance, plunging backward as my mayo sandwich flew in the air. I screamed because it happened so suddenly, but no one heard me because there was no one home.

I fell hard, back into the wooden dresser. The force of my body colliding with that solid piece of furniture stunned me. I fell forward on my knees. What the heck just happened? Everything was going so well, going as planned.

Using the palms of my hands, I rose unsteadily to my feet.

"Dang." My back and butt hurt like crazy.

I pulled up my T-shirt and twisted my head so I could see if I had a bruise. To my utter horror, there was a huge open gash on the left side of my behind. My brown skin was pushed in and I could see this bright, pink stuff. I guess it was the inside of my behind. I twisted my waist and head harder to get a better view. If I had a hole in my behind, where was the blood? None was seeping out from the deep butt crevice, there was nothing on the floor. I was puzzled and in pain.

Turning to the dresser, I thought maybe I would find blood, skin, or some of my pink insides plastered somewhere. But still nothing. I did notice that one of the round knobs on the dresser drawer had a wet, shiny, slimy feel to it as I ran my fingers over it. *What in the world?* I had a hole in my butt, caused by a knob on the dresser? This was crazy. I was scared and still a little shaken. I frantically looked around the room, trying to figure out what to do.

Ma would probably be home soon, and I wasn't going tell her what happened. She would make me go to the hospital, and I was deathly afraid of being left there all alone. Let me tell you why.

I had only been to a hospital once before, a couple of years earlier, when I had a high fever that wouldn't break. It was late one night when Ma took me to the hospital not far from where we lived. The nurses told Ma they had to put me in a bathtub of cold water to break the fever. I remember screaming and crying as the nurse and Ma took off my clothes and forced me into the ice-cold water. I kept reaching up for Ma, begging her to take me out.

After what I thought was an eternity, she took me out, dried me off, and put a little cloth gown on me. I had to lie in a bed that had metal bars on the side of it. Ma was probably exhausted herself from all of this, when she looked down at me and announced, "Pippa, I'm going out to get some cigarettes. I'll be right back."

I panicked. The thought of being left alone in this strange place, with these strange people, was just too much for me. I started crying and screaming, this time trying to get out of that hospital prison bed. Two nurses came over and were helping Ma to restrain me. Ma told the nurses she had to run out and would be right back. As they held me down, Ma looked at me and said in a tired voice, "Pippa, I'm just going to the corner; I'll be right back."

I was petrified of being abandoned as my mother disappeared from the room. I was also physically and emotionally drained. Shortly after Ma walked away from me, I cowered in a fetal position and sobbed myself to sleep in that strange hospital bed.

So, you see to me, hospitals were an unfriendly place where you could get lost in those long, endless hallways. Unsmiling people in white coats scurrying along like the roaches I'd seen in our apartment.

Hospitals were a place, in my mind, where parents could leave their kids and never come back.

I was not going to give Ma the opportunity to take me back a second time and leave me with some strange people holding me down. But now, what was I going to do? I was pacing back and forth in our little bedroom, still holding the twisted T-shirt up in my hands, when a voice from behind startled me. I jumped.

"Pippa, what are you doing?" My brother Ron was standing in the doorway.

I must have looked like a deer in headlights, standing there with my panties down and the oversized T-shirt pulled up.

"I-I hurt myself."

"What do you mean?"

By this time, he was walking toward me. I backed up, sheer panic setting in.

"Ron, I fell off the bunk bed and hit the dresser. I hurt myself."

Tears were streaming from my eyes, partly from the pain in my back and butt that were throbbing now, but mostly from the fear of Ron telling Ma what happened.

"Show me," he demanded, turning me around.

"Damn, Pip," he muttered as he looked at my behind. "How the hell did you get a hole in your butt?"

"I fell back and think I hit the dresser drawer knob. Please don't tell Ma," I begged. "She'll, she'll leave me at that hospital again." I stuttered in between heaving sobs.

My brother looked at the dresser knobs and back at my butt, slowly shaking his head. He grabbed me by the arm and said, "Let's go to the bathroom. We gotta cover this up."

"Don't tell Ma." He half-dragged, half-pulled me behind him. "Don't tell on me, Ron," I wailed.

"Come on, girl," he commanded. "I don't have time for this."

Once inside the tiny bathroom, he scrounged around, looking for supplies to cover up the damage to my behind. He found gauze, tape, and a pair of scissors.

"Turn around and lean on the sink."

I didn't think to be embarrassed or modest as my brother worked on patching up the gaping hole I had in my backside. He cut long swatches of gauze, folded it several times, and pressed it on the open wound. I winced from the pressure but didn't say anything. At least he was helping me.

"Put your hand back here and hold this in place," he directed.

I felt the thick wad of gauze. Ron was busy, methodically cutting tape and plastering it to my rear end.

"Pippa, we gotta change this every couple of days and don't get it wet," he finished.

I pulled my panties up and the T-shirt down.

"You not gonna tell Ma on me, are you?" I whispered.

"Girl, I don't have time for you and this mess. But you better find me to change that patch," he ordered.

"I-I will, I promise."

Ron had already put the evidence away and was heading out of the bathroom. I turned my back to the mirror and tried to look at his handiwork. You could see a little bulge in my panties, but when I pulled the T-shirt down, you couldn't see a thing. I felt relieved. This whole ordeal would be a secret between Ron and me, and I would not have to go back to that dreadful hospital. No more trips to the top bunk either. Nope, not for me. I found the bread ends of my mayonnaise sandwich, threw them in the kitchen garbage can, and returned to watch cartoons from the bottom bunk.

Ron changed my bandages every other day. Ma never noticed that I wasn't taking a bath. She would just ask me, "Pippa did you get in the tub tonight?" To which I always replied a quick, "Yeah, Ma."

One evening, there was no one left in the house but Sloppy Joe and me. I don't know where Michael was, probably over at his girlfriend Beverly's house. My three older brothers, Kevin, Ron, and Anthony were with this man named Mr. Boyd, who I guess was a friend of Ma's. Mr. Boyd would often come around and take the boys out. Googie was with his godparents, Mamma Louise and Uncle Steve. I stayed in my room watching TV, with my baby brother sleeping contently, nestled in the rumpled bunk bed sheets and covers. When the last cartoons were done, then shows like *Lassie, The Honeymooners,* or *Dennis the Menace* came on. I'd laugh out loud while snacking on penny candy from the corner grocery store.

By the time these shows were done, it was late and dark outside. The light from the city streetlamp was illuminating my room with a soft glow. I turned on the one room light we had, located in the middle of the ceiling. That wasn't enough light for me. I felt an uneasiness and apprehension start to take hold. My brothers were gone, the baby was sleeping, and the scary TV shows with all those creepy night monsters were coming on soon. I didn't want to be caught alone in my room with them.

What was I to do? I know, I'll sneak in Ma's bed and go to sleep. We rarely did this, because there were so many of us, Ma would have kicked us out anyway. I pulled the blanket over my sleeping brother and tiptoed to Ma's room. As usual, I had on my favorite bedtime outfit, a pair of panties and one of my brother's T-shirts.

By this time, Ma was in the kitchen entertaining Jitter, so she didn't see or hear me as I slipped into her darkened room. I climbed into the large bed, got under the sheet, and pulled the covers up over my head. I curled myself up in a tight ball and prayed that she wouldn't notice the little mound on the edge of her bed. Within a few minutes, I could feel my body starting to relax as I drifted off to sleep. I could hear chatter and laughter coming from the kitchen. I was safe, warm, and not alone.

Sometime later, I thought I felt the bed bounce and the covers pulled and ruffled. I didn't dare move; I didn't want Ma to kick me out and make me go back to my bunk bed, where night monsters might be lurking. The room was pitch black; I couldn't see a thing, but I was wide awake, lying there on the edge of the bed. Suddenly, Ma asked in an irritated voice, "Pippa, why you in my bed?"

"I was scared of the dark and the monsters on TV," I said from underneath the blanket.

"Child, go back to sleep." She pulled me closer to snuggle up next to her. Suddenly, she blurted out, "What is this on your butt?" Her hand had swiped across my backside and felt the mound of gauze and tape.

51

"I-I hurt myself, Ma. I fell on the knob on the dresser in my room," I whispered, suddenly scared.

She flung the covers and sheets back, got out of bed, and turned on the light. "Let me see, sit up." I did as I was told. Ma got behind me and pulled the top of my panties down. "Who put this on you?" she demanded.

"Ron helped me," I whispered, getting more nervous by the second. She took her fingers and pulled back the tape. I could hear her catch her breath at the sight of the large wound in my butt.

"What in the name of Jesus! Ronald knew about this and didn't tell me?" She raised her voice and continued with her interrogation and the examination of my butt.

"I didn't want him to tell you cause I-I was scared you were gonna take me b-back to that hospital and leave me." I tripped and stuttered over my words. I was petrified by now.

"You better be glad this thing is not infected and almost healed." With that, she covered the huge sore and pressed the tape back into place.

"Go back to sleep. No need to go to the hospital now," she muttered, turning off the light and getting back into bed.

She didn't snuggle up against me this time, but she didn't kick me out either. For that I was relieved and grateful. It didn't take long for me to hear her even breathing and light snoring. I knew she was asleep, so I drifted off again.

Hours later, I felt more movement in the bed. Still hugging the edge of the mattress, with the covers completely over my head, I didn't move. I felt the creaking of the box springs; jostling side to side of the uneven, lumpy mattress; the sheets and covers being stretched and pulled off me. Then, there in the dark, I realized Ma and I were not alone in the bed.

A man's voice said, "Open your legs, Ruth. Stop playing, open your legs."

I recognized the high-pitched, distinctive voice. It belonged to one of Ma's male friends who came to her card parties.

"I can't. Pippa is here in the bed."

More movement, more shaking of the mattress.

"Woman, open your damn legs," the voice ordered in the dark.

I was frozen, scared to move an inch. They thought I was asleep, and I wanted to keep it that way.

"You gonna wake up the baby," Ma said.

"Pippa ain't no damn baby, and she's sleep," the man with the high voice said.

By this time, the headboard was hitting up against the wall. *What in the world was going on?* I thought. They weren't playing, because neither one was laughing, but they weren't fighting either.

"Ruth, I came all the way cross town for this. Now open your legs."

"But Pippa," Ma said.

"But Pippa nothing, wider Ruth … that's it … wider," he said with a muffled voice.

The headboard began hitting the wall in an even sort of rhythm. Thump, thump, thump, thump. Ma got quiet letting out an occasional whimper; the man moaned like he was in pain.

I remained still, motionless there in the dark.

7

During this time, Ma was still having her house parties, with crowds of people coming and going. About the only thing that may have seemed different in my young mind was that Mike came around less often. When he did, he and Ma would always end up arguing so loud that my brothers and I quietly retreated into the safety of our bedroom. We would cower together on the bunk beds in the dark. Whatever they were talking about always seemed to end up with him screaming and cursing about her card parties, other men, and money.

Then, over time, the yelling began to morph into something much more sinister.

"Get over here, Ruth," Mike would bellow.

We could hear a clicking sound, the sound of him locking the front door. Ma was literally trapped in there with this big, white, crippled man. My little, petite mom with no way to escape. We could hear him shuffling around the kitchen with his cane, dragging his feet. Apparently, Ma would try to get out of his reach, from the sounds of kitchen chairs and the table being shoved around.

I'd drape my arm around one of my younger brothers in a feeble act of protection. But we were all subjected to the onslaught of anger coming out of Mike's mouth.

"What the hell did I tell you about having all those damn people in here, Ruth?" With this came the sound of a loud slap. Was that his hand or belt? I couldn't tell.

"Ahhhh, no Mike, stop!" My Ma crying, wailing out loud like a little child? Another slap! Then a sound, a hard thud like Ma had fallen on the floor. We could hear chairs being toppled over and the sounds of pots falling, crashing to the floor.

"Mike, noooo." Long, anguished sobs were coming from Ma. Knocking and slapping sounds. Cries of pain and agony making their way from the kitchen to our frightened ears. Accusations and vile curse words spewing from Mike.

There was nothing we could do but huddle in the shadows, of our room. Petrified, terrified. Hoping and praying that whatever made Mike so mad, he wouldn't come and take it out on us. We felt cornered in that little space, trapped like Ma was in the kitchen.

"I needed the money, Mike. The kids needed shoes and food."

Ma was pleading her case as our father moved around the room and she tried to stay out of the reach of his cane and hand. All kinds of awful words were hurled from his mouth. Words I had never heard before, "You bitch, slut, goddamn tramp!" I didn't know what they meant, but I knew they were not good.

"You need to know your damn place, and that's here with these kids, not out in the goddamn streets all the time."

What had Ma done to deserve this? Mike didn't hit us; he didn't curse us. He was always very attentive and caring toward me. We were confused and very, very scared. We didn't dare move or utter a sound. We wanted to become invisible to his wrath, praying that he would forget that we were there in the back room, listening to and witnessing what we would come to know much later as the physical, verbal, and emotional abuse of our mother.

As quickly as the onslaught happened, it would be over with the sound of the front door being unlocked and Mike shuffling out. The slamming door caused me to jump. We could hear Ma quietly sobbing. Gingerly, one by one, we would venture out of the bed and make our way toward the kitchen. By the time I got up enough courage to head that way, Anthony, Ronald, and Kevin had already slipped out the front door. Googie stayed in the room with the baby.

I found my mother sitting at the kitchen table with her head in her hands, still shaking and crying quietly. Her hair and clothes were disheveled. I placed my hand softly on her shoulder.

"Ma?"

When she did raise her head to look at me, my eyes teared up, and I started crying. My mother's eye was swollen almost shut, and her bottom lip was fat and bleeding.

"It's all right, Pippa. Go get me some tissue from the bathroom."

I did as I was told and returned with a big wad of toilet paper. Feeling helpless and not knowing what to say, I just gently rubbed Ma's shoulder.

"It's gonna be okay," she managed to get out as she dabbed at her lip. "Go take care of your brothers."

Ma stood up painfully, slowly. She began picking up chairs and broken dishes strewn around the kitchen, as I retreated to our back room.

Even at six years old, I started to question, who really was Mike? What was this I was witnessing? How was it affecting me, affecting my brothers? What would be the emotional damage, the toll of all that loud arguing, yelling of vile curse words, screaming insults, accusations, and the physical violence?

What happened in front of us began to be a regular occurrence. But nobody talked about it. My brothers never brought it up, I didn't bring it up, and Ma never uttered a word about it. She never bad-mouthed Mike, at least not in front of us. After each of his visits, Ma would straighten the house up, then herself. She would tend to whatever cuts or bruises Mike would leave behind. Then, as if nothing happened, life would go on.

I was left confused, tussling with conflicting mental information from these visits. Mike was still attentive and affectionate toward me when he came around. However, my two oldest brothers stayed away during these encounters. It left the remaining five of us to be held hostage, right along with Ma in that tiny two-bedroom apartment.

Each time, Mike would come, shuffle to a chair, and settle in. But inevitably the atmosphere would change shortly after he and Ma started their kitchen conversations. When she could sense that things were about to change, she would send us all to our room in the back. I guess she didn't want us to watch what was surely going to unfold. Something was brewing, changing from a routine summer shower to a massive, destructive hurricane in a matter of minutes. Right in our kitchen.

There was a sense of tugging going on in my head. On one hand, I found myself caring deeply for this man who treated me so well. Then I would feel a ground swell of guilt because I wanted to hate him for treating Ma the way he did. How could he laugh and play with me, take me places, buy me nice things, then turn around and beat and abuse the woman who made me, who I looked just like?

I began to think that Mike was like the monsters we watched every night on TV. Many of them started out as one thing and then changed into something evil, hideous, and deadly. The wolfman went from being a good-looking, kind man to a raving, howling, killing machine whenever the full moon came out. *Maybe Mike didn't like full moons*, I thought. Or Count Dracula, who stayed quiet, unseen, and sleeping peacefully during the day, but was a blood-sucking, throat-ripping beast at night. Did Mike need more rest? Was he working too hard during the day? Whatever the case, something was causing him to turn into an angry, raving madman whenever he came to our house.

There was no one for me to talk to about this. No one to explain to me why two people who made lots of babies together could not get along. No one to help me understand why the dynamics between Ma and Mike were so different from Sam and Mattie, or Ozzie and Harriet on TV. Why did Mike keep coming around if Ma made him so mad, so angry? Why did Ma keep letting him in? Why didn't we just move far away? So many unanswered questions. So many conflicting feelings and emotions. Who was my loyalty supposed to be to? Which one was I supposed to be angry at? Which one to love? It was a constant tug of war that never seemed to end.

8

One early-afternoon visit, Mike changed things up. He came in, spoke to Ma briefly, giving her some dollar bills, and then turned to me.

"You wanna go out, Pippa?" he asked from his kitchen seat. I was passing through on my way outside to play. I stopped in my tracks and looked at him, then at Ma. She didn't look upset or distraught. There were no signs of new cuts or bruises. I was relieved, because if there were, I was going to choose to stay home, close to Ma.

"Can I, Ma?" I begged, with the whining voice of a spoiled child.

"Yeah, go in the back and get a jacket," she answered softly while puffing on her cigarette.

I did as I was told, quickly running to the bedroom. I was elated; this was just like old times. Mike and me hanging out, just the two of us. This was the man I cared for, the one who was gentle, quiet, and affectionate with me. The man who would let me sit on his lap and play with his big dog. The same one who filled my piggy bank and my Christmas stocking. I could skip, spin around, and have all kinds of fun with Mike looking at me with a twinkle in his eye.

Where was the other half of this Dr. Jekyll and Mr. Hyde team? The one who caused my brothers and me to run and cower in our bunk beds? The monster who inflicted torture and pain on Ma? I didn't know and didn't care to find out. I didn't want to do or say anything that would provoke the furious Mr. Hyde to appear.

Mike and I left the apartment to begin our short stroll to the subway station. We took our time because he was using his cane and couldn't walk fast. This gave me time to take in my surroundings. As usual, I could see grownups and kids were everywhere. I could see them, all ages. People leisurely hanging out or scurrying to their next destination, laughing and talking loudly, or quietly intent and focused on whatever was in front of them. Lots of cars, taxis, and buses traveled up and down the streets. Periodically, some man or lady would call out to Mike, "Mike, what was last night's number?"

"Hey, Mike, what's up, what's new with you?"

"Who's that cutie pie with you, Mike? Your girlfriend?"

We continued our way down the sidewalk to the 125th Street subway station. Along the way, we passed long rows of brownstone houses like the one our apartment was in. As we made our way toward the middle of the block, we could see a small crowd of people up ahead. There an ambulance and police car were double parked in the street.

"Oh, oh," I blurted out loud half to myself, half to Mike. "Somebody's hurt."

He never said a word, just kept carefully and methodically making his way along the cracked, uneven sidewalk. Then suddenly, without warning, a strong, foul smell hit me! Something reeked, the smell so powerful and disgusting, I thought I was going to get sick on my stomach. The odor hung in the air like a huge, poisonous cloud.

"What is that smell?" I yelled out, dramatically screwing up my face and pinching my nose shut.

"Do you smell that?" I asked, looking at Mike.

I couldn't even compare it to Sloppy Joe's doo-doo. This was different, something I had never experienced. It wasn't like the stink of my burning hair or the gas that came from the top of our stove or the black exhaust from the city buses. I had nothing to compare it to.

As we got closer, the smell grew in intensity. I thought I was going to gag. Mike made his way to the outer core of the crowd, and rather than push through, he stepped out into the street to go around. I followed him. But my eyes stayed focused on the throng of people. They were all looking upward, some pointing toward an open second-floor window. Walking past the group, I could hear snatches of conversation.

"Yeah, up there. That's where they found him."

"Poor guy."

"I wonder how long he been in there?"

"Who found him?"

"Nobody, somebody complained about the smell and called the cops."

"What a way to go, all alone."

By this time, Mike and I were passing the ambulance, which had its back doors swung wide open. An officer standing near the police car was writing something on a small pad. Another was standing, keeping watch from the middle step of the brownstone. Suddenly, one yelled out in a take-charge voice, "All right everyone, back! Move back! Let 'em through!"

The crowd took a few steps back. Just then, the front doors of the building opened, and an even stronger blast of foul, pungent air descended on us. Two men dressed in all white were carrying a covered stretcher gingerly down the steps. People were covering their faces with their hands, arms, caps, pulled-up shirts, or whatever else they could use. No one, including me, was standing there acting like we were breathing in fresh summertime air.

Mike had never stopped walking, but I was paralyzed. What on earth was that huge bulge under the white sheet? Was that what was causing the horrific smell? The men in white made their way down the steps. Control cop was in front of them, ordering the people to, "Move back! Outta the way!"

I didn't move, mesmerized by the whole scene.

Suddenly, I heard, "Pip, Pippa, get over here!"

I shook my head, snapping back to attention just as the stretcher was being loaded into the back of the ambulance. Mike had made his way to the front of the emergency vehicle and was ready to step back up on the curb.

"Get over here, I said," Mike yelled out to me.

I turned, ran toward him, and hopped on the sidewalk.

"What was that smell? Did you smell it? What happened? They said it was a man under the sheets. Was it, Mike? Was it a man? Why did he smell like that?"

I blurted out questions rapid fire style, not giving him the opportunity to answer one before I shot off another. He kept walking, looking ahead. I was by his side now, keeping pace with him, waiting for an answer.

"Did somebody hurt him? Was he dead like the people in the monster movies on TV?" I continued my interrogation.

Finally, Mike stopped to catch his breath and looked down at me. Sighing, he began to slowly explain, "Yeah, Pip, that was a dead man under the sheets. He had been dead a long time in that house. That's why it smelled like that. He probably didn't have any family. Sad."

I realized the seriousness of the situation from Mike's demeanor and grabbed his free hand.

"Yup, that's very sad. I feel bad that he didn't have any family."

We walked in silence until we arrived at the subway station. It had been a long time since I had ridden one with my brother Michael and Beverly. I perked up as Mike got the tokens that we needed from the woman behind the glass partition.

"Where we going?" I was curious.

"You'll see. It's a surprise."

"Tell me, tell me!" I pressed, getting excited.

"It's somewhere you've never been. Now that's all I'm saying," Mike answered as he put the token in the turnstile, and I pressed my stomach against it and pushed my way through. He did the same.

We walked along the subway platform with the crowd of people until we came to a bench against the wall, where we sat down. A few minutes later, I could hear the train approaching from the blackened tunnel. Loud, rumbling sounds, then I could see the bright light from the first car. The train slowed as it entered the station. Everyone stood up or stepped forward as the train finally screeched to a loud stop. The double doors slid open, and Mike and I stepped inside, while others who were inside pushed their way out.

Settling on the hard subway seat, I pressed my body next to Mike's. Looking back, we were probably a sight to see. The little Black girl laughing and chatting away, sitting next to the older, white crippled man. Nobody stared, and nobody commented, at least not out loud. I was oblivious, in a world of my own.

We rode for about an hour, I think. With each passing stop, the train got more crowded, with people standing too close in front of us, hanging on to the leather straps above our heads. Everybody was shifting, leaning, and shaking, in time with the moving train.

"Okay, we're here," Mike announced as the train slowed then jerked to a stop.

We got off, and everybody seemed to be going in the same direction. Exiting the underground tunnel, we followed the masses outside into the blaring sunlight. We walked for about five or ten minutes, then I saw it! The outline of a huge, colorful entrance with flags, clown faces, and balloons.

"Coney Island! Coney Island!" I squealed, jumping and dancing around as much as I could while Mike held on to me with his free hand. I had only heard about this magical place from my brother Michael and Penny, Dot's son. I guess they were old enough to go to Coney Island by themselves. But Ma had never brought us here. I was thrilled, excited beyond belief.

There was so much to do! So many rides to pick from, so many strange things to see, so many games to play, and so many food vendors to taste the goodies they were selling!

"Okay, little girl, where do you want to start?"

Mike stood in a line and bought a roll of tickets. I tried to do it all. We played shoot the duck, bust the balloons with darts, basketball throw, and several other games. I was competitive, of course, thanks to my brothers, and thought I could beat Mike at everything. As we strolled up and down the lanes, there were fun rides on each side. I wanted to try them all—the Ferris wheel, caterpillar, spinning saucers, bobsled, merry-go-round, and flying swings. Mike did not ride but waited for me by the exit gate of each ride. In between a host of games and thrill rides, I indulged in hot dogs, pizza, candied apples, and ice-cream cones.

It was a full day and night of fun. Right before it was time to go, Mike said he was going to get on one ride. I was surprised but elated. We walked a little further and got in at the end of a long line.

"What is this ride called?" I wanted to be sure I had all the names, so I could brag to my brothers.

"It's the Cyclone," he answered.

Well, that word didn't mean a thing to me with my still-developing vocabulary. Now, if he had said roller coaster, I would have known what he was talking about. At least I heard that term from my brothers, but not Cyclone.

Slowly the line moved forward, and we neared this extremely tall, wooden structure. When it was our turn, we gave the man our tickets and walked to the nearest empty ride seats. After settling in and securing the leather strap and bar around our waists, the line of cars lurched forward. Up, up we slowly climbed. Looking over the side, I could see all the bright lights and action below. *This is amazing*, I thought!

Then, without warning, the ride plunged downward, catching me totally by surprise! Speeding down the tracks, knocking the breath from me, whipping my head back. I was petrified as I gripped the metal bar in front of me and tried to bury my face in Mike's shoulder. If I was going to die, I didn't want to see how. My body lurched from side to side as we sped down the rails, the wind ripping across my face, my eyes tightly shut. I was frozen with fear, but I could hear Mike laughing.

Up, down, around twists and turns, when was this torture going to end? Abruptly, the cars screeched and jerked to a stop. We exited the ride, and I made my way down the ramp on trembling legs. My whole body was shaking. When we cleared the crowds, Mike finally paused and looked down at me.

"Did you like the ride, Pip?"

"I-I never wanna, wanna go on that ride again." My chest heaved as tears welled up in my eyes.

My response was water trickling down my shaking legs, forming a small puddle at my feet, as I peed on myself.

9

When I was around the age of seven, my mother took me to a crowded clinic, where a lady in a long, white jacket stuck a needle in my left shoulder. Ma said I needed to get vaccinated in order to start school. P.S. 24 was a few blocks from our house. Ma enrolled me in first grade, as the school didn't have kindergarten. She showed me where my class was and introduced me to my teacher. I remember she was a very dark-skinned lady named Mrs. White. I thought that was so strange, as her name did not match her skin color.

This was the school that my brothers Kevin and Ronald went to. They were used to walking back and forth by themselves, so I just tagged along. My first few weeks were uneventful as I settled into the daily routine. So many rules. No talking. Raise your hand. Walk quietly in the halls. Keep your hands to yourself. Don't touch anyone else's belongings. Color inside the lines. On and on and on, so much stuff to remember.

What I do remember is those darn Dick and Jane books. I hated those books. Blond-headed, happy, little white kids running around all day chasing that dog named Spot.

"Come, Dick. Look, Dick, see Spot run! Run, Spot, run. Spot can run." I thought this was ridiculous. Nobody I knew spoke like that, and for the life of me, I couldn't understand why those poor kids spoke like that either.

School life dragged on, with me learning about the cheerful life of Dick and Jane and trying to memorize a long list of rules. One day, the teacher told me to stay in my seat after she had dismissed the rest of the class. I was puzzled, of course, but did as I was told. A few minutes later, standing there in the classroom doorway was Ma. *What in the world was she doing here?* I thought. I knew I hadn't done anything to get into trouble, at least not at school.

The two of them approached my desk, Ma glaring down at me and the teacher looking perplexed.

"I don't know what's wrong with your daughter, Ms. Paige. She won't answer to her name!" Mrs. White stated.

With her hand on her hip, Ma said in an irritated voice, "What do you mean she won't answer?"

"Every time I call on her, she just ignores me."

Ma looked at me, incredulous, shaking her head.

"What's wrong with you? Why aren't you answering when the teacher calls on you?"

Now I was confused. "Ma, she never calls on me. She always calls on the other kids, but not me," I said, my eyes wide, looking at Ma.

With that accusation, Ma turned to Mrs. White for her explanation.

"Ms. Paige, I call on Lutricia just as much as I call on any of the other kids. What she is saying is simply not true."

Hearing that, I looked at Ma. "Who is Lu-Lu-Lutricia?" I stuttered.

They both looked at me. The teacher was stunned, and so was I.

"Oh, now I see what the problem is, Mrs. White. We all call her Pippa at home. Her brothers couldn't pronounce Lutricia, so they nicknamed her Pippa."

"Well, that's the name on her school records, and that's what we will have to call her," Mrs. White said definitively.

I stood up and looked both of them in the eye and said, "I ain't answering to no Lu-Lutricia or whoever that is. My name is Pippa!"

"I don't know what you are going to do, Ms. Paige, but I will have to continue to use her legal name. We don't use nicknames for our students."

Resigned, Ma said, "I'll work with her. I'll see what I can do."

I never did learn to spell or write Lutricia on my papers. I continued to put Pippa at the top of every sheet. By the end of that school year, Ma told me she had changed my name to Carolyn. I didn't like that name much better, but I could handle it, and I did. I was Pippa at home and Carolyn at school.

My time at P.S. 24 remained uneventful until one day I was walking home after school by myself. I had mastered the route, and Ma trusted me to make it home on my own.

Suddenly, from behind me down the street, I heard a group of kids yelling.

"There she is! Pippa, we gonna whip your butt! Get her!"

I turned to see three girls and a boy running in my direction. They were from my school and a little bit older than me.

Not knowing what to do, my flight instincts kicked in, and I took off running like my life depended on it—because it did!

"When I catch you, Imma kick your tail," somebody screamed.

"You just wait, you just wait." The screams were getting closer, and I was getting out of breath.

I could tell they were gaining on me, and I wasn't going to be able to outrun them. Stopping in the middle of the street, I turned and faced them as they ran up and surrounded me. I was scared out of my mind. Four against one wasn't exactly an even fight.

One girl got up close in my face and pointed her finger.

"You lying dog, you lied on my brother," she hissed, "and Imma whip your tail."

"Yeah, you lied, and your brothers jumped him," the smallest girl chimed in.

"You gonna pay for that!"

I turned around in circles, not knowing who the first blow was going to come from.

Then I looked at the boy and recognized him. He was a neighborhood kid who played with Kevin and Ronald. I ran into him one day in his apartment hallway, as I was on an errand for Ma. He had stopped in the dimly lit stairwell, turned around, and asked me if I wanted to see something. Of course, curiosity took over, and I said sure. At this he unzipped his pants and pulled out his pecker. I remember recoiling in disgust and telling him I was going to tell my brothers what he did. When I got home, I told four of my brothers what happened with the stinky pee-pee boy. Knowing my brothers, they did catch this kid and whip his tail.

There I was, surrounded by three angry girls and one guilty boy. He wasn't saying anything, just pacing back and forth like a nervous, caged animal. We looked at each other. He knew he deserved whatever justice the Paige brothers had inflicted on his stink behind. He wasn't going to fess up, and there was no sense in me pleading my case. They had already made up their minds that I was lying on their brother.

Without another word, the biggest girl in the group grabbed me by my hair and started pounding my head and face with her fist. I knew I wasn't going to survive this onslaught. If she got tired, another one would just pick up where she left off. What was I going to do? She was swinging me around like a little rag doll. Not being able to withstand another blow to my head, I lunged at her as she pulled me closer for another hammering blow. Opening my mouth wide, I bit into her chest. I chomped down as hard as I could, getting a mouthful of blouse and skin. Holding on for dear life, I felt her release the grip she had on my head.

"She's biting me!" the bully screamed out in agonizing pain.

Yes, I was, as hard as I could. I finally opened my mouth and released her. She stumbled back, grimacing with a look of utter surprise on her face as she clutched at her chest. My sudden attack caught them all off guard.

"She bit you. She bit you?"

The other three couldn't believe it, crowding around her as she pulled up her blouse, crying in agony.

I took this as my cue and turned to run, since their focus wasn't on me. Racing down the street, I was determined to make it home in one piece. But that wasn't going to be the case, as they were after me again. I wouldn't survive another brutal beating, which I was sure all four would probably take part in, since the first beat down hadn't gone the way they planned.

By the sounds of the yelling, screaming, and cursing behind me, I knew I wasn't going to make it to the safety of my house and protective brothers. Up ahead was a school that had an extremely high chain-link fence enclosing a courtyard. I took a gamble and started to climb up, higher and higher. Straddling the top of the fence, I turned and looked down into the courtyard. If these bullies climbed up, I would be forced down into the courtyard and cornered, with no way out. Panic set in, but I stayed precariously perched on top of the fence, one leg on each side.

"Come down here, and we gonna whip your ass," one of my tormentors screamed.

"You gotta come down, and when you do, Imma finish what I started," the overweight, injured bully yelled.

"Yeah, you made my sister bleed. You gonna pay for that," the nasty boy snarled.

I looked down at that hostile little crowd of bullies and thought to myself, *Please don't let them be able to climb up here.* But they didn't. Apparently, everybody in that group was afraid of heights. Not one of them put their feet on that fence to climb up. They continued their ranting and raving for about ten minutes—me not coming down and them not coming up.

Finally, the big girl said while still gripping the front of her blouse with both hands, "Imma tell my mother, and she gonna come over your house and whip you and your momma's tail."

With that, she turned on her heels and started marching back up the street with her two friends and nasty brother.

I guess all that running, chasing, and climbing I had been doing with my brothers paid off after all.

10

Months rolled on, life continued up and down the block and in our house. Ma's house parties and her beatings by Mike were a part of our life. They were almost routine, a sad part of our day-to-day reality. It was a roller-coaster way of life that we had grown accustomed to. It was the only life we knew. That was about to change soon.

Early one evening, a few buildings down from our house, I was challenging my friend to see who could jump from the highest step. There were about ten steps, and we each took turns showing off, as we dared each other to go higher. We started at about the fourth step from the bottom. She made it to the sixth step, and I was determined to beat her. I looked down at her from the seventh step.

"I bet you can't do that," she taunted me.

"Watch me!"

And with that, I bent both my knees, swung my arms back, and propelled myself off the steps. Oh yes, I made it! But I landed in a crumpled heap, twisting my ankle and hollering out in agony. She ran over, trying to help me up. I could barely stand and put any pressure on my right foot. The pain was intense. All I could do was lean on her and try to balance on my other foot.

There was a man and woman on the next stoop, watching all this unfold.

"What's up, why she crying like that?" the man asked in a deep, husky voice.

My friend answered, "She hurt her foot and can't walk."

"Bring her over here. We'll take care of her." The lady came down the steps where she had been standing, smoking her cigarette.

My friend held on to me as I limped over. The two grownups met us in front of the gate leading to the ground-level apartment.

"We got her." The man waved his hand. "Go on now," he said, dismissing my friend.

The woman took me by my underarm and guided me into a dimly lit apartment. She told me to sit down, as the man closed the door behind him. He stood by the door like he was guarding it. The lady handed me a cold, wet rag and told me to put it on my ankle. Then, without taking her eyes off me, she backed up to the door where the man was still standing.

Suddenly, that familiar feeling of fear began to sweep over me. They stood there looking at me for a few seconds, neither saying a word. The woman was puffing on her cigarette, the man with his arms folded across his chest. My eyes darted around the room, with the realization that there was no way out. They were standing in front of my only possible escape. I didn't know these people, and Ma and my brothers didn't know where I was.

"What do you want to do with her?" the woman asked, still staring at me.

"I don't know, I'm thinking," he responded, long and slow.

At this, panic really started to set in. My ankle was throbbing, but my heart was pounding! What in the world were these people gonna do with me? I looked from him to her, the door was closed behind them. I could tell from the light coming in from the windows that it was starting to get dark outside.

"What's your name, little girl?" she asked in a monotone voice, holding the cigarette in one hand and slowly tapping her cheek with her finger.

"Pippa," I whispered. "Ruth's my ma, and Mike is my dad."

At this, they both stood up a little straighter.

"Mike? Big Mike is your dad?" the man said in a surprised voice. They both looked at each other. The man backed away from the door and opened it.

"Get her butt outta here. I don't want no shit with Mike."

The woman came over and helped me up. She walked me out the door and back to the sidewalk. The man never moved; it was like something had spooked him. I didn't care. I was just glad to be outside, free, and not cornered in that apartment with them. A flood of relief washed over me as I slowly hobbled home.

When I finally made it to my house twenty minutes later, it was dark outside except for the city streetlights. Still walking with a pained limp, I made my way inside to our front door, which was slightly ajar. Pushing it open, I saw that all the lights were out. It was quiet, so I knew no one was home. I slowly made my way across the kitchen floor to where I knew the light switch was.

Suddenly, my foot hit something hard, and I toppled forward. I landed on a body, in the dark, in the middle of my kitchen. I screamed at the top of my lungs as I pushed myself off the person lying on our floor. I was crying out loud, trying to stand up and make my way back to the front door, which was still wide open.

I was a mess! This was too much in one day. Hurting my ankle, being held hostage in a strange house, and now falling over a dead body in my own kitchen. To say I was terrified would be an understatement. I was traumatized.

As I backed closer to the door, someone appeared with a flashlight. It was the elderly white lady from across the hall. Clutching her bathrobe tightly, she aimed the light at my face.

"Why are you screaming, Pippa? What happened?"

"There's, there's a dead man on the floor, right there." I pointed downward in the direction of the body.

"Wait right here. I'll turn on the light," she said, moving to the wall where the switch was located.

As soon as she turned on the light, we both looked down. She moved toward the heap on the floor, but I stayed pressed up against the wall.

"Pippa, it's your mother." She looked at me. I started crying all over again.

"Is-is she all right? Is she all right? Is she d-d-dead?" I stuttered.

The neighbor kneeled beside my mother and gently shook her. "Ruth, Ruth can you hear me?" Ma let out a soft moan but did not move.

At this I yelled out, "Ma, Ma, get up. It's me, Pippa." She still didn't move. The kind lady stood up and straightened her robe.

"She's just sleeping. Come on, you can spend the night at my house. I'll leave the light on, so your mother can see when she wakes up."

We left Ma there on the kitchen floor and went across the hall. I spent the night in the biggest, softest bed I had ever seen. Late the next morning, the kind lady made me some poached eggs. That was my first experience with poached eggs. I didn't like the way they looked or tasted but dared not say anything. I sat at her huge wooden table, which had lots of tiny statues on it. On the walls were painted pictures of birds, fruit, and forest scenes. The apartment was crowded, with lots of old-looking things I had never seen before. As I ate my poached egg and toast, I wondered how in the world she got all this stuff in her tiny apartment.

When I finished eating, she said, "Okay, young lady, let's go see if your momma is home."

Ma was home, sitting at the kitchen table. That was a relief for me, just knowing that she wasn't still lying on the cold floor, passed out.

"Ruth, I kept Pippa with me last night."

"Thanks. That was real kind of you. I had a bad headache last night."

The old, white lady who had shown me so much kindness turned and left.

"Ma, where's everybody at?" I asked.

Rubbing her head, then lighting up a cigarette, she slowly responded, "Well, I guess your baby brother and Googie are with Momma Louise and Uncle Steve. And the rest of your brothers are with Big Gardiner somewhere."

Momma Louise and Uncle Steve were Googie's godparents. They lived down the street in an apartment over the neighborhood deli. For some reason, they took a special interest in Googie and treated him like he was theirs. They spoiled him with extra gifts when it was Christmas and his birthday. He could go over their house anytime he wanted, to eat, sleep, or play. He even had his own room at their house.

Big Gardiner was a city cop, I think. His grown-up name was Mr. Boyd. All the young guys around Kevin and Ronald's age loved him, but my brothers were the only kids who could call him Big Gardiner.

He was not married and did not have any kids of his own. I never knew what the relationship was between him and Ma. And I don't know why my baby brother was named after him.

Whenever he came to our house, he didn't ask Ma if my brothers could go with him; they just grabbed their things and ran out the door. He took them to the movies, the park, and the swimming pool. When it was cold outside, he took them to a nearby gym to play basketball. He bought them gifts and clothes.

I could sense that this man did not like me, but I didn't know why. He never spoke to me or even looked at me when he came to the house. I remember distinctly the day he came into our bedroom where we were watching TV. He had a brown paper bag full of huge cookies, the kind I used to see at the deli that Mike took me to. All my brothers except the baby crowded around, clamoring about like he was Santa Claus. He made a fuss, holding each cookie up in the air as my brothers jumped and reached for it. One by one, he gave each of the boys a cookie. When he finished, he looked around satisfied and walked out. He never looked at me or offered me a cookie.

One evening, everyone was gone, just Ma and me left in the house. I did my usual thing. I retreated to the comfort and solitude of our bedroom, relishing the fact that I had it all to myself. Hour after hour and TV show after show, I entertained myself, while eating bologna sandwiches, until I drifted off to sleep.

At some point during the night, a loud slamming door jolted me awake. I was disoriented at first, looking wildly around my darkened room. Then I heard it. The bolting of the locks on the apartment door. Shuffling feet and kitchen chairs sliding across the floor.

"No, Mike, no." It was Ma's voice. She was pleading again and scared.

Mike bellowed, "What the hell did I tell you, Ruth? You don't know where the hell your damn kids are."

I could hear him moving about the kitchen. Ma must have been trying to get out of his way when I heard a solid thud. She screamed out in agony.

"Mike you don't have to do this. Don't hit me no more."

I heard another hard-cracking sound as Mike's cane struck something. I could hear the sound of someone pushing the table across the kitchen floor, toppling more chairs.

"You got seven goddamn kids and don't know where the hell they are. And taking money from me every week. For what, Ruth? For what?"

Dishes were breaking and things being knocked off the counter. Covering half my face with a blanket, I crouched in the corner of my bottom bunk bed and pressed my back into the wall. The feeling of terror took over me. Just like when I was in those strangers' house the other day, but this time more intense. I felt trapped again. No way out but through the kitchen where Ma was being brutally beaten by Mike. I was scared to death, didn't know what to do, didn't move. Paralyzed.

I heard a loud, agonizing cry of pain from Ma and more vile words coming out of Mike's mouth.

"Get over here bitch. I'm not through with you yet. You got some more of this coming."

I could hear his cane slapping into objects, then a very loud crash like he tripped and fell on the floor.

"Shit, you wait till I get up off this god-damn floor, you just wait."

More bumping and banging sounds when Ma threw open my door and screamed, "Pippa, get up!" Before I could move, she reached out and snatched me by the arm.

"Come on." She had a long, open split on her nose. Blood was streaming down her face and all over the front of her blouse.

Were we going right back to the kitchen where Mike was going crazy? Thoughts flew around my head but were quickly answered, as Ma rammed her fist into our bedroom glass window struggling to open it. She was like a wild woman, possessed, with one thought in mind: escape. The shards of glass ripped through the skin on her fist and arm, causing more blood to spew out. But she was determined to get away from her abuser, her tormenter, the man who made her life a living hell.

She lifted me up and pushed me out the window. As I turned around, she was coming through. We were both panicked as we heard Mike's voice at the bedroom door.

"Ruth, where the hell you going?" he roared. "You not taking Pippa with you."

But Ma never looked back, and neither did I.

11

After that last violent incident at the house, things changed. Mike didn't come around anymore. If I wanted to see him, I would run over to Sam's Barber Shop. He never asked about Ma or the boys, so I never brought them up either. The conversation was usually about school, what I watched on TV, or where we were going to grab a bite to eat.

At home, my older brothers stayed away from the house much more often. I'm not sure why. After school, Ronald and Kevin went straight to the cop's house and didn't come home until it was time for bed. Most days, Googie was over at Momma Louise and Uncle Steve's house. So, Ma, baby Sloppy Joe, and I were usually the only ones home. She kept busy writing numbers out on little slips of paper, smoking, and drinking her beer.

There were no more house parties. Jitter and Dot came around less often, and I didn't get my hair done as regularly as I used to. My brothers weren't there to make me a hot grilled cheese sandwich in the afternoons. The baby and I ate lots of cold cereal and mayonnaise or ketchup sandwiches during this time. Ma always seemed quiet and distracted, so I tried to stay out of her way as much as possible.

Christmas Eve finally came, and I was so excited. Mike hadn't been buying me new clothes or toys in a long time. So, I knew Santa Claus was going to be quite generous this year, to make up for the lean times.

Ma, my brothers, and I walked to a nearby corner lot where men were selling trees of all sizes. We got a tiny Christmas tree with multicolored bulbs and set it up in the living room. I decided to sleep on the couch, which was right across from the tree. I was going to stay up all night and wait for Santa Claus. The house was quiet as I lay there waiting and waiting, afraid to close my eyes.

Santa Claus never came that night. He didn't drink the small glass of milk or taste the two cookies I left on a plate for him. That was so strange to me. Why did he skip over our house? I had been good and hadn't gotten a whipping in a long, long time.

When Ma finally woke up, I asked her, "Where's our presents? There's nothing under the tree. I waited up all night for Santa Claus." I remember the look in her eyes.

"Pippa, there's no Santa Claus, and I don't have money for presents. Y'all not getting anything this year."

That was too much reality for me to comprehend. No presents; no fat, jolly old man with reindeer; nothing. Surprisingly, I did not have a temper tantrum or bust out crying hysterically. I sat alone stunned, in disbelief, on the living room couch, looking at the little tree with the brightly twinkling lights. Not one wrapped present for me or anyone else was under our tree. A sad, empty feeling washed over me as tears trickled down my face.

Shortly after my life-altering knowledge about Santa Claus never visiting our house again, we had a new, real visitor enter our world. His name was Ray. Apparently, he was Ma's new boyfriend. He'd appear around dinnertime and was often still there when I fell asleep.

Ray was dark brown, medium built, had short hair, and smelled like something he called Old Spice. He was quiet spoken. I liked that, no drama. He didn't raise his voice or curse often when he talked. I used to think to myself, *He is so different from Mike. Maybe that's why Ma likes him.*

Apparently, Ray had a job, because when he spent the night, he had to get up in the mornings and leave. When he returned, if Ma hadn't cooked, he would get in the kitchen and start rattling pots and pans. He loved to fry pork chops with onions. The house smelled good from the aroma of food cooking. We licked our fingers, while feasting on Ray's delicious meals.

Often, I'd hear Ray and Ma talking about the day's number and what they wanted to play. Taking money out of his pocket, he would tell Ma what number to play for him and to be sure to buy him some Ballentine Ale. I don't know who drank the most, but when they both were drinking, the whole room stunk with the smell of beer. I couldn't stand it when they talked loudly or had a big laugh, because the foul beer odor rushed out of their mouths and filled the tiny room.

I stayed out of Ray's way because he was still an outsider to me. I didn't like him, nor did I dislike him. I guess you could say I tolerated him as much as a little kid could. In my opinion, he was just a man who came in and out of Ma's house, often overextending his visits. If he wasn't in the kitchen whipping up some sausage and eggs or smothered chicken, I had little use for him. Plus, Mike was still a part of my life. I felt a tug of allegiance to him, even though he and Ma were no longer together. Ray didn't laugh or joke with us. He didn't play games or take us anywhere. Unless we were running to the store to pick up something for him, we all kept our distance as much as possible in that small apartment. He seemed to make Ma a little happier when he warmed her bed at night or gave her money.

One rare Sunday evening, most of my brothers were home. We all had our fill of Ray's cooking and were watching whatever shows came on TV. The boys were in the back room, and I was in the living room, where the larger black-and-white TV was.

I had on an oversized T-shirt that belonged to one of my brothers and settled myself on the couch. Eventually I dozed off and fell asleep. I awoke to someone lifting me off the couch. The living room was dark, except for the light coming from the TV. I could hear Ray saying, "Pippa's sleep," and Ma somewhere in the background saying, "Take her to her room, Ray."

I was still a little groggy, but I remember being cradled in Ray's arms as he moved slowly toward the hallway. My head and shoulders were in the crook of one of his arms. My legs were draped over his other arm, when I felt it. I didn't have any panties on. His hand was between my legs, his fingers slowly moving. The light was off in the hallway; it was dark. Ray didn't see that I had opened my eyes. I was totally aware of where I was at that point and what was being done to me. Ray pushed his finger in my private part and rubbed hard. I jerked and squirmed. He quickly removed his hand and bent down to lay me on the bottom bunk bed, where my two younger brothers were sprawled out. He turned and left.

Lying there in my dark bedroom, I was wide awake. What just happened? Did he really do that to me? Rub his hand on my bare butt, then push his finger in my tootie? He wasn't supposed to do that. Why did he do that? Do I tell Ma? Would she believe me? Or would she get mad at me? Shouldn't she get mad at Ray if I told her?

A thousand thoughts seemed to crowd my mind. I didn't know what to do. The more I lay there in the dark thinking, the madder I got. I had to do something, but what?

The house was quiet; someone had turned the TV off in the living room. Eventually I stood up and tiptoed down the hallway toward Ma's bedroom. The door was open, and I could hear her and Ray snoring. I slipped into the kitchen, flipped on the light, and looked around. Feeling betrayed, violated, and angry, I wanted to grab a knife and kill this man. But I was too little; that plan was not going to work. What to do, what to do?

Then it hit me. Ray had to go to work in a few hours. He always kept his khaki-colored work pants hanging in the hallway closet. I opened the closet door, found the pants, and took them out. One by one, I gripped the opening of the pants in my hand. I leaned against the wall for support, raised my leg and put my foot in the middle of the zipper, where I knew his private thing hung in his pants. I pulled and ripped. *How dare he touch me down there! That's nasty; he's nasty. I'll show him.*

I made sure each pair of pants had a large tear, either in the front or the back. When I was finished with my revenge plan, I carefully folded each pair of pants along the crease and hung it back on the hanger. I put them back in the same spot inside the closet and quietly closed the door. Making my way back to my bedroom, I thought to myself, *That'll show him. He won't mess with me no more.*

A couple of hours later, I heard Ma and Ray arguing in the hallway.

"Look at my damn pants, Ruth. How the hell am I supposed to go to work?"

"Well, Ray, I don't know what you expect me to do."

"Wake Pippa up. She did this shit."

"You don't know that, Ray."

"Yes, I do, she did this to my work pants. All of them."

"Ray, you don't know that. You just can't blame Pippa when there's seven kids in this house."

"She did it, Ruth. Pippa did this shit."

"Why would she do that, Ray? Tell me. You don't have any proof that she did that."

They went back and forth like this for several minutes—Ray yelling and cursing, Ma trying to reason with him, which sounded logical to me. If you have proof, spit it out. If you don't, shut the heck up and go on to work.

Needless to say, Ma never questioned me about the ripped pants, and Ray never touched me again.

PART TWO

Hell

12

It was a weekday morning in late autumn. The temperature was falling, and there was a cool crispness in the city air. It was a few weeks before my eighth birthday, and I should have been in school, but Ma didn't wake me up. There was muffled movement and talking coming from the kitchen. Making my way in that direction, I heard Dot's voice.

"I'll keep the baby till you come back, Ruth. Don't worry about him."

"This is a mess, Dot. I don't know what I'm going to do."

"Let me know how it goes. Everything will be all right."

"They gonna try and take my kids from me, I know it." Ma was shaking her head as she paced from one side of the kitchen to the other.

I was standing in the hallway as Dot, cradling my fully clothed baby brother in her arms, walked out of the apartment.

Turning to me, Ma said, "Pippa, go wake up Googie, and y'all get dressed. We gotta go downtown."

"What's the matter, Ma, what happened?"

Ma snapped, "Just do what I said."

An hour later, the three of us were piled in the back of a yellow cab, making our way through the city streets. My face pressed into the passenger window as I took in the busy morning sights. Ma looked at Googie and me. I could tell by her demeanor all morning that something serious was bothering her. I didn't know what it was or where we were going.

In a quiet, solemn voice, she finally said, "Pippa, Googie, listen to me. Some people want to talk to us. They want to talk to y'all." We both turned and looked up into Ma's face.

"These people are gonna ask y'all a lot of questions. Questions about me, you, your brothers, and what goes on in our house."

"What people?" I asked, puzzled.

"Why, Ma?" Googie said.

"Somebody called downtown and said some bad things about me. About me and Mike. Now these city people wanna talk to me and you kids. They gonna be asking lots of questions."

The cab got on the highway, then picked up speed.

"Well, that's okay, right, Ma? You gonna be there with us, right?" I looked at her for reassurance.

"I don't know. I don't know how they do these things." She was rubbing her hands together and pulling on her fingers. If I didn't know any better, I could swear that Ma was scared.

"Just listen to me," she said, her voice cracking just a little. "Don't you say anything about Ray being over the house, or my card parties, you hear?" We both nodded. "And if they don't ask you about Mike, don't say nothing about him either."

"Why can't we talk about Mike?" I ventured to ask.

"Because I said so. Because he don't live there."

She was getting more agitated. Googie's eyes got big.

"Can I talk about Momma Louise and Uncle Steve?" he said barely above a whisper.

"Yeah. If they don't ask you nothin', don't say nothin'. Whatever they ask you, just say everything is good." We both looked at her, puzzled.

By this time, the cab had pulled off the highway and was making its way through the streets, crowded with buses, cars, and other taxis. We pulled in front of a huge gray office building. A lot of people were going in and out. I had never seen anything like it. Ma paid the driver and turned to us as we stood waiting on the sidewalk. She pulled both of us closer to her and bent down with her face almost touching ours.

"Now you remember what I said in the cab. Don't tell them nothing they don't ask you. And don't tell them nothing bad, you hear me?"

There was a sternness in her voice. When neither one of us responded, she grabbed us by the shoulders and shook us.

"Do you hear me?" She raised her voice.

We both nodded. I'm sure my brother was just as perplexed as I was. We were confused by this whole situation and scared to death of being questioned by people we didn't know.

Ma looked at us, and then it came out.

"If y'all say the wrong things, they gonna try and take you kids from me." Her eyes were wide with a kind of fear that I had never seen before.

So, there it was. That was what had Ma spooked, nervous, and snapping at us. Somehow, she thought if we said the wrong things, some people were going to take us away. I tried to wrap my head around that thought as we made our way into the massive entrance of the building.

Ma stopped at a huge circular reception desk for directions from the uniformed attendant standing behind it. Walking across the wide foyer, we stopped in front of a shiny metal wall. Ma pushed a little red button. I was busy staring at my reflection on the mirrorlike façade, when suddenly the walls parted. I stepped back, startled. A few people came out of the small, enclosed box, and then we stepped in. As the doors closed, Ma reached out and pressed the number four on the inside wall. We took our very first elevator ride, up to the fourth floor. A pleasant-looking older lady greeted Ma, they exchanged a few words, and we were directed to a seating area.

Once we sat down on the cushioned seats, Ma leaned in and said, "Now Pippa, Googie, you remember what I said. You hear me?"

We both nodded in agreement. But I was already confused. What to say, what not to say, who I could talk about, who not to talk about, say only good things, no bad things. This was just too much stuff to remember. Like all those darn rules in my teacher's class.

Finally, two nicely dressed ladies in dark suits came over and told Ma they wanted to talk to her alone. The shorter lady took my brother and me to a little playroom that was full of toys, dolls, puzzles, books, blocks, and anything else to keep a young child occupied. Within a few minutes, we were both absorbed in our individual play and had almost completely forgotten about Ma.

After a while, the tall woman who had been talking to Ma returned to the playroom and said sweetly, "Carolyn, James, we are ready for you. Can you come with us please?"

Reluctantly we stood up and looked around the room. Clearly, we were not ready to leave.

"Oh, don't worry, you can each bring a toy with you."

Googie had a red fire truck in his hands, and I had a beautiful Raggedy Ann doll. This made interrupting our play a little more tolerable.

Once in the outer area, the tall woman who had been with Ma took me by the shoulder and said, "Come with me."

The short lady had walked up to Googie and was acting like she was interested in his toy truck. We moved down a hallway, past some offices that were enclosed by glass panes. As we walked by one, I looked inside and saw Ma. She stood up and came to the door as we were passing. She said, "Pippa, don't forget what I told you."

Tall lady had her hand firmly on my shoulder so that I couldn't turn around to respond to Ma.

Once inside a brightly painted little room, I sat at a table and chair that was made just for small kids like me. There were cookies and tiny bottles of Coke on the table. Tall lady sat down with me. Another lady with a pen and clipboard came in but sat in a grown-up chair by the door.

Tall lady said to me as I tried to look over her shoulder, "Oh, don't worry about her, she's here to watch me, observe me. Just pretend that's she's not here."

And that's how it started. Getting me to slowly relax with the doll, then offering me as many cookies and sodas as I wanted. Making me comfortable with her as she asked about school and what I liked about it, my first fight with the four bullies, what fun things I liked to do with my brothers, and what kinds of games I enjoyed playing outside. She seemed genuinely interested in everything I had to say, nodding and smiling the whole time.

Then ever so subtle, so easy, so smooth the conversation branched out into other territory. One question seemed to lead into another. About me hurting myself in the bedroom that I shared with all my brothers, going to the city park alone, riding on the back of the big transit bus. She smiled with awe and wonderment at my escapades.

Then gently, in a quiet voice, she began to ask about Ma. Did she always cook for us, was there enough food in the house, what were those exciting card parties like? Did I ever go to the store to get beer or cigarettes for Ma? Who was Mike? How did he treat me, my brothers? How did he treat Ma?

"I'm so sorry if he scared you at times," she'd say. "Ray? Who is Ray? Oh my, he touched you. Can you show me where on your little Raggedy Ann doll?"

I don't ever remember sitting with a grownup who was so eager to engage me in conversation and interested in hearing everything I had to say. Offering me snacks and letting me play while we talked. I almost felt like I had made a new friend. It was so easy to talk to Tall Lady. She smiled, nodded, and laughed as I rattled on. I was really enjoying myself. I didn't notice that the lady with the clipboard had silently slipped out of the room.

And then it was over. My new, tall lady friend stood up.

"Well, thank you so much, Carolyn. You have had an exciting little life. You are so smart and brave. I've enjoyed listening to you and everything you've had to say." I smiled up at her, still carrying the Raggedy Ann doll.

We exited the room and walked back down the hallway. As we got near the glass office where Ma was earlier, I could hear loud talking. Someone was arguing. It was Ma.

"No, no, you are not taking my kids. You aren't taking my damn children from me."

"Ma'am, ma'am, calm down. Calm down please." It was a different woman in there, along with two men, both of whom had on uniforms.

I moved toward the door that led to Ma, when my tall lady friend firmly took my shoulders and said, "No, Carolyn, you can't go in there with your mother right now."

She pushed me along the hallway just as Ma caught a glimpse of me.

"Pippa, Pippa. What did you tell them? What did you say to them?" Ma yelled out of the open office door. At this point, she was struggling to get past the two big, uniformed men, who I guess were cops. She couldn't get around them.

"Damn it, let me go. You are not taking my kids from me. Pippa, I told you what to say. They gonna take you and your brothers from me."

Ma was screaming at the top of her voice. I could hear her sobbing and crying behind me. I was scared. Why wasn't this lady taking me into the room with my ma? Why wouldn't those men let her out? Where was my little brother? Where were they taking me?

I struggled to turn and run back to Ma. But the second lady rejoined us and helped escort me to the elevator and back down to the lobby.

"Where am I going? I want my ma. Where are you taking me?"

My crying and questioning now fell on deaf ears. They took me outside and over to the curb. There was a black car parked in front. I pulled back and tried to fight to get loose, when one of them opened the car door.

"What are you doing? Where are you taking me?"

Tall lady finally looked down at me and said, "I'm so sorry, Carolyn, but you can't stay at your house tonight." With firm hands, she guided me into the back seat of the car and got in beside me. The other short lady got in the driver's seat.

I was heaving, crying, and scared out of my mind. As the car began to pull away, out into the congested traffic, I turned around in time to see Ma running out of the building. She had a frantic look on her face. I screamed out her name, not knowing if she could hear me. Running toward the curb, she caught a glimpse of me in the back seat of the car. Screaming my name, "Pippa, Pippa," she dropped, collapsing to her knees on the hard city concrete.

That image of Ma crying in the streets was burned into my memory. I felt her pain, her anguish at having her kids ripped from her life. My own unfathomable fear of being abandoned and left all alone had a firm grip on me.

I didn't see Ma for the next six years. The first few months after Child Protective Services took me away, I was shell-shocked, trauma-tized, and depressed. All my fears and insecurities flooded back and took over. Fear of the dark, of being abandoned, of being bullied, of being killed and left in the streets. I retreated into myself. I didn't speak unless someone asked me a question. When I did answer, my stutter-ing came out with a vengeance, giving way to another reason to tease and bully me, which caused me to go even deeper inside my world of isolation.

13

The two caseworkers in the car with me said very little. It felt like I had just been kidnapped by these fake, pretend friends. The one next to me offered some tissues as I continued crying. They drove me to the side door of a big building; told me it was an emergency shelter for girls and that I would be spending the night there. Someone finally came to the door, the adults exchanged papers, and the two ladies patted and rubbed my back, then left.

The next three nights, I slept on a cot in a huge auditorium type room with dozens and dozens of other young girls. The woman in charge gave me some sheets, a blanket, and a pillow and told me to put my jacket on a cot, so I would know it was my new bed. She then called two older girls over and directed them to show me where the bathroom and showers were.

Once we were alone in the bathroom, the bigger girl said to me, "You're the new kid on the block, so you're supposed to get your butt kicked tonight."

I clutched the little pile of washcloths, towel, soap, toothbrush, and toothpaste that I had been given. Scared as hell and stammering, I looked at my new tormentor, "F-for what? I haven't d-done anything."

The other girl just laughed and said, "Leave her alone, she can't even talk. We'll get her later."

The next two days, I stayed to myself, didn't speak, didn't join in any activities. I just got in line and followed whatever rule was barked out over the bullhorn by the lady in charge.

"Time to get up, make your cots, take a shower, breakfast time, independent reading time, line up for dinner, movie hour, time for bed, lights out." Easy enough, just leave me alone.

This was my think time. Time to wonder if I had gotten Ma in trouble. Did I do something wrong? Should I have lied to that nice lady when I didn't lie to Ma or Mike? Time to wonder about where my six brothers were and if they were as miserable and lonely as I was. Time to think about how long I was going to be in this God-awful place and when these people would let me go home. And time to wonder about why Ma or Mike hadn't come to see me, to see if I was all right. Yes, I had a lot of time to think, and I had a lot of unanswered questions.

On the fourth day, a few of my questions were answered. A middle-aged white lady with glasses came to see me at the shelter. She said she was a social worker and had found a foster home for me. My perplexed expression made her explain that I would stay with another family until my mother was ready and healthy enough to care for me. Ready? Healthy? What did Ma have to do to get ready to bring me back home? She wasn't sick when I was with her; she looked fine. Okay, I was still confused.

The social worker then tried to assure me that I wouldn't be with these new folks for long, that they were a nice family, and it was only for a short period of time. I still didn't like the sound of this, but my ears perked up when she said my younger brother Googie would be there with me. Now that did make me feel better, to have a familiar face in the new house with the temporary family. I was so ready to get out of this dreadful emergency shelter with all their army-like rules and gangs of bullies.

Googie and I were introduced to an older, slow-moving Black lady and her overweight teenage son. They lived in a single-family two-story house in Queens. I had my own room, with my own bed for the first time in my life. My little brother shared a bedroom with the son. Foster Mother had her room. On the first floor, in the living room was a huge old piano with a wooden bench in front of it. I marveled at that. It was the first time I had seen a real piano up close. It took up almost the whole room. I gently touched the black and white keys every time I walked past it.

There was also an old, rusted swing and slide set outside in a small gate-enclosed backyard. We never had a backyard at home in the city, so this was really exciting for us. To be able to come out back whenever we wanted and swing to our hearts' content was awesome. Foster Brother never came out back with us. I guess the swing set belonged to him, way back in his younger, skinnier days. Foster Mother also let me ride a red bicycle that was leaning up against the house in the backyard. We never had a bike before. I guess with seven kids, trying to buy seven bikes was out of the question for Ma and Mike. Googie was scared he was going to fall off, so he wasn't interested in trying to ride the bike. I didn't have to share it with anybody; I had it all to myself. Yes, I fell off during my first few feeble attempts, but that didn't deter me. After two or three unbalanced crashes into garbage cans, light poles, and wrought iron gates, I was flying down the sidewalk like a pro.

"Be careful, Carolyn, don't go far." Foster Mother called out behind me, as she headed back into the house to prepare dinner.

"I won't," I called over my shoulder, already knowing I was going to ride as far as I could down those streets without getting lost.

Foster Mother took us to the dentist and eye doctor before she enrolled us in school. I had to get glasses. Shucks, I didn't know how much I had been missing until I got my new dark-brown plastic glasses. The world was much clearer.

Each day Foster Mother walked us to our new school, which was about five blocks away. Googie was in the first grade, I was in third. In the afternoons Foster Brother would meet us in front of the school and walk us home. The trip took about fifteen minutes.

One morning, as the three of us made our way toward the school, Foster Mother asked if we thought we could walk home by ourselves. Of course, we said yes. It was going to be an adventure, just like old times back home. She made sure we had her address memorized. We both said it over and over out loud until she was satisfied.

The next day, we went to school with our two-piece snowsuits on because the weatherman on TV had forecasted snow. That afternoon,

Googie and I met up at the usual spot on the steps in front of the school. We began our journey home, trudging through the steadily falling snow.

At each corner, we'd look at one another and ask, "Is this the way? Are you sure?"

After thirty minutes of walking past blocks of houses that all looked the same, I said, "I think we are lost, and I gotta go to the bathroom really bad."

He looked at me. "We gotta keep walking. It's cold out here."

We walked another block or so, and nothing was looking like Foster Mother's house. My stomach was cramping and felt bloated.

"I gotta go. I can't hold it," I said, gripping my stomach and squishing up my face.

"We're not there yet. You gotta hold it."

I don't know if it was the grilled cheese, chocolate milk, or ice-cream sandwich I had at lunch, but it all came out of me. Right there, on the city street.

"Googie, I doo-dooed on myself," I said leaning back on an iron fence in front of a house. He stopped walking, turned, and looked at me in astonishment.

"You did what? For real, Pippa?" He was clearly amused that his older sister had gone to the bathroom on herself in the middle of the street.

"I told you can't hold it. I gotta go for real," I rocked back and forth, gripping my stomach.

We both looked around. No one was coming in either direction. There were some garbage cans on the curb. They had piles of black plastic bags full of trash on top of them. I ducked behind them, took the bottom of my snowsuit off, then my pants. I cleaned myself as best I could. Balling up the soiled pants, I said, "Here, throw these in the garbage can."

Googie gingerly reached out and took the stinky evidence, opened the lid on the nearest can, and threw the clothes in. And yes, he had a look of disgust on his face. I couldn't blame him.

I struggled to put the snowsuit bottoms back on and pulled my coat as tightly around me as I could. The stench would surely give me away if I wasn't careful.

"What are we gonna do now?" he asked, looking around. The sky was thick with snow clouds and it was starting to get dark. The lightly falling snow was beginning to stick to the pavement.

"Come on, follow me."

I walked right up to the next house and rang the doorbell. A lady opened and was clearly surprised to see two little kids standing there.

"Hi, can I help you?"

"Yes, we are lost and don't know how to get home," I said.

"Oh my, that's awful. Do you know your address?"

Googie nodded, as I immediately gave the full address to Foster Mother's house.

"That's not far from here. It's in the other direction. I'll show you." We were relieved. She grabbed her coat, hat, and gloves and walked with us down the snow-covered city streets.

Foster Mother thanked her profusely. I had already run past them to the upstairs bathroom. It was time to wash my stink butt. And Googie, bless his little heart, never said another word about it.

Sometimes after dinner, I would stop by the huge piano, sit on the bench, and pluck at the keys. There were so many of them. Not like the little toy piano back home that Mike had bought me. One evening, Foster Brother heard me pinging away on the keys and walked up quietly behind me.

"You like my piano? I can show you how to play if you want."

I nodded eagerly. "Yeah, show me."

At this, he came closer, and I scooted over on the bench. He was so big, there was little room left on the bench for me. Putting both hands on the keys, he began to play. He played songs that I never heard of. I was amazed at how quickly and easily his fingers moved up and down the keyboard.

"Wow, that's nice. You're so good!" I was amazed.

Then he played some tunes that I knew, "Three Blind Mice" and "Twinkle, Twinkle Little Star." We sang them as he played. I was having a great time. Then he said, "You want me to show you how to play?"

I looked up at him with all the excitement of a new adventure in my eyes and said, "Yeah, yeah, show me."

"Okay, but you'll have to get in front of me so I can show you where to put your fingers." With that, he edged me off the end of the bench and pushed it back a little.

"Here, get in front of me."

He reached over, grabbed me by the arm, and positioned me in between his legs. As I stood there facing the piano, his tree-size arms encircled me. He put my hands on the black and white keys, then placed his huge hands over mine. His fingers pressed down on mine one at a time, to the tune of another familiar nursery rhyme.

I could feel his hot, awful-smelling breath on the back of my neck. He was like a gigantic bear that had me cornered on all sides. That slow, dark feeling of dread began to creep over me. He was too close to me. But we kept playing a few minutes more.

"This is not working," he said. "I can't get your fingers the way I want them. You'll have to sit on my lap. Then I can show you better."

With that, he quickly lifted me up and placed me smack-dab in the middle of his lap. Yes, right there on top of his zipper, where underneath I knew was his private thing.

His arms encased me once again, and I felt the weight of his fingers on mine. Pressing, playing the cute little nursery rhymes that I knew. But something else was going on, something else was happening. He was playing the piano; he was quietly singing the songs. But he was also making little circular motions with his hips and legs. He was pressing his private part into my behind. I guess he thought, or he hoped that I would be too involved, too enthralled with my new piano lessons to notice what he was doing. Nope. By the end of the song, by the end of the third or fourth intrusion on my backside, I hopped off his lap.

"That's enough for today," I said as I squeezed past his mammoth thighs to freedom.

He was turning his huge body around on the bench as I made my way past him.

"Are you sure? I can show you some more."

"Nope, I've had enough."

By that time, I was bounding up the stairs to my room. I was done with piano lessons for good.

14

I n early spring, Foster Mother told Googie and me that another social worker would be visiting, to talk about a new, more permanent home for us. I remember feeling a little twinge of disappointment, because I was just getting used to this home, the neighborhood, and my school. The sting of not seeing Ma and the rest of my brothers was wearing off just a little more with each passing day. After all, I had Googie to keep me company.

The social worker came one day after school. She was sitting in the living room with Foster Mother when we came charging through the door, laughing loud and pushing each other.

"James, Carolyn, this is the social worker I was telling you about. She is here to speak to you."

We put our metal lunchboxes down, along with the few schoolbooks and notepads that we carried every day. We sat next to each other on the piano bench, facing the two women. I felt a twinge of anticipation, mixed with a dab of anxiety, not knowing what new changes were about to take place in my life.

"I have some news for the both of you," she started.

She talked quietly, hands folded in her lap, looking from me, then to my brother.

"James, your godfather and godmother, Mr. and Mrs. Stevens, have agreed to take you and let you live with them."

"Oh boy, Momma Louise and Uncle Steve! I miss them," Googie said, hardly able to contain himself.

I sat up a little straighter as I focused on the social worker's next words, which were surely going to be great news for me too. Maybe I was going with Googie. I just knew they wouldn't separate us again.

"Carolyn, you will be living with a new family upstate," she said.

I was puzzled, because I knew Momma Louise and Uncle Steve lived in Harlem, so what was this upstate stuff coming out of her mouth? She saw the look of confusion on my face and continued.

"You and your baby brother Gardiner will be together. Your new family also has a son around your age, someone you can make friends with and play with."

Googie and I looked at each other. I grabbed his hand, then looked back at the social worker.

"You mean w-we are not gonna be together anymore?" I needed clarification. I refused to believe they were going to split us up again.

"I'm so sorry, Carolyn. No, you will not be with your brother James, but you will have Gardiner with you."

"Why? Why can't I go with Googie? Why can't I go with him to Momma Louise and Uncle Steve's house?" I pressed, feeling my bottom lip start to quiver and my eyes begin to well up.

The social worker continued in her slow, quiet, uncompromising voice, "I understand how you feel. I know you love your brother and want to be together with him. However, the Stevenses could only take one of you. They only have room in their apartment for one child."

Small tears trickled down my cheeks, as the realization began to sink in. Momma Louise and Uncle Steve made a choice, and it didn't include me.

Googie felt so bad for me. I could tell by the way he was squeezing my hand and leaning on me. He looked like he wanted to cry.

"Don't worry, Pip, I'll ask them if you can come and stay with us too."

But I already knew the answer; the decision was made years ago. Way back when Googie was the only one of us who went to Momma Louise and Uncle Steve's house to visit, to play, to stay. He had his own room then. He was always the chosen one.

I pulled my hand away from his and jumped off the piano stool. Looking at the two women, I whispered in a shaky voice, tears streaming now, "It's not fair, it's just not fair."

I knew my brother was happy. I wanted him to be happy, but I wanted to be happy too. I wanted someone to want me, the way the Stevenses wanted my brother.

Three days later, I was all packed and riding in a new-looking station wagon with my little brother Gardiner yapping away next to me. When the social worker arrived that morning, she had him with her. I was glad to see him and gave him a huge hug, lifting him up and swinging him around. He was still chubby, just like I remembered, but no longer baby Sloppy Joe in diapers. I was thrilled that he was so happy to see me, squealing out "Pippa!" when he saw me.

A different social worker had come to get Googie the day before, to drive him to Momma Louise and Uncle Steve's house. I didn't get a chance to see him off because I had to go to school. We spent the evening before he left huddled together, talking and playing one last time in the backyard. We promised to write each other, and he promised to ask Momma Louise if I could come and stay with them.

I didn't have a hard time saying good-bye to Foster Mother. She was always nice and kind, but I didn't allow myself to get attached to her. After all, in my mind she was not my ma. Her nasty son was nowhere in sight, and that was fine by me. I wouldn't have looked at him or said good-bye anyway. I knew I would miss having my own room and playing in the backyard. But that's about it.

Riding in the car, I thought about what new and different things were in store for us. How was my life going to change, or would it be the same, or possibly even better? I pressed my shoulder into the car door as I stared out the window at the changing landscape. We drove along on the highway for about an hour. Gardiner was busying himself with a few small toys and some animal crackers he had to snack on.

The busy New York City skyline with the tall skyscrapers came into view and then disappeared in the distance behind us. We exited the highway and started driving past busy intersections with businesses, restaurants, and gas stations on both sides. But it was different, not as crowded as the streets I was used to, and it seemed cleaner, the air fresher. There were no yellow cabs, subway stations, transit buses, screaming fire trucks, or police sirens blaring.

"We're almost here," Social Worker said as she navigated the unfamiliar streets.

"Where are we going?" I finally asked.

"We're in the city of White Plains now, but we are going to a section called Greenburgh."

I had no reference point for any of that, so I turned and continued looking out my window.

We continued over a four-lane highway, and then things really changed. Traveling down a long road, I saw one- and two-story private homes. Each had a manicured front yard and blossoming trees and flowering bushes out front. The yards ended where the road began. There were no sidewalks like I was used to in the city. Each driveway had a mailbox with numbers on it. The homes were different sizes, shapes, and colors. No two were alike.

Very few people were visible. Occasionally I saw someone walking on the side of the road in the grass, a woman checking her mailbox, or a man watering the lawn with a long snakelike hose. This was different even from the foster home that I had just left. I was mesmerized.

Finally, we made a right turn on a street called North Road. The brightly colored front neighborhood sign that hung on two wooden posts said Parkway Gardens. We rode past streets named after the presidents of the United States. Washington Place, Adams Place, Jefferson, Madison and so on.

"These are the presidents," I said. "Is the house on one of these streets?" I sat up even straighter in anticipation, because these homes were even nicer than the ones we had been passing.

"Just a few more blocks, up this hill and we are almost there."

She drove past four more presidents, then made a quick left turn and a fast right into the driveway of a brown, split-level house sitting on a corner lot. The lush green grass was freshly cut, with neatly trimmed bushes decorating the front of the house.

We walked up the few steps to the front door. I carried our few meager possessions in four, large store paper bags. After Social Worker pushed the bell a couple of times, a light-skinned middle-aged, slightly overweight woman answered the door. She had soft black hair, which was pulled tightly back in a bun. A pretty, multicolored teal-and-green blouse hung over her torso but could not hide her huge breasts or thick hips. Dark-green pants complemented and finished off her outfit.

She smiled pleasantly at Social Worker, as she stood back to let the three of us enter what was the formal living room. I put our bags down as she motioned for us to have a seat on the plastic-covered couch.

Introductions were made. Her name was Mrs. Thompson. She informed Social Worker that her husband was working in the city. I think she referred to him as a detective. Their son, Donnie, who was a year younger than me, was still at school. She graciously gave us a quick tour of the house, allowing us a peek into several rooms. There was a nice kitchen with a table that was attached to the wall with chairs on three sides. Over the sink and counter was a row of windows that looked out into the backyard. The dining room had a full set of formal furniture in it. We passed a door, which she opened and merely said, "That's the basement, it leads to the garage."

Then up five or six steps to the bedroom section of the house. She pointed out the full bath on the left and a small bedroom right opposite it.

"Carolyn, this will be your room."

It was quite tiny, with a brown chest of drawers, a small wooden nightstand, a twin-size bed, and a closet. I saw a small, boxed window, draped with thin beige curtains.

We walked down the narrow hall to the next room. It had two twin beds that were separated, one on each wall. There was a much larger chest of drawers, with books, small balls, and green plastic soldiers on top.

"Gardiner will share this room with my son," she said as she turned, and with her extended hand pointing toward the stairs, let us know the tour was over.

We were not shown her daughter's room or the bedroom she shared with her husband. Both of those doors were closed, which told me they were off limits.

Once back downstairs in the living room, Mrs. Thompson and Social Worker exchanged a few more tidbits of information that neither

Gardiner nor I was interested in. We had regained our positions on the sticky plastic couch and were busy looking around, taking in our new home. Everything looked so clean, the tan walls trimmed in white paint, right down to the soft, thick, beige carpet we walked on. The plastic-covered furniture, large and small paintings, lamps, and various glass statues of animals, everything had its place. There was a pristine neatness and order to this house, inside and out. Sunlight and soft breezes came in from the open windows, the crisp smell of fresh-cut grass mingled with scented rose bushes, and birds could be heard chirping outside in the trees.

We were to quickly find out that things were not quite as peaceful and serene as they seemed.

15

After Social Worker left, I busied myself putting my few belongings in the drawers and closet. Mrs. Thompson called me. "Carolyn, come here. I'm going to show you the rest of the house."

I came down the stairs and found her standing by the door that she had told us earlier led to the basement. She turned on a light inside the door that illuminated the steps as she carefully descended, with me following.

The basement was a rectangular room with two long, narrow windows facing the front of the house. It had a back door with tiny windows that opened to another screen door, then to the yard outside. Along the longest wall was a ledge that jutted out about three inches. It was lined with album covers of black singers and musicians—Count Basie, Duke Ellington, Johnny Mathis and more. I was studying the faces on each cover intently wondering what their music sounded like.

Mrs. Thompson moved across the room to another door, which she yanked open and simply said, "This is the garage." I quickly noticed that it was a mess, with tires, piles of newspapers, bicycles, cardboard boxes, lawn equipment, and pieces of furniture everywhere. I wondered how a car could possibly fit in there.

"I'm going to need you to help me straighten this up," she said, nodding more to herself than to me, then turning back to look around the small basement.

There was an old, faded plaid couch with sunken cushions; a small nightstand-looking table with a black-and-silver record player on it; and shelves on the opposite wall with lots of albums stacked up, with a few dusty books next to them. At the bottom of the stairs, in a small, indented area, sat a square table with two folding chairs.

"Can I p-play your records?" I asked.

"After you do your chores," was her dry response.

Chores, like jobs I did at Ma's house, helping my brothers to make our beds, or probably sweeping the kitchen floor after dinner like Foster Mother had me doing. I rolled the idea of doing chores in this new house over in my head. While those thoughts were attempting to take shape, Mrs. Thompson said, opening another door that was in between the steps and square table, "This is the subbasement; you can do the laundry down here."

She moved back a little as I squinted to make out what exactly was in a subbasement. All I could see were rows of rope going from one side of the room to the other. Sheets, shirts, pants, and socks were hung on five or six ropes with clothespins. The floor was gray concrete, and the only light came from a cobwebbed, dirty window, and two little bare bulbs in the middle of the ceiling.

"Come on, let's go back up in the kitchen. I'm going to show you how to do the dishes after everyone is finished eating."

Cleaning the garage, doing laundry, washing dishes—none of this registered with me … not yet, but it was going to.

Mrs. Thompson's son came home from school about the time my personal tour of the house was complete. He was a skinny, brown-skinned boy with big eyes and a close haircut. There really was nothing interesting about him. He didn't speak much, so neither did I. He ran straight to his room to meet and inspect the little kid who was going to occupy the other bed in his room.

The three of us ate dinner at the little kitchen table. Gardiner tried to make little babbles of conversation, but I was too shy to open my mouth. Mrs. Thompson busied herself between the stove and sink, scraping pots and organizing dishes. That one meal in the kitchen, on my first day in the Thompsons' house, was the only time in the five and a half years we lived there, that I ate with my little brother.

After the boys finished, she said, "Go upstairs and play in your room."

I'm sure Gardiner was happy, because our new foster brother apparently had a wooden chest in his room that was full of toys.

As I got up from the table to empty my plate, she turned to me and asked, "Do you know how to wash dishes?"

"Yes, y-yes, Mrs. Thompson," I said as respectfully as I could, still holding on to the plate.

She had a dish towel in her hand and stopped drying the pot that she held. Looking down at me from across the kitchen, she stated in a matter-of-fact way, "Carolyn, I want you to call me Mom, not Mrs. Thompson."

I was surprised and puzzled. Cocking my head to the side, I thought maybe I misheard her.

"Mrs. Thompson, you're not my ma. The only person I call ma is my ma."

I thought my explanation would clear things up, because apparently, she must be a little confused.

She put the metal pot slowly down on the counter. "I know I'm not your mother. Nobody in this house calls me Mrs. Thompson. So, I want you and your brother to call me Mom."

I looked at her with disbelief. I just met this lady, and she wants me to call her Mom. *That's ridiculous*, I thought.

She took a step toward me. "Did you hear me? Do you understand what I'm saying?"

I thought I would try to reason with her one more time, "Mrs. Thompson, I h-hear you, but I d-don't call anybody mom but my ma."

My voice didn't come out as strong and confident as it sounded in my head, but at least I told her. She had to understand.

No. No, she didn't understand, and I didn't see her raised open hand coming toward my face until it was too late. Mrs. Thompson struck me so hard that my glasses flew off and hit the table behind me. I dropped the plate that I had been holding and grabbed the side of my face in utter disbelief. The stinging was immediate, the tears filling up in my eyes about to overflow.

"I said you are to call me Mom. Do you understand?" She drew out the last words in a low, menacing voice, leaning in closer to me.

I backed up a step, shaking my head no and opened my mouth to protest again. But before a word could come out, she landed another forceful slap to the other side of my temple. Oh yes, tears were streaming now. I couldn't believe what was happening. This lady was knocking my head off my neck because I didn't want to call her mom. I gawked at her with my mouth still open, standing there shaking, trying to make sense of this senseless situation and this sudden onslaught of violence.

She glared at me and in slow motion raised her arm, getting it in striking position again. I backed up.

"What did I tell you to call me?"

I wiped the tears with my fingers, and the snot that was beginning to run down my nose with the back of my hand. I gave in. Barely above a whisper, I said, "Mom."

"What did you say? I can't hear you." She took another menacing step toward me.

"Mom, you said to call you Mom." Just like that, I was defeated, broken, beaten into submission.

"Good. Now clean up this mess on the floor and wash these dishes. Do you hear me?"

I thought about it for a split second. Should I say, "Yes, Mrs. Thompson," like I wanted to, like the brave Pippa would have said? Somewhere in the distance, I heard a frightened little girl simply say,

"Yes, Mom."

Late the next afternoon, Foster Mom took me to Old Tarrytown Road School and enrolled me in Ms. Luddy's third-grade class. On the way back home, she stopped at the corner of South Road and Van Buren Place. It was two blocks from her house. She pointed to the street sign and said, "This is where you are going to catch your bus tomorrow morning, do you understand?"

Looking out from my back-seat window, I tried to stamp the image of the pretty white house with black shutters in my mind.

"Yes, Mom," I dutifully said.

"Humph, good." She slowly turned the car in the direction of her house.

Once we arrived, I went straight upstairs to my room. My brother Gardiner had been left at home with her son Donnie and Mr. Thompson, who I guessed was in his room sleeping because he worked at night. When Gardiner heard us coming upstairs from the basement, he stuck his head out of the bedroom to greet me. He had a huge smile on his face.

"Hey there, Sloppy Joe," I said in a cheerful, animated voice.

Before he could answer, Foster Mom came up behind me and said to Gardiner, "Get in that room, and don't come out unless I tell you."

The happy expression on my baby brother's face faded as he ducked back into his bedroom.

I never went in his room; in fact, I didn't dare venture down the hall past the bathroom or my room. The scope of my movement around that house was limited to those two rooms, the kitchen, and the basement. In all the years I lived there, my eyes never saw the inside of Foster Mom's room or her daughter Barbara's room.

When Foster Mom called me out of my room for dinner, Donnie and Gardiner were already at the kitchen table eating. They looked at me, but neither said a word. I noticed that the third chair was no longer at the table. I wondered where I was supposed to sit, certainly not in the fancy dining room. Foster Mom turned from spooning out food on my plate and turned to hand it to me.

"You can eat at the table downstairs," she said in a casual voice.

I was puzzled as I stood there holding my plate, not moving. The boys had stopped eating, their forks extended in midair between their plate and mouth, as they looked at us. Foster Mom, sensing my bewilderment by the look on my face, moved from the kitchen, past the steps, and opened the door that led to the basement. Holding the door open, with her eyes still trained on me, she motioned with a slight nod of her head. Then it registered, it hit me like a punch in the gut. She wanted me to eat in the basement, by myself.

This revelation was incredulous; with plate in hand I walked to the door and down the steps. I heard the wooden door closing behind me with a click of the lock. Placing my food on the square table, I stood there for a few long minutes, looking around. I had lost my appetite. Me, Pippa, who was used to loud, raucous, fun-filled meals with six mischievous brothers, was in a dimly lit basement, eating alone. I didn't know it at that moment, but soon enough, the realization would become apparent that this was going to be my new normal.

Alone, isolated not only from the rest of the people in this house but from my baby brother. My mind was racing to find a logical reason for this. What had I done to deserve this kind of treatment? What had I done that would warrant me being placed in such a dire situation? Finally, sitting on the edge of my seat, I began picking at the food, somehow knowing in advance that if I didn't eat it, there would be hell to pay.

The next morning after eating my solitary breakfast of cold cereal and milk in the basement, Foster Mom yelled out, "It's time for y'all to catch the bus. Carolyn, bring your bowl up here and put it in the sink. Y'all better not miss that bus."

I grabbed the metal lunchbox with Snow White and the Seven Dwarfs on the lid, along with a black-and-white composition book and some pencils that Foster Mom gave me. She had directed me earlier to use the basement door that led out to the yard as my way of coming in and out of the house. Going around the side of the house and making my way to the driveway and road, I heard the front door opening. Foster Mom was bending over Donnie, giving him a kiss good-bye.

That's odd, I thought. *Why isn't he using the back door like me?* We met up by the mailbox and started walking to our bus stop. When we got to the next corner called Harrison Place, Donnie crossed the street and continued on it past the first house.

"Wait a minute, where are you going?" I asked him, thinking he was clearly suddenly confused as to where his bus stop was.

"I'm going to my bus stop," he responded, surprised that I would ask such a ridiculous question.

"The bus stops on Van Buren Place." I pointed down the street.

Donnie looked at me and said as he kept walking, "Your stop is down there. Mine is closer."

Okay, that didn't make sense to me, but I was going to where Foster Mom had clearly shown me the stop was. I walked the next two blocks and waited by myself for the bus to come. About fifteen minutes later, the bus pulled up, stopped, and a smiling female driver opened the door.

"Good morning, young lady. You must be new. Welcome. Sit any-where you like."

As I walked down the center of the bus looking for a choice seat, I spotted Donnie looking out the window like he didn't see me. Stopping as I approached him, I said, "Donnie, why weren't you at the bus stop?"

He turned his head and looked up at me. "I was at my bus stop. Mom said we couldn't be at the same stop."

And with that, he turned his head and continued studying whatever he was staring at outside the window. I took a seat a few rows behind him. This was another puzzle I couldn't figure out. We go to the same school, ride the same bus, but Foster Mom didn't want us together at the same bus stop.

After a couple of weeks, I had become resigned in my mind that I was not going to be seeing much of my brother. I saw Barbara, Foster Mom's sweet, soft-spoken older daughter only on a few occasions. Mr. Thompson—or *Dad*, as I was instructed to call him—made even rarer appearances than his daughter. He was a very good-looking man with a head full of hair, with slightly graying edges and a thick mustache that almost hid his entire top lip.

Late one night, Foster Dad opened my door and came into my darkened bedroom. I immediately felt my body tense up because initially I thought it was that wicked Foster Mom. But when I saw his silhouette outlined by the bright hallway light, memories of Ray touching me when he thought I was asleep washed over me. I could feel my adrenaline rushing and the need to run, escape. That old feeling of being held hostage, with no way out magnified my fear that much more. Foster Dad walked over to my bed. Looking down, he could see that I was awake, my eyes were wide open. He bent down toward me and said, "I came in to say good night," his head coming toward mine.

I turned my face to the wall as he planted a slight kiss on my cheek. I never said a word to acknowledge him or his peck on my face. He walked out, gently closing the door behind him, and never came in my room again.

The rest of my school year was uneventful except for one small incident. I stole. Yes, I stole again for the second time in my life, but for a different reason: self-preservation. I honestly thought I was slowly starving; I was always so hungry.

Each school morning, Foster Mom gave me a small bowl of cereal and a cup of milk. One day, on my way down the basement stairs, I lost my balance on the bottom step, dropped the bowl of cereal, and spilled some of my milk. After placing what was still left of the milk on the table, I got down on my hands and knees to try to scoop up the mess I'd made. Running the palms of my hands across the dusty floor, I gathered up most of the cereal and put it back into the bowl. Stopping on the top step with my bowl, I knocked on the closed door. A few seconds later, Foster Mom opened it and with an annoyed look on her face said,

"What is it?"

"Mom, I spilled my cereal on the floor by accident. But I tried to get most of it up, so can I have another bowl of cereal? Please?" I thought I did a good job of explaining what happened.

She reached out and took the bowl.

"Wait here."

She returned with a different bowl, full of cereal, and handed it to me. *Okay*, I thought to myself, *at least she's not mad.* I returned to my table to quickly eat, before she yelled out that it was time to catch the school bus. I poured what was left of my milk over the cereal, picked up the spoon, opened my mouth and was about to take a big scoop. Moving my head closer to the bowl, I thought I saw something, something darker than the cereal. Then a few more specks appeared, floating on top of the milk. Some thin-looking strings rose, wet, and covered in the white liquid. It was hair. Hair, dust, and dirt were now easily discernable mingled in with the cereal. Then the stark realization hit me. Foster Mom didn't give me more cereal; she simply poured the cereal that I had scooped up from the nasty floor into a different-colored bowl. Shaking my head in disbelief I emptied the contents in the nearby bathroom toilet. Yes, I went to school that day hungry, again.

In my lunchbox each day, Foster Mom would pack a sandwich with one slice of cheese or bologna, but never both. No mayonnaise, no mustard. Other days, it was a grape jelly or peanut butter sandwich, but not both together. Many days, my sandwich was made using the ends of the bread. I remember thinking to myself, *How many ends can one loaf have? Because I'm always winding up with these darn hard end pieces.* Along with my skimpy sandwich, Foster Mom put in a juice box and an apple.

When Ms. Luddy called out snack time around midmorning each day, the kids pulled out chips, cookies, animal crackers, bags of popcorn, peanuts, and all kinds of fruit. If I ate my fruit at snack time, I only had a sandwich and drink for lunch. So, most days I would either have half my sandwich for a snack or pretend I wasn't hungry and more interested in finishing up my classwork.

One morning, our class was on the way to recess outside. Halfway down the hall, I ran up to Ms. Luddy and asked if I could go back to the class to get my sweater. She said of course, and I made my way back to the room, over to the open cupboards where we hung our outerwear and book bags and stored the lunchboxes until it was time to go to the cafeteria. My stomach was growling like an angry beast. I had unrelenting cramps from a gnawing need for something to eat. My eyes fell on a brightly colored Cinderella lunchbox. I couldn't resist; the emptiness in my belly was too great. Quickly snatching the container from the nearby cupboard, I unlatched it and found pure gold—a turkey-and-cheese sandwich on rye bread. I freed it from the clear plastic wrap and quickly devoured it. Snatching my sweater, I threw the telltale wrapping in the trash can by the open door and ran to rejoin my class outside.

At lunchtime, my classmate was distraught upon learning that half her lunch was missing. One of her girlfriends tried to console her. "Maybe your mother forgot to make it."

A boy sitting nearby offered, "Or maybe she made it and forgot to pack it. It's probably on your kitchen counter."

Ms. Luddy was so kind, she offered my classmate half of her own sandwich and invited the little girl to sit next to her at the lunchroom table. I kept my eyes glued to the poor excuse of a sandwich in front of me, but my stomach, for once, had ceased growling.

I felt so bad about stealing my classmate's food. The guilt ate at me like a relentless gnat that I couldn't swat away. But the incessant daily hunger from too little food wouldn't go away either. I had to do something, but what? Asking Foster Mom already proved to be a wasted effort, and stealing from my classmate weighed too heavy on my heart.

There was one solution. In the subbasement was a long, white freezer all the way in the back on the concrete floor. I didn't see it the first time Foster Mom gave me my private tour, because there were so many sheets handing on the numerous clotheslines. But since I had inherited the added chore of hanging up the wet laundry for the entire family every weekend, I discovered the gigantic freezer. Upon inspecting, it I found dozens of frozen desserts and treats—Twinkies, Moon Pies, individual apple and cherry pies, chocolate eclairs, flavored ice Popsicles, and vanilla ice-cream sandwiches. Every day after my solitary dinner, I'd sneak down into the subbasement, quietly open my newfound treasure chest, and indulge myself in a different delectable daily dessert.

No, I didn't see it as stealing. I saw it as self-preservation, one small benefit for having to spend countless hours in that basement isolated and alone.

16

Time dragged on in the Thompson house. I had become used to being left alone in my room or in the basement with no one to talk to, day in, day out. I never saw Foster Dad, and Barbara their daughter had moved out to live with her boyfriend, Ralph. Donnie never had anything to do with me; it was like he had a superior, snobbish attitude and I was beneath him.

When I did see my brother in the kitchen or hallway, I could tell something in him was changing. The smile that lit up his face when he used to see me was gone. He didn't talk, even when I tried to engage him with a short, familiar "hey, Sloppy Joe." He looked sad, withdrawn, like the life was slowly being sucked out of him. Then I noticed something else. Whenever Foster Mom appeared near him, he tensed up, stopped moving altogether. He'd stand still, motionless, like a miniature statue. My baby brother was scared, terrified of Foster Mom. He couldn't tell me, couldn't verbalize it, but I knew. I knew because I felt the same way. It pained me that I couldn't help him, couldn't protect him. He was trapped, alone in this house all day with her. There was nothing I could do except imagine what twisted, horrible things might be happening to him by this wicked witch of a woman who pretended to be something she wasn't.

When I wasn't in school, my time was spent in my room, reading fairytale books I'd signed out from the school library. I read until it got so dark outside that the light coming in my window made seeing the words impossible. During the spring and summer, Foster Mom told me I better not turn on the light in my room. When it got too dark to read, I'd listen to the little plastic AM transistor radio that Barbara gave me. The program announcer was somebody named Cousin Bruscie, who played all the latest songs of the day from the Beatles, the Rolling Stones, and Tom Jones.

For the most part, I spent every Saturday and Sunday after church in the basement. By fourth grade, Foster Mom had me washing clothes for the whole family in a large, white utility tub in the subbasement. She showed me how to separate, wash, and rinse endless piles of clothes, sheets, and towels. She had an old-fashioned wringer. I had to feed the wet clothes through two rolls of wood attached to the top of it and turn a handle to squeeze out the excess water. Afterward, I hung each item on the rows of lines behind me.

When that was complete, she made me clean the half-bathroom in the basement, dust the ledges and bookshelves, and sweep the floor. If that was done to her satisfaction, she always found something for me to clean, dust, stack, sweep, or rearrange in the garage.

When it was warm enough outside, she'd make me pull weeds around the back and side of her property. I worked, down on my hands and knees in the dirt for hours at a time. No water to drink, in the direct, blazing sunlight, pulling whatever she deemed was undesirable growth. She called me inside around noon, to eat my peanut butter or jelly sandwich. Then it was back out in the heat, to sit in the dirt, inching my way around the perimeter of her property, pulling weeds.

I kept my mouth shut and my head down, feeling every bit like Cinderella in my fairytale books. I didn't ask any questions and certainly made no attempt at small talk with Foster Mom. I dutifully tried to memorize everything she wanted me to do and how she wanted it done. I didn't want her to have to repeat herself, for fear of being the target of her wrath. Desperately I wanted to become invisible and hope to God that she would forget that I even existed.

The bulk of my late Saturday afternoons and evenings were spent taking down the dry clothes and folding them into neat piles according to who they belonged to. Foster Mom produced an ironing board with a faded, burnt flowery cover on it, which she set up in front of the sunken couch. I had to learn to iron fast. Yes, by age ten, I ironed everybody's clothes that needed to be ironed: hers, her husband's, her son's, Gardiner's and mine. Her blouses and Foster Dad's shirts had to be hung on hangers.

It didn't even faze Foster Mom when I touched the scorching-hot face of the iron and burned a huge swatch of skin on my forearm. When I went to the top of the stairs and knocked on the door to show her, I thought the sight of my shriveled, burnt skin would elicit a motherly, concerned response. But it didn't. She left me standing there, returning momentarily with some butter on a paper towel.

"Here, put some of this on it." She closed the door and left me standing on the top step.

So, it goes without saying that the next time I had an unfortunate accident, I didn't bother her with it. And it did happen, some months later. I had been doing various chores all morning and ironing for hours into the late afternoon. I was exhausted and beginning to doze off. Back and forth, up and down over Foster Dad's long-sleeve shirts. My eyes briefly closed from exhaustion, but my hand holding the hot iron slid off the edge of the board and fell on my bare thigh, frying my flesh like one of Ray's pork chops. I screamed from the pain, jumped up, and knocked over the board, clothes, and iron. A large four-inch piece of skin was burnt, but I didn't even bother the wicked witch with this latest mishap because I knew it wouldn't garner any sympathy. Covering the burned area with a washcloth dipped in cold water offered soothing, temporary relief.

Hour after hour, week after week, this was my routine, my new normal, my life. I spent so much time by myself in the basement that I had to figure out ways to entertain myself. Foster Mom did not let me go outside to play, like I was used to doing back in the city. Even if she did, there was no one for me to play with, as she never, not once in five years, allowed me to invite any classmates or acquaintances from church over to the house. There was no TV for me to watch, so my favorite TV shows and animated cartoons were long gone, in the distant past.

After frequently dusting the albums that were stacked on the bookcases and lining the wall ledges, I became curious as to what the music sounded like on the flat, black vinyl twelve-inch records. Taking a calculated risk that I wouldn't get a negative response, I asked Foster

Mom if I could play the albums on the old record player while I did my chores. Much to my surprise, she said yes, as long as I didn't break any and put them back inside their right covers.

My long, lonely hours of domestic drudgery were made more bearable when I listened to the jazz, blues, or comedy albums that inhabited the dreary basement with me. During my elementary school years, I got to know the incredible music and songs of Louis Armstrong, Count Basie, and Duke Ellington. I pretended to sing along with beautiful Black women like Ella Fitzgerald, Billie Holiday, and Lena Horne. The funny, off-color jokes of Moms Mabley made me think of Ma, Jitter, and Dorothy during my happier days. I later found out from Barbara, that Moms Mabley lived right down North Road, near the entrance to Parkway Gardens. Why, I was practically rubbing elbows with someone famous, right here in the neighborhood.

Every Saturday morning, even in bad weather, Foster Mom would give me fifty cents and make me walk by myself to the business section of Greenburgh, to buy a pair of stockings for Sunday church. I didn't mind the long, lonely trek that was at least a mile and a half each way. It gave me time to get out of that awful house and into the freedom of fresh air.

I passed the familiar eight presidents, each lined with beautiful homes and manicured, lush lawns. I made my way down North Road to the intersection of Hillside Avenue, where Moms Mabley lived. I walked another mile on the side of the street in the grass and dirt, as there were no sidewalks. Crossing over the highway, I knew I only had a short distance left to get to the row of stores and shops on Tarrytown Road. The pleasant shopkeeper recognized me from my weekly trips to pick up my French coffee-colored stockings. I didn't have any extra money for a soda or snack, but that didn't bother me. I was relaxed and free for a few hours.

Going and coming back during my weekly march to get stockings, I hummed the tunes I memorized from the many music albums in the basement. My absolute favorite was "To Dream the Impossible Dream" by Johnny Mathis. Something about those words inspired in me a glimmer of hope for the future. If I just held on a little while longer, if I just believed that something wonderful was in store for me despite how hopeless my life felt right now, if I just dared to dream an impossible but brighter dream, eventually my life would be better. Keeping that song and positive thoughts in the forefront of my mind, I sang, swung my arms, and skipped along those tree lined Greenburgh streets.

In school, I was basically failing everything, but Foster Mom didn't seem to care, so neither did I. She never asked me about school, if I had any homework, needed supplies, or needed help with my assignments. And because of my deprived look, due to outdated, often too-large clothes and unkempt, nappy hair, I was often the target of cruel jokes and relentless teasing.

This daily onslaught of taunting and teasing was led by a classmate name Sheila. Now, Sheila herself was nothing to look at, being short, with a huge head and kinky hair worse than mine. She resembled a miniature football linebacker with a helmet attached to a body without a neck. She didn't dress any better than me and lived in a poorer section of Greenburgh. But what she did have was an unnerving way of instilling fear in anyone she targeted, and for some reason, she picked me. Daily during lunch, outside on the playground, in the halls and girls' bathroom, she glared, pointed, threatened, and made me the butt of her jokes.

The other kids were secretly afraid of her too, so to stay on her good side, they laughed along with everything she said or did. I was constantly humiliated because of my clothes, thick glasses, big nose, the huge gap in my front teeth, and unruly short hair. But the most intense pain I felt was when she and the rest of the kids mercilessly howled with laughter, each time I opened my mouth to speak in class, only to uncontrollably start stuttering and tripping over my words.

I retreated into the comforts of a deep, dark, silent depression. Intimidated and fearful at home, taunted by a foster mother who silently opened my door in the middle of the night and then forcibly slammed it shut without a word, jolting me out of my sleep. Bullied and harassed at school by groups of kids too numerous to defend myself against. Separated from my family and people who cared, and wondering if they ever thought about me, where I was, or how I was doing. To me, it felt like an unhappy, no-win situation with no end in sight.

It was then that Mr. Chesden, my fifth-grade teacher, honed in on something even I didn't know I possessed, a knack for creative writing. One day, he gave us a simple writing assignment. He had cut out an assortment of pictures from numerous newspapers, magazines, National Geographic books, and flyers. Each picture was glued on a colorful sheet of construction paper. The homework assignment was to use your imagination, to make up and write a story about the picture you selected. He wanted us to write a beginning, middle, and ending for our story.

That shouldn't be too hard, I thought, *not with my love for reading fairy-tale books, making up games, and playing by myself all those months in the basement.* I took Mr. Chesden's one picture assignment and created an intricate, complex story that was pages long. I included multiple characters with dialogue, humor, surprise, and suspense.

The next day, when Mr. Chesden asked for volunteers to read, I did not raise my hand, for fear of stuttering and being laughed at. Eventually, everyone had to stand up in front of the class and read their story, because it was going to be graded.

I was the last to read. After asking permission to tape my picture to the black chalkboard, I shyly, timidly opened my mouth and began to read. Turning my pages over from one side to the next, I got involved in my own story, gaining confidence as I moved along, hearing my classmates laughing at a funny line or inflection of my voice. I did not stutter or stammer. At the conclusion of the last page, I looked up and said, "The end." Much to my surprise, the class, along with Mr. Chesden, erupted in applause.

"Wow, Carolyn, that was really good. I can tell you put a lot of time and effort into your story, and I loved the way you tied in your picture."

No one had ever complimented me on anything I did in school, not my ma, or the first foster mother, certainly not the current one, and not one single teacher, in five years of schooling.

Mr. Chesden was the first. He encouraged me by saying positive things and giving me pointers on how to make my stories better and

117

improve my penmanship. He let me stay in during recess if I didn't finish my work at home. In addition, he gave me extra paper and pencils when I ran out of supplies. He kept me motivated by letting me visit other classrooms to read my stories, as those students listened intently and looked on in amazement at how I tied each story to a single picture. Mr. Chesden sparked my first real interest in school and bolstered my self-confidence. Maybe there was something I was good at after all.

O n Wednesday afternoons, several kids in my class left early for religious instruction at their church. Laura, one of my classmates, lived about five streets down the road from me and attended the same church as my foster family. She explained that it was a cool way to get out of school and have a little fun. So, I asked Foster Mom if I could attend religious instruction with my newfound friend. The school bus would take us to the church, and her mother would bring me home. She agreed, I suspect, as it would not inconvenience her in the least.

I started receiving Bible instruction at Grace Episcopal Church on Main Street every Wednesday afternoon. The white pastor and his wife ran the classes. Their kids were also schoolmates of mine. They seemed to be a loving family who had fun together.

This was the first time in my life that I learned about God, the Ten Commandments, and the stories in the Bible. I was intrigued and interested so much that I even completed the voluntary homework assignments they gave us each week.

Laura sang in the children's choir and suggested I join also. She thought it would be fun, but in my mind, I felt it would be another wonderful way to be out of the house and away from Foster Mom if only for a few extra hours each week. I asked the pastor if he would please call Foster Mom to get permission for me to join the choir. One call from the pastor, and I was in, taking part in choir practice, after religious instruction every Wednesday with about twenty-five other kids.

It was exciting and different to learn how to sing the religious songs, chants, and responses that I heard on Sundays during the regular church service. Marching into the church, up to the altar, and sitting in the pews reserved for the choir was something I'd never experienced before. Being that close to the pastor, assistant ministers, and altar boys carrying the cross and candles made me feel like I was part of something special. Taking direction and cues from the choir master as to when to stand, turn, genuflect, kneel, sit, bow your head, or make the sign of the cross was intriguing to me.

Once our choir marched reverently into the sanctuary, we were expected to be quiet and perfectly well behaved during the ninety-minute service. This we could do, but Laura and I thought of a way to communicate as we sat across from each other in our pews, on opposite sides of the altar. We decided to learn sign language and spell out with our fingers what we wanted to say during the church service.

One Sunday morning, we became too engrossed in our finger antics. We started silently laughing, giggling, and making faces at each other across the pews, when we should have had our heads bowed in reverent prayer. The choir director saw this and was not happy. He made calls to both our parents immediately after the church service.

"So, you thought it was funny making faces and playing hand games in church, huh?" Foster Mom hissed at me like a serpent, as soon as I walked in the door after being dropped off by Laura's parents.

I kept my eyes peeled on the floor, too afraid to give her eye contact, for fear of being thought of as obstinate. The idea was to try as much as possible to avert another hefty slap to my face.

"I'll show you what's funny. You're under punishment for the next two months, and no more choir practice for you," she added.

I didn't respond; there was no use. I was guilty, but two months? That was the whole summer, since school would be out soon.

"Go upstairs to your room, and don't come out unless I call you."

I thought about that as I made my way to my room. Sitting on the edge of the bed, gazing out the little window, I reflected on what Foster Mom said. Shrugging my shoulders, I laid back on the pillow, studying the corners of the ceiling. *Okay, so I have to stay in my room and don't come out unless she tells me to.* Bedroom, bathroom, basement. That was the story of my life anyway, so what difference did it make? I already felt like a condemned prisoner, in jail for life. Truth be told, Foster Mom's punitive sentence didn't really faze me. It was just her verbalizing what she had been doing to me anyway.

That entire summer was spent with me cleaning, washing and ironing clothes, and picking imaginary weeds. After doing dinner dishes, I'd take a bath, put on my pajamas, and retreat to my room to listen to the radio or read. This was usually around 7 p.m. The sun was still shining bright, but I was ready for bed.

Laura and her younger sister trudged up the hill one hot afternoon and yelled to my open window.

"Hey, Carolyn, can you come outside and play for a while?"

Getting off the bed, I pressed my face against the screened window.

"No, I'm still under punishment from church," I tried to answer in a low voice, so Foster Mom would not hear.

"What, from church?" Laura said with wide eyes. "That was weeks ago. You still in trouble for that?" Her voice rose; she couldn't believe it.

"I'm on punishment for the whole summer." I tried to say in a loud whisper.

"Girl, I'll see you when school starts. Bye." And with that, the two sisters turned and headed back down North Road toward their house, five blocks away.

Spending the whole summer in my bedroom prison, I got to see and hear some things that were incredibly painful for me. Things I probably wasn't supposed to be witness to. I saw undeniable proof of the hell and torture my baby brother was being subjected to at the hands of Foster Mom.

Whenever she wanted him, she would scream his name out in a loud, piercing voice, "Gaaad-neeer," coming from her bedroom, the kitchen, or whatever part of the house she was in. I could hear the rustling and the patter of feet as Gardiner would scamper out of his room to rush to wherever the call was coming from. The way she yelled out his name unnerved me, so I know it tore him to pieces.

Coming out of my room one afternoon, to head down to the basement for my daily drudgery of chores, I passed the open bathroom door. Looking in, I froze. Foster Mom had her hand on the back of Gardiner's neck and was pushing his head down in the toilet. With his back bent over and his hands straddling the rim of the toilet bowl, I couldn't see his face at all, just the back of his black, curly hair.

He was sobbing his heart out as she held his head down.

"Do you see it? Do you see what I want you to clean?" she demanded.

Through muffled sounds, sniffling, and crying, I heard my little brother say repeatedly, "Yes Mom, yes Mom."

"Yes what?"

"Yes, I see it," he whimpered.

Her back was to me, but she must have sensed my presence. She turned and glared at me as she slammed the bathroom door shut. When I got to the basement, I went into the half-bathroom, sat on the covered toilet, and buried my face in my hands and began to sob. Crying for my defenseless baby brother and the incredible feeling of helplessness that washed over me. Looking up at the light coming in from the bathroom window, I said out loud,

"Why, God, why?"

On another occasion, after my solitary meal in the basement, I went up to the kitchen to wash dishes. Passing by the hallway, a movement caught my eye. Turning my head, I saw Gardiner standing in the middle of the hall with his hands clasped above his head, as he tried to balance himself on one foot. For an instant, I thought he was playing around until I saw the look in his eyes. I stood at the bottom of the steps, looking up at him. I was puzzled, what in the world was he doing.

Then I heard, "Gaaad-neeer." Foster Mom came out of the hall bathroom with a house slipper in her hand. Gardiner was teetering back and forth. She slapped him several times with the slipper, each time causing him to flinch, lose his balance, and hit his elbow on the wall. She hit him again and again with the slipper. Tears were streaming down his face.

"Put your foot down one more time, and I'll slap you again." She held the slipper close to his face.

I silently slipped into the kitchen and turned on the faucet. Shaking my head, I tried to erase that awful scene. But some things are etched into your memory forever. I knew for sure that these traumatic, horrific experiences inflicted on my brother at such a young, vulnerable age, would haunt him for the rest of his life.

My friend, cycle, period, menstruation, monthly, it had so many darn names, came at the most inopportune time at the end of the school year with Mr. Chesden. One of my snickering male classmates announced to me as I was walking by his desk, "Ha, Carolyn, you started your period."

I stopped walking and turned to face this little twerp.

"How do you know? You don't know nothing," I said with an indignant tilt to my head.

"Yes, you did. You can't lie. There's a red spot on the back of your pants."

It didn't help that I had on white shorts that day. I was mortified when my menstrual cycle had decided to make its first grand appearance in the middle of Mr. Chesden's fifth-grade elementary class. I was so grateful the gym teacher had separated the boys from the girls last year and showed us filmstrips about this "natural female occurrence," as she called it. So, I knew it was going to happen eventually, but I wasn't ready for the big reveal in Mr. Chesden's class.

Thank God for the gym teacher educating me on this natural fact of female life, because Foster Mom never said a word about it or anything else that would help prepare me for the transformations that were happening to my body. Hair began to appear under my arms and private parts. My breasts were beginning to swell and ache every month during my period.

The only feminine hygiene information came one evening after I had taken my nightly bath. Foster Mom entered my room with a small red jar, saying as she unscrewed the top, "This is Tussey deodorant. You need to put some under your arms every day to keep from smelling."

With that, she scooped out a large mound of the white cream with her finger and started smearing it on my back. If it belonged under my arms, why the heck was she putting it on my back? But I didn't say a word. She put the red top back on the jar and slapped it down on my dresser.

That was the full extent of my emerging adolescent education from Foster Mom. When I announced to her that I started my period in school, she appeared at my bedroom door with a sanitary belt and a box of white, cushioned sanitary pads.

"Do you know how to use these?"

"Yes, Mom, we learned about that last year in fourth grade," I answered.

Thank goodness for my gym teacher, I thought, *because you sure didn't tell me a darn thing about this period stuff.*

By the time I started seventh grade at Woodlands School, I had been having my period for a year and a half. During that time, it was coming every month like clockwork, accompanied by painful, debilitating cramps. I tried to tell Foster Mom how much agony I was in. But she honestly didn't care, dismissing my distress like I was a worrisome fly circling her head. She said in a dry, unfeeling voice,

"Get used to it. You're not staying home from school."

One day, the female administrator in the lunchroom quickly ushered me to the nurse's office, after I puked in the middle of the cafeteria floor. The nurse was so nice and concerned. She listened attentively, her eyes never leaving my face, as I told her about the agonizing cramps that assaulted me every month. There was a look of surprise on her face when I said, "No, don't bother to call my Foster Mom. She already said I can't miss school because of my period."

"How often do you throw up, Carolyn?" she asked in a quiet voice.

"During the first two days of each cycle. I can feel my stomach cramping, and I try to make it to the bathroom. But this time it happened too fast. I made a mess in the cafeteria; I'm so embarrassed. Sometimes like today, I don't make it all the way to the toilet. I've thrown up on the bathroom floor or in the trash can …" My voice trailed off.

I lowered my eyes and started crying. Sitting in the chair, gripping my abdomen, I rocked back and forth, then bending over trying to alleviate the incessant rolling pain. The nurse listened with a sympathetic look on her face. She could sense my utter distress.

"That's okay, Carolyn. Don't worry, I'll put a note about this in your charts, and I'll give you a special pass to come here whenever you are having severe cramps. We don't want you getting sick in class, the hall, or the cafeteria anymore. You can lay down on my cot anytime you need to."

With that, she guided me to a small back room and motioned for me to lie down. She put a blanket over me and said as she turned off one of the ceiling lights to dim the room, "I'll call you in time to catch your bus home. It's going to be all right, dear."

Empathy. Compassion. Understanding, from someone I didn't even know. It was an unexpected, wonderful gift, a present of kindness that I didn't see coming but was ever so grateful for. I felt a wave of relief that I didn't have to suffer each month alone, that I had at least one understanding ally looking out for me. And again, it was at school.

Jesse was in one of my classes. He was tall, light skinned, and had a thick head of jet-black soft hair. His slightly slanted eyes were framed by full, unruly eyebrows. We were attracted to each other immediately. Me, because he reminded me of my brothers with his good looks and mischievous smile. What drew him to me, I wasn't sure. Maybe because I was quiet and kept to myself. Or maybe it was because I had six brothers and was comfortable being around boys. It was quite easy for me to talk to him. And it was easy for him to approach me, as I didn't hang around with other groups of girls for fear of being teased.

Jesse carried my books and walked me to class when our schedules allowed. At the end of the day, he also escorted me to where my bus was located before heading off to catch his.

He was so much fun. We laughed, joked, and talked about how different our home lives were. I was thrilled to have someone my own age to talk to, someone who thought I was special. We were experiencing our first school crush.

When Jesse found out that I walked every Saturday from Parkway Gardens into Greenburgh to get stockings, we realized his house was only a couple of blocks away from the main road I traveled along. He asked his mother for permission for me to stop at their house, so he could walk with me the rest of the way to the store, then part of the way back to my house. To our surprise, she said yes. This gave us some private time on Saturdays to be together.

The back of their house was situated facing Interstate 287. I had to walk across the Hillside Avenue Bridge above the highway to get to the business section in town. Since I came about the same time each Saturday, Jesse's mother or sisters could see me out their back windows.

"Here she comes, Jesse, get ready. She's almost here," one of them would yell.

About five months into our relationship of being boyfriend and girlfriend, Jesse asked me to go to the movies with him on a Saturday afternoon. I gingerly broached the subject with Foster Mom.

"One of my friends wants me to go to the movies on Saturday. Is it okay?" I asked after cleaning the basement, washing, ironing, and folding everyone's clothes.

"Hmmm, with who?" Foster Mom inquired as she picked up a pile of folded garments.

"His name is Jesse. He lives in Greenburgh, right over the bridge. He goes to Woodlands and is in seventh grade like me."

She lifted some of her husband's shirts that were on hangers. Inspecting them, she said, "You can go next Saturday, but you'd better be ready to finish all your chores on Sunday after church."

I was elated. Around noon the following Saturday, I made my weekly pilgrimage down Hillside Avenue to meet up with Jesse, get my stockings, and go on my first date.

Once I secured my stockings for church, we boarded a bus and rode into White Plains, where the movie theater was located. We had a fantastic time, giggling, holding hands, and kissing in the darkened theater. When we got back to his house late that afternoon, his mother invited me to stay for dinner. Wow, the thought of that was too good to pass up. Having dinner with a real family, around a table full of people talking and laughing nonstop was a treat. Jesse's sisters were about the same age as me, and his cousin Midge was in some of my classes. We had a wonderful time. In some small way, I felt like I was a part of this tight-knit, boisterous family, if only for a few precious hours.

It had been years since I ate a meal in the company of others. Only Jesse knew that I ate alone in the basement of my foster parents' house. It was so easy to talk to him and share the private details of my life. He knew about my family situation and didn't judge me. He genuinely cared about me.

When it got dark, his mother told him he had to walk home with me. The hours had passed so quickly that I completely lost track of time. Foster Mom had not given me a curfew, but I knew darn well I should have been home hours earlier. I was probably going to be put on a long, arduous punishment again, but I didn't care. For one day, I was free and having the time of my life, with a happy family who wanted me around.

Walking in the dark, his arm draped over my shoulders, we talked about the day's events. Jesse was astonished at how far I walked every week. It was his first time being in Parkway Gardens. When we finally made our way up North Road, past my seven presidents to Foster Mom's house, I still wasn't ready to let him go. We stood across from the house under a streetlamp, quietly talking and holding on to the moment. About thirty minutes later, we crossed over to the back of the house, where he planted one last kiss on my lips.

"I hope you don't get in too much trouble. I'll see you Monday at school." With that, he turned and started his own solitary, long walk home.

Pulling open the screened entryway, I gently knocked on the inside door. I felt my body tense up as I heard the latch turning. There in her night bonnet and bathrobe, Foster Mom hissed,

"Don't be standing under that streetlight for all the neighbors to see you. You should've been home hours ago."

I didn't know what to say, so I mumbled, "Yes, Mom." I followed her up the stairs and turned to go into my room.

I turned on the little AM radio in the dark and held it close to my ear. A few minutes later, the announcer said, "It's eleven thirty-five." Turning the plastic dial to silence the radio, I pondered over the day's events and the harsh retribution that was sure to come.

The next day, after church, while I methodically ironed piece after piece of clothing, I was lost, deep in thought. I was barely twelve years old and had been gone all day and night, almost eleven hours on my first date, with a boy that Foster Mom had never seen or met. She never said another word about it. It was like it never happened. I was dumbfounded. Each time she called me or I passed her in the house, I was ready, waiting for her to drop the hammer of wrath on my head. But nothing.

I had been out for hours with a boy, but wasn't allowed to have female friends over to the house. I was puzzled. Something was wrong with this picture, but I couldn't figure it out. Why wasn't she saying anything? Why wasn't she levering out a lengthy, unbearable prison sentence, and why wasn't she coming up with a litany of impossible chores for me to complete?

I decided to leave well enough alone, keep my head down, and continue to be submissive. Maybe for some unexplainable reason, I wasn't in trouble. I sure didn't want to do anything to make waves.

Over the next few weeks, I never mentioned Jesse or asked to go out again. We stuck to our routine of seeing each other in school and him meeting me on Saturdays for my weekly walk to get stockings for church.

Early one Saturday spring morning, Foster Mom woke me up asking, "Do you know where Alexander's is, across from the church?"

"Yes, Mom," I said sitting up in the bed, while rubbing the sleep from my eyes.

"You need an overnight bag. The smallest size they sell in their luggage sets. Do you know what I'm talking about?"

Nodding I responded again, "Yes, Mom."

"Get dressed and eat your cereal. I'm going to give you money to get one." She turned and pulled the door shut behind her.

Alexander's was a big department store right across from our church on Main Street. I had only been inside a few times, but I loved looking at the beige mannequins in the display windows. They were always dressed in beautiful, expensive-looking outfits, posing in lavish seasonal scenes. Alexander's and the church were at least another mile and a half further than where I got my stockings. It was going to take me twice as long to walk there and back, past many busy intersections and a lot of traffic. But I didn't care. It was another reason to get out of the house for a longer period of time.

About an hour later, Foster Mom came to the top of the basement stairs, holding one of my light jackets.

"Here, put this on."

Walking up to the top step, I took the jacket from her outstretched hand.

"This is twenty dollars. It should be more than enough for you to buy one of their small overnight bags," she said, folding a bill and stuffing it quickly into the top pocket of my jacket.

"You better not lose it," she said in a threatening tone.

"Yes, Mom."

With that, I turned, went down the steps, and out the side basement door to begin my even longer, solitary trek to downtown White Plains.

She hadn't said anything about me using some of the money to catch the bus once I made it to the busy thoroughfare that led into town. The same bus that Jesse and I took to the movies. I wouldn't even know where to get change for a twenty-dollar bill, and if I spent money on the bus ride, would I have enough to pay for the overnight bag? As these thoughts circulated in my mind, I ambled down North Road on the first leg of my journey.

Humming and singing some popular radio tunes, I was feeling relatively happy as I took in the familiar streets and homes that I passed every weekend. About thirty minutes later, I crossed the bridge not far from Jesse's house. I knew I couldn't see him. I was sure his mother would not let him walk all the way into White Plains with me.

As I approached the intersection of Hillside Avenue and Tarrytown Road, I passed the Carvel ice-cream shop on the left corner. Gazing at the few customers waiting in line, I thought how much I would love to have a vanilla-and-chocolate cone. But again, I knew I couldn't spend an extra dime on anything until I paid for the overnight bag. With that thought, I patted my hand on the top pocket of my jacket where the folded twenty-dollar bill was.

But I didn't feel anything, not the outline of money that should have been there. Stopping in the street, I stuck my fingers in the pocket to retrieve the money. But nothing. Nothing was inside the pocket. Right away, I started to panic, pulling open the pocket so I could peer inside. I saw nothing but the blue inside lining. Where was the money? I knew I didn't lose it, because I had not put my hand inside the pocket once Foster Mom deposited the folded bill there. Ripping off the jacket, I held it in front of me to look inside again and again. What in the world was going on? Where did the money disappear to? I knew for sure that I didn't drop it, because I never touched it. The last thing Foster Mom said was that I'd better not lose it. And it was gone, just like that. But how?

I started walking again, feeling confused, then distraught. Waiting for traffic lights to turn green, crossing busy streets, passing more and more business establishments, I didn't know what to think. As I neared the huge, beautiful gray-white expanse of the Westchester County Center, a hideous, sinister thought crept into my mind. I stopped and gazed at the magnificent architecture of the building and thick, lush foliage adorning the grounds in front of it. The thought forming in my brain became as crystal clear and as sharp as the edifice in front of me.

Foster Mom never put the twenty-dollar bill in my pocket. She lied to me. She wanted me to fail, to not come back with the piece of luggage. She wanted to accuse me of losing her money, the very last thing she told me not to do. I was mortified, almost physically sick at the thought of her doing this to me, then punishing me in some twisted, dark way for returning home without the luggage or her money. She had given me an assignment that she knew I could not accomplish, a test that I was destined to fail because she had callously stacked the odds against me.

Making my way toward downtown, I racked my brains. What was I going to do? What could I do? She was going to beat me, punish me, or kill me. Whatever, the outcome was not going to be good. Looking at the front of Grace Episcopal Church, I stood still and thought to myself, *God please forgive me. I'm desperate and about to break one of your commandments.*

I entered Alexander's around midmorning. The store was relatively empty, as it was still early. I casually walked through the different departments on the first floor, as though I had all the time in the world, as I browsed the display cases and racks of clothes. To an onlooker, I'm sure I appeared to simply be examining the various items on sale, gently touching this, turning over a price tag for that. Blouses, pants, pocketbooks, shoes, umbrellas, and yes, luggage.

To my surprise, the luggage department was right near an exit leading to the street outside. I circled the numerous displays of various matching luggage sets. Most of them had the smaller, overnight version that Foster Mom told me to buy. I knew what I was going to do. I had already asked God to forgive me before I walked into the store. I would rather steal and risk getting caught by the store's security guards than go home empty-handed to a wicked, perverted foster mother who had set me up to fall short of her despicable scheme.

Glancing around the entire section of the store that was within my scope of vision, I did not see any clerks or customers. Walking through the rows of luggage, I slid my hand across the handle of a small, floral print overnight bag. Without bending down or breaking my easy stride, I gripped it and walked straight out the exit door and onto the sidewalk. No alarms went off. No one behind me screamed the words *stop, thief.* Without looking back, I casually crossed the street to the church. As I passed it, I slowed down to look up at the gray stone steeple and mouthed the words,

"I'm sorry, dear Lord."

Somewhere during the slow, arduous two-hour journey home, I ripped off the price tag and dropped it on the street. To the people who passed me in their cars, vans, trucks, or on the buses, I'm sure I must have looked like a confident little girl, carrying her pretty overnight bag as she made her way to wherever her final destination was.

When I finally made it to the brown split-level house on North Road, I was filled with remorse and self-loathing. I had sinned, broken the seventh commandment, thou shalt not steal. But I was also feeling intense anger and hatred for the woman who I felt put me in this degrading and shameful predicament. Steal or be humiliated, verbally abused, and unjustly punished. Both choices were horrible; it was a no-win situation.

Foster Mom of course looked surprised when I entered, carrying a pretty, brand-new piece of luggage.

Fingering it, she asked, "How much did it cost? Where is the receipt?"

I looked her straight in the eye and answered, "It was right at twenty dollars; I must have dropped the receipt on my way home."

She didn't say another word about it, and neither did I.

19

Life for me dragged on like one of the scratched records in the basement of my world, constantly skipping and repeating itself. School, church, chores. Repeat. Keep my head down, be submissive, stay out of trouble, don't speak unless spoken to, and don't ask any questions.

I only caught occasional glimpses of my little brother, even though we lived in the same house. As time passed, we never spoke to each other or even smiled at one another. We were both beaten, broken, and worn down by a woman who got pleasure from inflicting verbal abuse and physical pain on us.

No one seemed to notice or care. Not her husband, her daughter, or the social worker from the agency who visited once every year or so. To the outside world, Gardiner and I probably appeared like perfect, well-behaved foster kids. We were like miniature robots, standing at attention, only moving or talking when directed by Foster Mom. Maybe if someone took the time to talk to us alone or even look closer at the blank expressions on our faces, they would have gotten an inkling that something was wrong. Something was off with these two children with the bland look in their eyes and expressionless faces. No one observed the deep sadness lurking just underneath our outward façade. It felt as if we didn't exist, merely moving through life unseen, unnoticed, invisible.

One of the last times I saw my brother was when Foster Mom barged into my room in the middle of the night screaming, "Get up. Get up. I want you to see what your nasty little brother did."

She was standing in my doorway with the hallway light outlining her frame. With hair sticking up wildly about her head and wearing a long, dark robe, she looked like one of the monsters I used to watch on TV a long time ago.

Stumbling out of bed, I followed her down the hallway. Her son, Donnie was standing there in his pajamas, covering his nose with his hand. Foster Mom walked into their bedroom, pushing me in front of her. There was an awful smell, which I immediately recognized as poop. My brother was standing in the corner of the room, disheveled and crying.

Foster Mom pointed to one of the beds. The sheets were pulled all the way back and halfway hanging on the floor. I wasn't sure why she made me come in there or what I was looking at. But I didn't have to wonder for long as she screamed and pointed,

"Your brother shitted on the floor over there in the corner and wiped his butt with the sheet."

Behind us in the hallway I heard her son say in a whining voice, "Yeah, and the smell woke me up outta my sleep."

I looked at my brother, who was petrified, sniffling, and cowering in the corner. He was shaking, rocking from side to side, scared to death. There was nothing I could do or say to help him.

"Carolyn, take these sheets off and put them in the basement sink with some soap and hot water. Gaaad-neeer, you gonna scrub this floor tonight, and then I'm gonna whip your nasty ass."

She reached out with one hand and grabbed him by his face, inserting her thumb in his mouth and gripping his chin. He screamed out in pain and sounded like he was choking on his tongue and spit. I backed up, as she pulled my brother by his mouth, past me and into the hallway. He was crying uncontrollably and gagging. I saw blood oozing out the corner of his mouth. Foster Mom's fingernail had ripped into my brother's mouth, causing it to bleed. I was horrified at what I was seeing, and felt a stab of intense hatred boiling over inside me.

I was paralyzed, glued to the same spot until they were no longer in the stench-filled room. It was only then that I moved to do as I was directed, pulling off the soiled sheets and bundling them in my arms. Making my way down the two sets of stairs to the subbasement, I thought about what was happening at that moment. I knew exactly the debilitating fear my little brother was feeling. He was literally too scared to come out of his room to go to the bathroom, and he certainly better not call out for Foster Mom in the middle of the night to wake her up. She had ingrained that rule in both of us early on. Once you go in your room for the night, you don't dare come out, for any reason. I was already a nervous wreck from her opening and slamming my door shut at random times during the night, so I certainly didn't venture out.

I was at least five years older than my brother, so of course I had better control over my bladder and bowels. Well at least most of the time. There was the one occasion I had to pee really bad in the middle of the night. But like I already said, we were too terrified to come out of our room once we were sent to bed. So, my solution was to squat and pee into the little potted plant that decorated the top of my dresser. I don't think the yellow liquid killed the plant.

However, my brother's bodily functions were too strong for him to control, and the fear instilled in him by Foster Mom crippled him from venturing out into the hall to go to the bathroom. Years later, he would tell me, she made him believe if he came out into the darkened hallway, a monster would snatch him. Of course, being a young, impressionable kid, he believed what this evil adult told him.

Just like me, he felt he was forced into a no-win situation, no matter what he did. He was scared, shamed, and humiliated; then beaten and punished. How many times was he subjected to this type of treatment, over and over again? There was no doubt in my mind that his little life was also like a scratched, broken record.

We rarely took trips together in the car unless it was to see Foster Mom's parents, who lived somewhere in the outer boroughs of the city. When she had her son Donnie, Gardiner, and me pile into the station wagon early one Saturday afternoon, I figured that was where we were going. It was a silent ride as I sat in the back seat next to my brother. Three children in a car, and no one saying a word. We didn't dare. Donnie sitting up front playing with his toy robot. Gardiner and I looking out our respective windows at the city sights flying by. Every now and then, I would slide my hand across the cushion seat and graze my brother's thigh, patting it with a gentle, light touch. I couldn't talk to him, play with him, hug him, or protect him. Through the touch of my hand, I tried to communicate that I missed and loved him very much. I think he got the message. When he felt my hand, he turned from looking out the window and attempted to give me a tiny, barely noticeable smile. That was good enough for me.

About forty minutes later, Foster Mom was navigating her car through the congested New York City traffic lanes. Buses, yellow taxis, delivery trucks, and private cars were all honking their horns, as they tried to make their way down the overcrowded streets. Skyscrapers rose on both sides of us. I strained my neck and tilted my head against the car window in an attempt to see the tops of the magnificent glass-and-concrete giants. There were all kinds of businesses, shops, and stores. Masses of people going and coming, each looking like they were on a mission. Gardiner and I were mesmerized, glued to the enormous amount of activity that was surrounding us. Not even the downtown streets of White Plains had this much action going on.

I noticed the numbers on the corner street signs were going down—45th, 44th, 43rd, and then 42nd. The buildings weren't as tall, and these streets weren't as clean. We passed huge, colorful billboards that read Times Square. Foster Mom inched her way along with the rest of the city traffic. Up ahead, I saw rows of movie theaters, flanked by small businesses on both sides of the street, including cigar shops, camera stores, delicatessens, and souvenir outlets.

The people I saw now didn't appear well dressed like the fashionable, suited folks in front of the city skyscrapers. Those folks had jobs to go to. These individuals, in fact, looked dirty, ragged, and poor. Some were sitting on the street, drinking from bottles in brown paper bags, others meandering up and down with no obvious place to go. One man opened both sides of his jacket in front of two ladies as he showed them rows of watches hanging from the insides. It looked like he was trying to make a sale. I surmised he was a phony salesman. So did the women, as they skirted around him and kept walking.

Was Foster Mom taking us shopping or to see a movie? A feeling of anticipation came over me as I strained to read the theater marquees; there were so many of them. *My Erotic Fantasies*, *Sexcapades*, and *Ghetto Freak*. I read other brightly flashing neon signs that said *Sexy Ladies*, *Naughty Girls*, and *XXX Adults Only*. This was beginning to feel strange; something was off.

There was an open space in front of the movie theater where *Naughty Girls* was playing. Foster Mom pulled her car into the spot and turned off the engine. Everyone was clearly puzzled, but we didn't say a word. Why was she stopping here? This definitely was not a kids' cartoon matinee. In fact, there were no mothers strolling along with children anywhere. Instead, I saw plenty of unkempt men loitering about, but definitely no families of the Greenburgh-White Plains type.

Foster Mom crossed in front of her car, came along the passenger side, and pulled open the back door where I was sitting.

"Come on," she said, looking down at me.

"Donnie, you and Gaaad-neeer wait here. I'll be right back."

Doing as I was told, I climbed out of the car and started surveying the hubbub of street activity. Foster Mom slammed the door shut behind me and started walking toward the movie entrance. The sidewalk was dirty, littered with trash and grimy garbage cans that were overflowing. An intoxicated man eyed us as we walked past, his head bobbing from side to side as he licked his crusty lips. I glanced back over my shoulder and could see my brother and Donnie with confused looks on their faces. I continued to trail behind Foster Mom, who walked up to the lady in the glass-enclosed ticket booth.

"How many?" the lady asked as though she was bored.

"One," Foster Mom was digging for money in her pocketbook.

Hearing that, I looked from the ticket lady to Foster Mom. There must be some mistake. Why did she only buy one ticket? Why not four? One ticket for who?

"Come on," she said over her shoulder, making her way into the dimly lit concession area.

There was no one around other than the man wiping down the top of the candy display case. Foster Mom glanced around, then found the entrance leading into the inner theater, where a movie was in progress. Pushing the door open, we entered. The only light was coming from the movie screen. My eyes were straining to adjust to the sudden darkness. I could barely make out the forms of a few people scattered throughout the theater. Foster Mom approached the last couple of rows in the back and pointed to the seat on the end.

"Sit here. I'll be back to get you when the movie is over," I heard her say to me in the dark.

My eyes darted from her to the few lonely bodies inhabiting the nearly pitch-black theater. I was suddenly frozen with fear, unable to move. She gave me a push toward the end seat.

"I said sit down, and don't you move. I'll be back."

Sinking down on the edge of the hard seat, I looked up at her. Without saying another word, she turned and disappeared up the aisle and back through the door.

I panicked, feeling the same rush of fear, of being left alone, that I had experienced when living with Ma. That awful, heart-stopping feeling I got when I stumbled on her body lying in the dark on our kitchen floor. The heightened anxiety and sense of terror when I was dropped off at the emergency shelter. I was in the dark, alone and being abandoned, again.

My fingers gripped the back of the chair in front of me, my eyes straining to focus on the shapes of the ominous figures slouched all around me, scattered on the numerous, dim rows. I could make out clouds of cigarette smoke rising here and there from the solitary bodies in the seats. The figures talking and moving about on the huge screen cast gray and white eerie shadows throughout the expanse of the theater.

There was no way I was going to stay there, in the dark, by myself, watching the half-naked people squirming about on the huge screen in front of me. Foster Mom had not been gone sixty seconds before I jumped up and made my way out of that god-forsaken theater and back onto the city streets. Her car was nowhere in sight. Frantic, I looked up and down the curb where she had been parked. I couldn't believe it. But it was true, an inconceivable revelation slamming into my mind with the force of a sledgehammer. This lady had left me in a sleazy 42nd Street porno movie theater, where only drunks and derelicts hung out. Did she want me to get kidnapped or raped? Was this another one of her sick, perverted tricks? *Who would do this to their twelve-year-old kid?* I thought as I made my way inside a nearby electronics store. Approaching the balding salesman at the counter, I asked in a nervous, timid voice,

"Excuse me sir, can you tell me where the nearest subway station to the Bronx is?"

Looking over his wire-rimmed glasses and waving his arm, he said, "Make a left, and go down one block. You'll run right into it."

"Thanks." And with that, I was on my way to freedom, to Ma's apartment.

I knew where she was living now, from the few letters she had mailed me at Foster Mom's house. Feeling in my pocket, I had a few nickels and dimes left from money I should have put in the collection plate on Sundays. When I explain to Ma that I had been left alone in a movie theater on 42nd Street, she was going to hit the roof. I'm sure she knew what kind of lowlife people hung out down there. She probably would curse Foster Mom out, after I tell her all the terrible things that were being done to me and Gardiner. Ma would get my little brother and me out of that house of horrors. I was sure of it.

Back in the sunlight, I didn't feel as afraid. In fact, a little surge of confidence was growing inside me. I was going to ride the subway like I used to with my brother Michael and his girlfriend. Being by myself wasn't bad, even if I didn't know where I was, after all, I was used to walking miles alone every Saturday to get stockings. I had no problem asking for directions, because I was hell-bent on making it to Ma's house.

20

Ninety minutes later I was standing in Ma's two-room apartment.

"Pippa, it was dead wrong for that lady to take you down there and leave you. I don't understand why she would do something like that."

"Ma, I told you, she is crazy. She does mean stuff like that to Gardiner and me all the time."

Ma was leaning against the white porcelain kitchen sink, looking at me. This was the first time I had seen her since the social workers took me away six years earlier. She was thinner, had gray hair around her temples, dark rings under her eyes, and the first signs of wrinkles forming across her forehead. Ma appeared tired, worn out.

"I can't go back there, Ma. You gotta let me stay with you," I begged.

Relaying incident after incident, I tried to describe what life had been like for me since that day Googie and I were taken away. What my living hell was like, with this lady who forced me to call her Mom. I felt my throat starting to close, my voice sounding desperate, and tears streaming from my eyes.

"Pippa, I know it's hard for you, but I can't take care of you and your brother. I can barely take care of myself. Look at this place. Look where I live."

With that, she gazed around at her own dismal surroundings. Ma had seven kids, and we were all taken from her. She had no skills, no job, little education, existed on the New York State welfare program, and apparently no boyfriend at that time to help subsidize her menial government income. She was literally just barely surviving herself.

I didn't care about any of that, or the apparent downward spiral her own life had taken over the course of the years. All I knew was that she was my mother, my real family. I knew she loved me. I was her only daughter. Surely, she couldn't, wouldn't make me go back to that hell house in Greenburgh. Not after all that I just told her. But she did.

"I have to call your social worker or that foster lady and let someone know where you are."

Ma was quiet, sad, but she meant what she said. I wouldn't be able to stay with her. I was distraught, as she counted some change in her hand and walked out the door to the payphone on the corner.

I couldn't believe it—that familiar feeling of being abandoned all over again was seeping into my pores. But this time, it cut me to my core. I was being turned away by my own mother. She didn't yell and scream for me to stay like she did years earlier. She wasn't irate, as I thought she'd be when I described the horrific acts inflicted on my baby brother, at the hands of this fake childcare foster parent. In fact, Ma was subdued, drained, and overwhelmed with her own life problems.

When Ma returned a short time later, I hoped she had a change of heart. Maybe this dreadful situation would have an unforeseen, magical ending like the fairy tales I read long ago.

Instead, she slowly, methodically gathered a few belongings and told me she was taking me to the 125th Street station, to take the train to White Plains. She put some crumpled dollar bills in a small plastic snap purse and told me it was cab fare from the station to Foster Mom's house. I didn't know who she called or spoke to on the phone. She didn't say, and I didn't ask. At that point, it didn't even matter.

Ma held my hand tight, as we made our way across town to the familiar train station that Mike used to take me to when I was younger. Everything looked just the same; nothing had changed. Along the way, neither one of us spoke. I had said everything I could, to try to get her to understand the utterly horrible way we were being treated.

We walked up the stairs to the train platform. As the Metro-North locomotive approached and slowly ground to a stop, Ma gathered me in her arms and held me tight. The floodgates of my already red and swollen eyes opened again. This time Ma teared up also.

"I love you, Pippa. Be a good girl and kiss your brother for me."

About an hour later, as the sun was going down, casting long tree shadows on the back of the house, I timidly knocked on the door. Taking in a long, deep breath, I had already mentally prepared myself for whatever unspeakable punishment was surely coming. Seconds later, I heard the inside latch and lock being undone. The door swung open, and there she was, silently glaring at me. I tensed and braced myself for a hard slap, but none came.

After what seemed like an eternity, Foster Mom, with her voice full of venom, said, "The next time you run away, don't come back." She turned and left me standing there.

I entered slowly and cautiously, still not sure what to expect. The house was quiet. Tiptoeing, I made my way up to the bedroom, knowing better than to expect anything to eat or drink. Slipping off my clothes and putting on my pajamas, I got into bed and curled up in a fetal position.

One week later, much to my surprise, another social worker came to the house. I heard Foster Mom call up to my bedroom, telling me to come down. Her voice didn't have the normal, nasty hiss to it. It was more natural sounding, like she was calling her son.

An older white lady got up from the plastic-covered couch and walked toward me and extended her hand. I didn't know what to do. This was different; it felt weird.

"Carolyn, my name is Mrs. Bowman. I've been here talking to your foster mother for a while and asked her if I could take you out for some ice cream. Would you like that?"

"I-I guess so," I stuttered in a barely audible voice. Foster Mom was standing just behind Mrs. Bowman, who couldn't see the stern glare that was being hurled my way.

"Great. I think I passed an ice-cream place down on Hillside Avenue as I was driving here."

Twenty minutes later, Mrs. Bowman and I were sitting in her car in the Carvel parking lot. I was enjoying my first ever ice-cream sundae with bananas, whip cream, and chocolate syrup. She was sipping on a diet soda. We talked for the next two hours about my life with the foster family. I was quite hesitant at first, not sure what Mrs. Bowman intended to do with the information I shared with her. Was she gonna share it with Foster Mom, who of course would deny everything, then exact cruel and inhumane punishments on me?

I had been through so much hell; at that point I really didn't care. Taking in a deep breath, I opened up and started talking. I recalled how Foster Mom slapped the glasses off my face until I caved in and called her Mom. How I was made to spend years by myself eating alone at a small wooden table in the basement. Enduring long, harsh, isolated incarcerations in my bedroom with nothing but an AM radio and a few books to keep me company. Being on the receiving end of physical abuse and watching my baby brother go through so much worse. I showed Mrs. Bowman, the evidence of iron burns on my body because of sheer exhaustion from long hours of washing, drying, folding, and then ironing everyone's clothes in the house.

It was hard. I stuttered many times, got choked up, and cried. But I kept on. This may be the only chance I had to tell a social worker the honest, raw story of my existence in that house of horrors. Mrs. Bowman listened intently, nodding and taking notes on a yellow pad.

I was embarrassed when I recalled my history of stealing. Stealing from my classmate because I was hungry. Stealing frozen food from the freezer in the basement out of sheer desperation. And then stealing the piece of luggage from Alexander's because I was too scared to come home without it. I included in my account how I was made to walk from the house to downtown White Plains, alone. And pointing down the street from where we were parked, to show Mrs. Bowman where I had to walk every Saturday, rain or shine, to buy a pair of stockings for church. She continued to take notes, giving me an occasional nod, or saying in a quiet voice, "It's okay, Carolyn, go on."

I talked about my baby brother and told her how helpless I felt seeing him being pushed, slapped, hit with a shoe, or yelled at. I shared with her that we were both terrified of coming out of our rooms at night, for fear of more punishments. I thought I saw Mrs. Bowman's eyes grow wide when I followed up with my potted plant incident and Gardiner's bowel movement mishap in his bedroom. She needed to know that our fears were real and not just an exaggerated figment of my imagination.

She smiled when I told her about my new boyfriend and how welcome his family made me feel. I talked about the kind school nurse who helped me out every month during my horrific cramps and bouts of throwing up. I shared that Foster Mom never gave me medicine for it or let me stay home.

Mrs. Bowman stopped writing altogether when I told her about Foster Mom leaving me alone in a dark 42nd Street porno movie theater and how I got on a subway by myself to find my mother's apartment.

There were so many things that I didn't share with her, but after two hours had passed, I think she got the picture. I at least hoped that she believed me. When you are telling the truth, it's easy. You don't have to waste time thinking about what to say. It just comes out. And a great deal of it came out that afternoon, sitting in the Carvel parking lot with someone I had never seen before. A flood of tears and raw, heartfelt emotions were laid bare. I shared my brutal, truthful accounts of our hell on earth, at the hands of someone who was charged with taking care of us.

When you're twelve years old and have been in the foster care system for as long as I had been, you still don't know how things work, how they unfold. You don't know what questions to ask, or even who to ask. And out of fear of retaliation, you certainly don't know who you can trust to even tell your truth to. The average person in my life during that time would not believe the events that I shared with the social worker. It would be easier to think that I was a little liar, just making up stories on that nice, churchgoing family, in that idyllic-looking split-level house on the corner lot in Parkway Gardens.

Maybe it was the call Ma made that day when I appeared at her house. Or perhaps the conversation I shared with the new social worker. Or maybe someone contacted the school to verify my monthly ailments.

I'd like to think it was everything, all of the above, and the Man from above looking down on me. Since I started attending Grace Episcopal Church and going to Wednesday religious instruction classes, I had developed my own one-sided conversations with God. I talked to

Him when I was alone, and that was most of the time, in my room, in the basement, and on my long, solitary Saturday walks.

He knew all about my trials and hardships. He certainly knew about my shortcomings and bouts with stealing. And I think He knew about the pain and suffering that Gardiner and I were going through, because I brought that up every week. I also told God about my fifth-grade teacher who made me feel special, the junior high school nurse who helped me, and my first boyfriend crush and his family who made me feel welcomed. Sometimes I asked God about my brothers, Ma, and Mike. I wanted to know how they were doing. I told Him I missed them and to please take care of them. Even though I thought my life felt impossible, I told God that I still hoped and dreamed for something better.

About two weeks later, on a Friday evening, my simplistic but humble conversations with God were answered. Foster Mom barged into my room with no warning and walked over to the bed where I was sitting. She had a small pile of folded brown grocery store bags. Throwing them on the bed, she simply said,

"Pack all your things. That social worker is coming for you in the morning."

Plain, simple, direct. Just the way she had trained me during all those years. I didn't ask any questions, even though I had many. Where was I going? Home to Ma finally? To another foster home? To an emergency shelter? Nearby or far away? Would I be going to my same school? Was my little brother coming with me?

Everything I owned in the world except my winter coat fit into four bags and my one piece of stolen luggage. My brother was right down the hall from me, just a few feet away, and I couldn't even spend time with him. I wondered if he knew I was leaving. He would feel even more frightened, hopeless, and alone if he thought I left him without saying a word.

I stayed awake all night in anxious anticipation of what was coming. That demon foster mother did not open and slam my door that night. I don't know why, and I didn't care. I could feel that a change was coming, and I was hoping and praying that it had to be better than this unbearable nightmare that I had been damned to for the past six years.

Stiff and awkward, that's how it felt standing in that fake, plastic living room for the last time. Mrs. Thompson and Mrs. Bowman exchanged some verbal information as I stood by the front door, hugging my little brother. He looked lost and scared, just as I knew he would, upon learning of my sudden departure. All I could do was promise to send him a letter or postcard as soon as I was able.

Once in the car, I looked up at the front door. Gardiner was still standing there with his hand up, making little waving motions. I asked Mrs. Bowman,

"What's gonna happen to my brother? Is he going to another foster home?"

"No, Carolyn, I'm going to come back to get him on Monday. He'll be going to a residential treatment facility, to live in a house with other boys his age."

As we pulled out of the driveway and headed down North Road, past the familiar streets named after the early presidents, I was still thinking about Gardiner, feeling guilty that I had left him.

"Is the place far from where I'll be living? Will I be able to see him?"

"He will be in Yonkers, not far from you. But he needs to get settled in, and so do you. But I'm sure something can be arranged," Mrs. Bowman said.

That was good enough for me, for now. At the bottom of the hill, I turned to look at the wooden street sign, saying in my mind, *Good-bye, Parkway Gardens. I hope I never see you again in life.*

21

The Parkers were my third and last foster family. They lived about twenty-five minutes from Greenburgh in a residential section of White Plains. Their light-gray stucco three-story home with a slanted roof was located on a steep hill. The house was small and reminded me of those log cottages found deep in the woods, in my fairy-tale books. On top of the attached single-car garage was an outside patio area. The Parker home was nestled on a tiny swath of property engulfed by tall, green-leaf trees and lush foliage on three sides.

The entire family was there to greet us. Mr. Parker, tall, with leather-looking dark skin, spoke with an accent. He was from some island in the Caribbean. Mrs. Parker was just the opposite—short, noticeably light skinned, with piercing gray eyes framed by brown glasses. Her hair was light red with gray strands around the temples. She had the smallest nose I had ever seen on a Black person. The Parkers had two little boys. Martie, the youngest, was five, cute and shy, as he hid behind his mother's hips. Paulie, age seven, was more outgoing, as he extended his hand to greet me.

Mrs. Parker gave me a quick tour of their house with the boys trailing close behind. I had my own room. The twin bed was decorated with a pink-and-green plaid bedspread, with matching window curtains and sheer drapes over the door of my very own miniature balcony. The room had an all-white dressing table with a tall trifold mirror attached to it. A white-cushioned stool was in front of it. It was a beautiful room, the nicest I ever had.

A short time later, Mrs. Bowman and Mrs. Parker stood outside the front door on the sidewalk. I walked up to them.

"Well, Carolyn, I hope you will be happy here with the Parkers. I know they were excited about having you live with them. Do you have any questions for me before I go?"

"Yes," I said with a twinge of fear beginning to eat at me. "Will you make sure I know where my brother is, so I can write him?"

"That won't be a problem. I'll call back on Monday with the address." The two women continued to look at me.

"I-I just have one more question."

"Sure, what is it?" Mrs. Bowman asked.

I looked at her, then to my new foster parent. "What do I call you?" It was a whisper, and I'm sure Mrs. Bowman knew exactly why I asked. I wanted to get clarification on that point before she got in her car and left me there.

"What do you want to call us?"

"Can I call you Mr. and Mrs. Parker?"

"Of course, dear, that will be fine," Mrs. Parker said with a big smile.

I was so relieved as I gave Mrs. Bowman a quick good-bye hug.

It didn't take me long to get adjusted to my new family and surroundings. Mrs. Parker was surprised at the small amount of clothes I had with me. She was an avid seamstress and used the small room on the third floor to sew, while she watched her favorite daytime stories on a tiny black-and-white TV. There were rolls of fabric and material everywhere, along with hundreds of spools of colorful thread. A tall thin mirror, a headless mannequin, and a table with a Singer sewing machine were all on one side of the room. An ironing board was set up in a corner. This room was her very own tailor shop. Mrs. Parker offered to make me some matching skirt, dress, and pants sets. I was thrilled, as all my clothes were worn and outdated.

That first afternoon, she took me to a Woolworth's store on Mamaroneck Avenue and bought me a straightening comb with its own electric heating unit for my hair. Then she piled ribbons, barrettes, grease, combs, and brushes into the basket. Lotion, deodorant, sanitary pads, belts, new underwear, and a bathrobe rounded out our first shopping trip. I thought Mrs. Parker had just as much fun as I did that day. This was an entirely new, exciting experience for me. It felt like Christmas in April.

On Monday, I was enrolled in Highlands Junior High School, to finish out the last couple of months of my seventh-grade year. Mrs. Parker made sure I had plenty of paper, composition notebooks, assignment pads, pencils, pens, rulers, and crayons. The assistant principal gave me my schedule and showed me the cafeteria, library, gym, and where I would catch the bus to go home in the afternoon.

The school was a long, two-story gray building. All my classes were on the first floor and easy to find. I was still very self-conscious about my stuttering, so I didn't speak unless a teacher asked me a question. During that first week, I kept to myself, just trying to get used to a new home and now a new school.

Most of the kids in my classes had known each other for years and had been together at least since their sixth-grade year. They were comfortable with one another, had already formed cliques, knew the nuances of the various teachers and how to navigate around the school premises.

It didn't take me long to realize how far behind academically I was in my classes. I was not used to doing homework, taking notes, studying for tests, writing reports, or completing projects. The foster mother in Greenburgh never asked me about school. She evidently didn't care about the importance of my education, so neither did I.

I was shocked when Mrs. Parker asked me every day how school went and if I had homework. The teachers had given me textbooks for language arts, reading, science, social studies, and math. I also had gym and a home economics class, but thank goodness those teachers didn't use textbooks. Mrs. Parker told me when I got home each afternoon I had to start on my homework, and if I didn't have any, I still needed to read or study. The small vanity table in my bedroom also served as my desk.

I gave schoolwork my best effort, but I had no foundation, no sound established academic work habits to draw on. Day after day, I struggled with keeping up with the assignments, reports, and expectations from seven different teachers. It was a mess, and my end-of-year report card with five failing grades was a testament to that fact.

Mrs. Parker could not help me with my classes; after all, her first and only job was to be a good wife and mother, which she was. While she recognized that I was struggling, she was always supportive and encouraging. She told me things like, "Carolyn, don't be afraid to raise your hand and ask questions. Sit up front, so you can see the board and hear the teacher. If you know the answer, don't worry about stuttering. Just take your time and get it out."

I gave it a half-hearted attempt. Ma had never bothered me about school, and neither did the first two foster mothers. This was literally my first academic intervention from someone I lived with.

At home, the family ate dinner together every night. Mrs. Parker gave me the task of setting the table and then helping her with the dishes when we finished. In all honesty, I was intimidated by eating in the presence of adults. I found it painful to engage in the lively, everyday chitchat as we consumed our food. Eating alone in the basement for six years, compounded by a stuttering problem, hampered my ability to socialize and communicate with others, even on the most basic level.

Still, no one pushed or criticized me. I was not intimidated or humiliated for the slightest infraction. Other than keeping my room clean and straightening up the bathroom after I used it, Mrs. Parker did not add a litany of chores for me to engage in. When I questioned her about what chores she needed me to do, her response was,

"Carolyn, your only real job around here is to focus on your schoolwork."

The emphasis in this new home was on being together as a family unit. There was a lot of conversation and laughter. The boys felt free to run in and out of their parents' bedroom. Mrs. Parker welcomed me in there too, when I wanted to watch a new science-fiction show on TV called *Star Trek*. That is, if my homework was done. I hadn't been allowed to watch TV for six years, so to be able to do this was a huge treat. My new foster mother had a strange look on her face when I asked if it was all right to come out of my room at night to use the bathroom.

She also enjoyed answering my never-ending questions about her sewing machine, stacks of patterns, and fashion books. By the end of the summer, Mrs. Parker had shown me how to buy and cut out a pattern. Then together, we laid out and pinned the fabric and ended with me sewing my first simple sleeveless blouse.

Mr. Parker left for work early in the morning before I got up for school. He would disappear into the bedroom or basement as soon as dinner was over. He was a man of few words, and that was fine with me. The Parkers seem to have an easygoing relationship. I never heard either one of them raise their voice in anger. I guess their marriage was based on love and respect, both of which I found unique and refreshing. That was something I had not witnessed since the last time I saw Sam and Mattie when I was about five years old. During the sixteen months I lived with the Parkers, I never heard a cuss word pass between them. I was experiencing a lot of positive firsts being with this family.

Vanetta and Cece were two girls my age who lived around the corner and rode my bus to school. As time passed, the three of us became good friends. I was surprised when Mrs. Parker said yes, I could have them over to visit. And once she met their parents, I was able to go to their homes. This was monumental to me, having girlfriends over to visit in my room, on the porch or backyard. We roared with unbridled laughter at each other's jokes or whispered when sharing personal secrets. It was the most fun I had had in years. I was starting to feel alive again.

Vanetta's mom, Mrs. Bryant, was a single parent and the principal of a school in New York City. I was immediately impressed by the proper way she spoke and the quiet, sophisticated way she carried herself. She didn't talk much, but when she spoke, Vanetta listened with respect. Their house was always immaculate with everything in its proper place. All Vanetta's clothes and underwear were neatly ironed, folded, placed in their respective drawers, or hung up according to style and color.

I wasn't exactly sure how a person became a school principal or what the job responsibilities entailed, but I believe knowing that Mrs. Bryant, a Black woman, was in charge of an entire school planted the seeds of something deep inside me. Something I couldn't clearly articulate, other than saying to myself, *When I grow up, I wanna be like her.*

Cece lived across from Vanetta in a house with her parents, Reverend and Mrs. Rollins, and her younger brother, Metz. I loved being around this clan, because they always had something going on. Mrs. Rollins loved to cook and share her desserts and treats with the neighborhood kids. During the winter months, when it was cold outside, she had us shovel the snow off their driveway. Afterward, we would have snowball fights or build a snowman on the front lawn. Mrs. Rollins always treated us to hot chocolate with huge marshmallows melting on top.

It was clear to me that this family loved each other and enjoyed one another's company. So, unbeknownst to me, another seed was planted in my subconscious mind. This was how I wanted my family to be when I grew up—together, happy, and living in harmony.

The other thing I picked up from my two new friends and their families was their parents' focus on education and its importance. Both girls got good grades, took pride in their schoolwork, and were on the honor roll. I watched from the sidelines as the three parents questioned their school assignments, why they got the grade they did, what did they need to do better, and finally lavished lots of verbal praise on them when they were successful. This was all totally new to me, and I liked it.

My two new friends didn't tease me about being a foster kid, and they didn't question me about my family background. They didn't laugh when I stuttered or make fun of my hair, the gap in my teeth, oversized nose, or the glasses I had to wear every day.

By the time we entered eighth grade we had our priorities straight: school, clothes, boys, and music. Both Vanetta and Cece could play the piano and sing. Vanetta had been taking piano lessons for years, and I guess Cece picked it up from church, since her dad was a pastor, and her mother sang in the choir.

I didn't care for the piano, because I held on to negative memories of that nasty foster brother who was gyrating on my backside years ago. But maybe singing was an option. The girls persuaded me to try out for the school chorus. They had been in it since sixth grade, so they didn't have to audition each year.

I was quite hesitant and deathly afraid that the choral director would ask me to speak, maybe tell a little about myself. I didn't want to end up stuttering and being embarrassed in front of all my peers. But that was not what happened. On the afternoon of tryouts, I sat in the chorus room with at least sixty other nervous students. We were seated in long rows with the director standing in front by his piano.

"All right listen up. There's a lot of you in here, and that's good. But we are going to have to do this real fast, so I can get you all back to class in time to catch your buses."

Okay, I thought to myself. *At least he's not going to ask each of us to speak.*

"I'm going to point to you and play a note on the piano. You listen to it and sing what you hear. Like this."

He demonstrated by striking a key on the piano, then opening his mouth wide to belt out a long sound that was in tune with the piano.

"Any questions? No? Good," he said, surveying the excited group of youngsters before him.

"If you make it, I'll say write your name on the pad by the door. Then you leave and go straight back to your class."

With that, the tryouts started. Most kids hit their respective note on the first try. Some who were a little more nervous, he gave a second chance. To each one, he ended with, "Write your name." Up and down each row with rapid-fire speed. He was not fooling around; it was all business. Hit your note and return to class. I was in the third row. He struck the key on the piano, and I opened my mouth, letting out the sound I thought I heard.

"Okay, let's try that again," he said, looking at me and hitting the piano key. And again, I sat up straight, opened my mouth, and gave him my best shot. He shook his head. "I'll come back to you."

He moved on to the rest of the students in my row and then completed the whole row behind me, until I was the only one left in the room with him. He had told every single student, "Write your name."

Looking at me, he said, "Okay, young lady, let's try it again," and with that, he struck a note, and I repeated what I thought was the sound.

"Do it again," he instructed, and I did.

The choral director looked at me in utter frustration and struck the same key several times.

"Do you hear that? Can you hear that note?"

I nodded and in a little voice said, "Yes."

Finally, exasperated and shaking his head, he said,

"Young lady, chorus is not for you. You may want to consider some other club or extracurricular activity." And with that, he closed the hood on the piano.

I guess I was dismissed to go back to my class. My feelings should have been hurt. Maybe they were for a split second. Thoughts were flying around in my head. All that singing I did while listening to Cousin Brucie on the radio, while playing jazz records in the basement and belting out tunes walking for miles alone, along Hillside Avenue gave me a false sense of being able to do something that I clearly could not. As I walked down the hallway, this revelation was like a hot news flash going across the front of my mind.

I thought to myself, *Wow, I really can't sing, I was the only one in that whole room who didn't make the chorus. And according to the chorus director, I can't copy the sound of the piano key. So, if I can't sing, there must be something else I can do, and I'm going to find out what that is.*

Later that afternoon, when I told Vanetta and Cece that I did not make the chorus, they were just as disappointed as I was. But I still wanted to do something extra in school, just like they were doing.

Vanetta came up with another idea. "Well, since you like music, why don't you join beginners' band?"

"Yeah, Carolyn, you can do that. That would be great," Cece added.

"I don't know how to read music, and I sure don't play any instruments." My bubble of hope felt like it was going to burst again.

"Don't be silly, that's what beginners' band is all about. They teach you everything you need to know," Vanetta chimed in.

"Tomorrow when we get to school, we'll show you where the band room is. The band director, Mr. Porter, is a real cool guy."

During dinner, when I shared this newfound information with the Parkers, they were surprised. I backtracked and told them how I had tried out for chorus but didn't make it. So, I wanted to see if I could be in the beginners' band.

"What do we need to do to get you in there?" Mrs. Parker asked.

"I think you just have to call the school to get my schedule changed."

"No problem. I'll take care of that first thing in the morning," she said.

"Carolyn, we're very proud of you. It took guts for you to try out for the chorus. I'm sorry you didn't make it. You'll do good in band," Mr. Parker said, finishing up his last forkful of food.

That felt good, to have the support of two adults in my life. They were encouraging me to try something new. This was a big step for me. I was venturing into unknown water and had no idea what was ahead.

My classes were changed, so that I went to beginners' band every day instead of home economics. It was a small class with maybe fifteen other students who, like me, didn't know a thing about reading music or playing an instrument. Mr. Porter was kind and patient with all of us. He started me out on something called a recorder. It looked like a toy. It was plastic, long, and white, with little holes along the body. I started out reading and playing basic notes; then I moved on to elementary songs. I enjoyed it and didn't even mind practicing my recorder at home.

I was still struggling with my main classes, and the five-week progress report card reflected it. Despite my best efforts, I only passed band and gym. Raising my hand to ask or answer a question was still hard; I was so self-conscious about my speech impediment. If I stuttered, I just knew the other kids would break out in laughter. I hated when a teacher called on me to read a paragraph out loud or to stand up and give my response. It would have felt better if the ground just opened up and swallowed me.

In science class, we were working on weather maps. One of the assignments was to look at a picture of the United States that had a cold front of thunderstorms and severe weather moving from west to east. Our homework was to predict and then draw on a blank map how the cold front would look twelve hours later. The Parkers always got the newspaper every day, so when I got home, I scooped up a pile of them and tore out the daily weather maps. I laid them out side by side according to the days of the week. This gave me a visual idea of how far the weather fronts moved in a twenty-four-hour period. So, on my blank homework map, I took a colored pencil and drew in where I thought my weather front should be in about half that time.

The next day, much to my surprise, the science teacher held up my picture and said I was the only one in the class who drew their weather map correctly. He then asked me to explain to the class how I did it. I didn't want to stand up and talk, but since I was put on the spot I had to. Yes, I stuttered some, but I tried to take my time in explaining how I tackled the homework assignment.

Later, when the class was being dismissed, the science teacher called me aside and told me I did a great job and that I got an A on that assignment. That felt good, really good. Maybe if I tried a little harder, I could get some more high grades and get a passing grade in his class.

So, at home, I began to redouble my efforts. I copied the main ideas from chapters in my textbooks, and I rewrote them several times on flash cards or in my notebooks. Mrs. Parker encouraged me by making sure I had all the school supplies I asked for. And she rewarded me by sewing several new outfits every week for me to wear to school.

My renewed efforts were beginning to pay off. By the end of the first grading period, I had a B in band, gym, and science. I was thrilled. Moving from an F to a B was a major accomplishment in my mind. That was until, I heard the other kids who were seated near me talking about how many A's and B's they had. One girl was distraught because she received a B on an otherwise perfect report card. Another boy was bragging about making the honor roll every marking period since sixth grade.

The next day I spoke to my science teacher and asked, "What do I have to do to make an A in your class?"

He answered me, but not before asking about my grades in the other core classes. When I told him I was failing all of them, he said, "Carolyn if you made a B in my class, you could make a B in those classes too. In fact, young lady, there's no reason at all for you not to be on the honor roll."

I'm sure he could tell from the expression on my face that the thought had never entered my mind. Making a B in all my main classes, being on the honor roll—that was really stretching things. But he challenged me to try, to give it 100 percent, to try harder than I ever did in my life. This brought me back to long-buried feelings of the past. That feeling of excitement and anticipation of being challenged by my brothers. That feeling I use to have of never giving up and giving it my all.

That evening, lying there in my pink-and-green princess bed, I thought about that crazy idea of making the honor roll. Some of my classmates were appalled at getting just one C on their report cards. My two best friends were always receiving recognition for their academic achievements. The science teacher thought I could do it. I just needed to believe that I could do it, to achieve this lofty dream. This notion of doing well in school for the first time in my life was going to be the hardest thing I had ever done.

One by one, I approached each of my teachers and asked them what I needed to do to bring my grades up. I explained to them that I never had anyone at home to help me with schoolwork. I wasn't even sure if I knew how to study.

The eighth-grade teachers at Highlands Junior High School must have sensed my sincerity. They gave me tips on how to take notes in class and from the textbooks, using an outline format. They had lots of ideas on how to study for quizzes and tests, how to write book reports, and suggestions on doing class projects at home. Each teacher gave me a time I could come in for extra help, either during the school day or after school. I also spent time on the weekends studying with Vanetta and Cece.

In addition to all this, I checked out a book called *Spanish for Beginners* from the school library and started teaching myself basic words. We had a few Spanish kids in the school. They kept to themselves, but they used to give me a big smile when I said a few words to them in their language.

By the time I added in practicing music for my band class and doing tons of schoolwork, my whole week was full. I stayed up late doing homework and studying, long after the rest of the family had gone to sleep. Mrs. Parker didn't bother me with a set bedtime because she knew I was working and not playing around. Often, I was exhausted, but I plugged away at this new, lofty challenge. I was determined to give it my best shot and see what the result of my efforts might be.

22

In November of that year, the Parkers let me have a party on my fourteenth birthday. It was the first party I ever had. We decorated the dining room with crepe paper, balloons, and cutouts. Mrs. Parker fried chicken wings, had a homemade dip with chips, and bought me the prettiest birthday cake I had ever seen. I invited seven friends from school, all girls, who were in my main classes or the band.

The Parkers said I was too young to have boys over. That was puzzling to me because the last foster mother let me stay out all day and night with my first boyfriend and never said a word. And I was younger then. This fact was a point of contention, but I did not want it to ruin my party.

We were all dressed up in our finest birthday outfits. We ate, laughed, and sang while listening to the latest Motown records in the dining room. Martie and Paulie were not allowed to come, even though they wanted to. I did ask Mrs. Parker if they could join in when it came time to sing happy birthday and blow out my candles. It was important to me that they share in a little bit of the birthday festivities. I remembered all too well what it felt like to be left out.

Christmas was fast approaching. My two friends and I had steady boyfriends from school. We were trying to figure out what to buy them for a present. We all settled on silver name bracelets that we had seen in a downtown store. I had some birthday money left over that I planned on using.

My boyfriend's name was Nelson. He was about my height, dark-skinned, very muscular, and had thick, luscious lips. Nelson was quiet and always smelled good from two colognes called Brut and Aqua Velva. He lived in the Fisher Avenue projects with his parents. His folks were cool about him having a girlfriend. The Parkers, on the other hand, were not entertaining that dating idea at all. The only time I got to see him was at school or when Cece's mother allowed her to invite friends over to rake leaves or shovel snow.

I wasn't permitted to use the house phone to call him, so I did the next-best thing. The Parkers had a dog that Martie was too small to walk and Paulie too lazy. Most of the time, Mrs. Parker took the dog out, but I started to volunteer to walk him. Every day after dinner, I'd take the dog out for a long walk. Right down to the small pharmacy on Post Road, to use their payphone to call Nelson. Local phone calls were only a dime. When your time ran out, the operator interrupted and asked for more money if you wanted to continue talking. Most days before we left school, Nelson gave me money to call him, and we'd settle on an approximate time, so he would be home.

Oh, the excitement of our secret puppy love. It was a special time in my young life. I had two cool girlfriends, was starting to do better in school, and had a caring, supportive boyfriend who was so easy to talk to.

One afternoon, Nelson could tell I didn't look well. As we walked to my bus, he wanted to know what was wrong. Maybe I should have been ashamed or embarrassed to tell him, but I wasn't.

"I got sick in class and didn't make it to the bathroom," I confided.

"What do you mean, what happened?" I could hear the concern in his voice.

Taking a deep breath and looking straight ahead, I mumbled, "It's that time of the month, and I have really bad cramps." The words trickled out one at a time. At this he took my hand as we walked and said, "Okay, then what? The teacher wouldn't let you go to the girls' room?"

By this time, I was squeezing and releasing his hand in a nervous frenzy. We stopped in the middle of the hallway against the lockers. I couldn't look him directly in the eye, but I whispered,

"I knew I was going to throw up; it came on me so fast. All I could do was run out of class. I tried to make it to the bathroom but couldn't."

"What did you do, what happened?" He looked at me as though he was hurting, feeling my pain.

"I ran out the door at the end of the hall and puked all over the back steps."

He lifted my face with his hand, planted a light kiss on my lips, and said, "My older sister gets sick like that too. I'm just glad you're okay now."

With that, we continued out to the bus parking lot. It felt good being able to talk to him. I knew he wouldn't tell anybody my business, because he seemed to genuinely care about me. He didn't judge me but accepted me for who I was, with all my flaws.

Right before spring break, two major events happened to me. The first was my playing in the band during the annual school spring concert. I had been playing the recorder for seven months, and it was time for everyone to showcase their musical talent. Mrs. Parker made me a whole new black-and-white outfit, which we were required to wear during the performance. Our beginners' band played five selections that night. I was so proud as I sat there with my schoolmates, reading the sheets of music and playing the tunes. When we finished, the packed crowd in the audience stood up to whistle and cheer. I felt terrific because the whole Parker family was there to see me.

Smiling to myself, I thought, *Well, I can't sing, but I sure can play this instrument.*

The second noteworthy incident was on the last day of school, right before spring break. At the end of the day, my science teacher passed out report cards for the third nine-week grading period. He glanced down at the paper before handing it to me and said,

"Good job, young lady. There's still time to make the honor roll. I believe you can do it."

"I'm going to give it my best shot," I said in an earnest tone.

My eyes darted across the paper from line to line. I had three B's and four C's. I passed every one of my classes for the first time in my life. This was awesome, incredible. All my hard work was starting to pay off. I wasn't at the top of my class on the honor roll, but I certainly was no longer on the bottom. Vanetta, Cece, and Nelson were just as proud of me as the Parkers were.

I had nine weeks left in the school year. Nine weeks to try to do something that up till a few months ago, I didn't think was even remotely possible. I passed all my classes. In two and a half months, I had pulled four failing grades up to C's. The teachers said I had potential and could have excellent grades. The Parkers were incredibly supportive, and my three closest friends dared me to try harder.

During this last grading period, the band director wanted me to move from playing the recorder to the flute. This meant that I would be in the school's orchestra, learning a new instrument and playing harder music selections. Of course, I didn't have a new flute lying around the house, and when the director told me one cost about two hundred dollars, I was sure I wasn't going to get one.

While washing dishes and straightening up the kitchen, I shared this information with Mrs. Parker.

"Why, Carolyn, that's wonderful. That's a great opportunity. If you're serious about it, I'll look into it and see what we can do," Mrs. Parker said as she put away the last of the pots and pans.

"I'll call your social worker and see if they have any extra funds to cover special school items like this."

In less than a week, we were in a music store on Central Avenue that sold all kinds of instruments. I picked out a shiny, brand-new silver flute that had its own felt-lined black leather case. The store owner suggested a beginner's flute music book, which showed the proper placement of your fingers for each note. We also purchased two music songbooks for flute players. When I flipped through the titles of music selections in the more advanced flute book, I was surprised to see "The Impossible Dream," one of my favorite songs. I couldn't wait to learn how to play that one. I was ecstatic, and yes, it felt like Christmas had come early again.

My days were jam-packed. I was busy from the time I woke up to get ready for school until late evening, after long hours of homework, practicing my flute, walking the dog, and getting my clothes and hair ready for the next day. Captain Kirk and Spock on *Star Trek* gave me one hour of relaxation on Thursday nights.

On an occasional Saturday, Mrs. Parker would let me walk around the block to Vanetta's or Cece's house if they were home. But under no circumstances would she let me visit Nelson or let him come to the house. I was finding that my brief encounters with him at school and our short payphone conversations were not enough.

"Why can't I see him?" I pressed Mrs. Parker one day after dinner.

"He's nice, kind, and doesn't get into trouble at school. Plus, he makes better grades than me. His mother doesn't mind us seeing each other."

"I don't think girls your age should be seeing boys, that's all. Besides, you have your schoolwork, flute practice, and girlfriends to keep you busy."

"It's just not fair. I do everything I'm supposed to do around here and in school. It's not like I'm asking to go out somewhere at night with him. I'm just asking you to let him come over and visit." I was still trying to make my case, but Mrs. Parker wasn't budging.

"Vanetta and Cece's parents let them have guys over. Why can't I?"

"I have no control over what their parents let them do. That is their business," she said.

Standing face to face and looking at Mrs. Parker, I attempted one last line of reasoning.

"What about if I have a small group of my friends over here sometimes, the boys and girls all together?" I was just about begging at this point.

Wiping her damp hands on the floral apron that was tied around her waist, she looked at me with those light-gray eyes of hers and said,

"I didn't grow up having boys visit me in my house at your age. I'm sorry, the answer is no."

Once again, I felt my eyes start to water. My throat was getting that thick, tight feeling in it. I knew I was on the verge of a teenage breakdown and predictably I yelled,

"You never let me do anything I wanna do," as I stormed out of the kitchen and went up to my room.

Entering my dainty pink-and-green-colored room, I walked over to the one little window on the side wall. I pushed back the sheer curtains, unlatched and pushed open the window. A breeze was rustling through the leaves on the huge thicket of trees. The sun was shining bright across the forest of greenery in my backyard. I could see two squirrels scampering across the swatches of grass and up the trunk of an old tree. Birds were chirping back and forth as if they were carrying on a full-fledged conversation. Down below my window in the blooming rose bushes and flowering daylilies and chrysanthemums, I could see several colorful butterflies darting from plant to plant.

I took in slow, shallow breaths. And when I let the air out of my lungs, the tears started to cascade down my cheeks. Gripping the edges of the wooden windowsill, I pressed my forehead against the metal screen. Gazing outside at the peaceful scene of nature's beauty and the wildlife moving leisurely about, I looked up at the blue, clear sky and said out loud, my lips quivering,

"God, I feel like a prisoner trapped in this house, like a princess trapped in some high, dark castle."

I don't know if He heard me or not. I just resigned myself to having another one-sided conversation with the Man above.

There was no use arguing or trying to state my case for seeing Nelson anymore. I felt defeated and gave in to the fact that Mrs. Parker said no. She was quiet and absolute. That was that, case closed.

When I had tried weeks earlier to ask for permission to join an afterschool twirling club, her response was,

"No, Carolyn, that would take away from your homework time and flute practice."

I tried to emphasize, "This is really something new I want to try. Some of my friends are in it. I'm still gonna get my homework done."

She merely looked at me and said, "Anybody can twirl; not everybody can play the flute. I'm sorry, but the answer is no."

Several times throughout the year when I brought up that I wanted to see my mother and baby brother, the answer was always,

"No, dear, the social worker said it is not a good time."

"When is a good time then?" I'd press her for information.

"They'll let us know. Try and be a little patient."

So, there I was, completely still for about twenty minutes, thinking about all the no's that had been coming my way. I continued looking out my bedroom window that afternoon, feeling trapped without an escape. My eyes were bloodshot and puffy.

Standing, thinking, and talking to that invisible Spirit, up in the clouds somewhere, slowly something in me started to change. It really was like a dimmer on a light bulb, gradually making the glow brighter. It felt as if I was gradually waking from a bad dream.

Fuzzy, disconnected thoughts started to find each other and link up. I knew my favorite song said to "dream the impossible dream, to go where the brave dare not go." In that moment, I made up my mind to try something different, because this was no fairy-tale castle, and I certainly was no trapped, helpless princess.

I'm sure the Parkers saw an immediate change in me. During that time, I'm certain they would describe me as depressed, withdrawn, and sullen. It was easy for me to revert back to being virtually quiet and not speaking unless spoken to. After all, I had six years of ingrained practice of not talking to anyone, from being left alone in the Thompsons' basement.

They could not say that I was rude or disrespectful. I did whatever was asked or expected of me and no more. During mealtimes and the subsequent cleaning up of the kitchen, I didn't look at anyone or say a word. I walked the dog like clockwork without being asked, sneaking in an occasional call to Nelson whenever I had spare change. I did not go in the Parkers' bedroom any longer on Thursdays to watch *Star Trek*, and I definitely did not go up to the third-floor sewing room to engage in unimportant chit-chat.

What I did do was pour all my energy into schoolwork and flute practice. Hour after hour, day after day, until my eyes stung from the strain.

Every Saturday, I would approach Mrs. Parker and ask in a monotone, "Can I go to Vanetta or Cece's house?"

If her answer was yes, I'd simply turn, get my belongings, and walk out the door. If the answer was no, I'd turn and go back upstairs to my room. No drama, no fuss.

I knew from years past, there was no sense in me running away to Ma's house. She would tell me she couldn't take care of me and just send me back. Plus, I didn't want to cause the Parkers that kind of grief and headache, because they had been generous and kind to me, for the most part. Mrs. Parker had a good, loving heart and meant well. I just couldn't adjust to her being so strict on me. I didn't know if she didn't trust me, didn't trust young boys and girls together, or if it was just her own strict upbringing or religious beliefs. Whatever. All I knew is that she was stifling me. I was feeling like I was being suffocated. But my lifeline, my oxygen tank, wasn't too far away.

The school year was rapidly coming to a close. I took part in the musical extravaganza, playing my flute in the orchestra. The auditorium was jam-packed, standing room only, in the back and along the side walls for those who arrived late. That was an amazing experience. Cece and Vanetta sang in the chorus. The Parkers were there; however, I asked for permission to go with Cece's parents for pizza right after the concert.

The last few weeks in June were a whirlwind of school projects, reports, presentations, and final exams. I never worked so hard in my young life, writing notes to myself, making lists of things to do, accumulating pages and pages of outlines, studying vocabulary words on index cards, and penciling in dates to remember on my calendar.

On Friday, the last day of school, my science teacher smiled as he handed me my folded report card. He didn't say a word. I couldn't bring myself to look at the paper, saying,

"Can I go to the girls' room, please?" to which he nodded yes before calling out the next student's name.

I rushed down the hall and flung open the bathroom door. I glanced around to see if I was alone before going into the last stall. I unfolded the paper, my hands trembling. Glancing down the last column, which contained final grades, I saw straight B's. I had made the honor roll. Leaning on the back of the stall door, I busted out in a sea of tears.

"Thank you, God," I whispered several times. "I did it, I finally did it."

I made the honor roll for the first time in my life, something that I never dreamed of. Something that I never thought was even possible. But when that seed was planted by my science teacher, nurtured by the Parkers, and challenged by my best friends, I dared to believe that maybe, just maybe, it was not an impossible dream.

Later, after dinner, I pulled out my report card and handed it to Mrs. Parker. She put the plates she was holding on the Formica countertop. Adjusting the wire-rimmed glasses on her nose, she unfolded the paper. It was a written testament to my consistent hard work and determination over the past few months.

Looking up over the rim of her bifocals, she said,

"Carolyn, this is absolutely wonderful. I am so proud of you." Turning toward the basement door, she yelled out to her husband, "Lambert, Lambert, come here. You have to see this. Carolyn has some good news."

I stood still, listening to the heavy shuffle of boots, as Mr. Parker made his way upstairs. Entering the kitchen, he approached us.

"What is it?" he asked in his thick, island accent, as his wife handed him my report card.

After glancing over the paper, he looked at me.

"Congratulations, young lady, this is really good."

The corners of my mouth turned up slightly in my half-hearted attempt at being polite.

"What do you want to do to celebrate? We need to do something special," Mrs. Parker offered, her voice light and enthusiastic. They both waited for my response.

"Thank you." I nodded to the two adults standing in front of me. With a deliberate and slow voice, I said,

"I do want to do something special. I'd like to see my mother and move to wherever it is my baby brother is living. So, can you please call the social worker and tell her I want a meeting with her?"

From the raised eyebrows and surprised expressions on their faces, I'm sure that was not what they were expecting. Silence hung in the air for a few seconds. You could feel the uncomfortable tension in the room. I didn't stutter. I didn't waiver, and I didn't take my eyes off them.

Mr. Parker handed me back my report card as his wife quietly said, "All right, if that's what you want."

I nodded again.

"Thank you, that's what I want," and I headed upstairs to my pink-and-green princess room.

Less than a week later, the social worker and I met and shared a quiet but in-depth conversation on the Parkers' patio above the garage. She knew of the transformations I had made in my life during my year-and-a-half stay with the Parkers. Learning to play an instrument, performing in the school band, bringing my failing grades up to honor roll status, always going above and beyond to do chores around the house, and making new friends were some of the things we covered.

Since I had made so much progress, she was stumped as to why I wanted to leave. I told her I felt stifled and smothered by not being allowed to see my male friends, no matter what I suggested. I felt I had done everything I could to earn the Parkers' trust, but it was never enough. It was extremely hard going from one foster mother who didn't care if I had a boyfriend to another one who strictly forbid all contact with boys. My girlfriends, who the Parkers knew and liked, had more freedom than me.

I worked extremely hard at school and at home, doing all the things that were expected of me. In return, I felt I had earned some leniency, some loosening of the strict rules around here.

I shared that I asked repeatedly to see my mother and brother but always got excuses about why this couldn't be done. The social worker looked at me intently when I said,

"I know where my mother is and how to get there. If I am not allowed to see her, I will just start running away. I know where my little brother is, and I want to live at that same place."

PART THREE

Hope

23

The summer of 1966, I moved to Leake and Watts Children's Home in Yonkers, New York. I was fourteen years old and about to join 150 other kids, some younger, others older, who lived at this residential treatment facility. My little brother Gardiner would be there somewhere, and I was determined to find him. It had been almost two years since I last saw his sad, frightened face as I left him in Greenburgh with Mrs. Thompson, that sadistic, abusive foster mother.

The social worker who came to the Parkers' house to get me was Mrs. Dorothy Wesson. She was white, middle-aged, with short blonde hair with gray highlights. She wore clear, oval plastic glasses and had on a light-blue skirt suit with a floral blouse.

It was the middle of the week in early afternoon, so Mr. Parker was not there when I left. I gathered my belongings, which were considerably more than when I first arrived, thanks to Mrs. Parker sewing numerous seasonal outfits for me. I put my items in the trunk of the small black sedan. Turning to face Mrs. Parker, I had a flashback of my first time seeing her, standing right there in front of her house with the two boys on either side of her. I gave her a quick hug, saying,

"Thank you for everything. I really, really appreciate it. Please tell Mr. Parker I said thank you too."

"I'm sorry you're leaving, Carolyn. Please keep in touch." Her eyes puddled over with water.

"I will, I promise." I could feel my throat closing with that thick feeling, like I was about to cry.

Looking at the boys, I couldn't tell how they felt about me leaving, but I quickly gave Paulie a high-five and Martie a little squeeze.

Mrs. Wesson was already in the car with the engine running. I jumped in, turned, and gave a small wave, one last time to the Parker family.

Thirty-five minutes later, we were pulling into a parking space in front of the main building on the Leake and Watts campus. It was a long, two-story Gothic-looking building, made of burnt brownstone and brick and appeared to be a hundred years old. Several rows of long steps led up to the massive arched entrance.

Mrs. Wesson, who chatted incessantly during the drive, and chain smoked just as much, had filled me with lots of information as to what to expect. She wanted to show me where her office was located on the main floor of that aged building. We would be meeting together at least once a week in her small office, until I settled into my new surroundings and routines.

The sprawling campus was located on forty acres of rolling grass, dotted with massive oak, maple, birch, and cedar trees. The land, which used to be a farm, was just a couple of blocks off the flowing Hudson River. The complex was in the city of Yonkers, but it did not feel like or look like a city. There were no massive business enterprises rising to the sky like in New York City a few miles away. The tallest structures nearby were the five- or six-story apartment buildings just off Valentine Lane.

When Mrs. Wesson drove along Hawthorne Avenue, approaching the small road that was the entrance to the campus, she pointed out several individual one- and two-story houses on both sides of the street.

"These homes are part of Leake and Watts too, Carolyn. They are called cottages. Each one has about ten to fifteen kids living there."

Turning my head from left to right, I took in my new surroundings.

"They look like the houses in Parkway Gardens," I remarked and added, "They're really nice."

Mrs. Wesson was driving slower now around a curve, as the road had narrowed considerably. She pointed to a larger, older two-story home and said,

"That's where you will be living. That's Gould Cottage."

I looked over at what was going to be my home for the next four years. It was clearly the largest and oldest home we had passed so far.

It had a huge front lawn with a walkway leading up to the door. And right in the middle of the grassy area was a gigantic, black metal bell on a concrete slab. I sat up straight, staring hard at the unusual object that looked so out of place.

"Wow, Mrs. Wesson, there's a bell just like that in Mount Morris Park where my brothers and I used to go to."

I couldn't believe it. For some strange reason, that bell would always make me feel connected back home to the city and to the rest of my family still living in Harlem.

"Where's everybody?" I asked, looking around at the cottages, fenced-in swimming pool, office building, and parking lot.

"There's nobody walking around."

This surprised me, as it was late afternoon on a beautiful, summer weekday.

"All the kids are either down in the rec area or on field trips with their counselors," she answered.

I could feel some tingling of excitement growing inside me. An on-campus swimming pool, recreation area, and field trips with other kids my age? This certainly was not what I was used to.

A little while later, I was standing in the large foyer area of Gould Cottage, being introduced to Mrs. Brown, the head cottage parent. Ma Brown, as she asked all the girls to call her, had a huge, jovial, welcoming smile. She had caramel-colored skin and wore her hair in short curls with a part on one side of her head. She wore a long, loose, brown sleeveless jumper over a white, open-collared blouse, and had on flat, black, comfortable-looking shoes. Over the coming weeks, I would find that with some small variation, this was Ma Brown's favorite outfit.

I had set my small pieces of luggage and bags on the floor, inside the foyer. Mrs. Wesson sat down on one of the worn couches in the open living room, as Ma Brown took me on a quick tour. Downstairs was a huge kitchen with stainless-steel sinks and enormous pots and pans on the counters. Just off this was a large room with numerous tables and chairs. This was my new dining room, where I would share meals with my cottage mates. The girls would be called down in the mornings by Pa Brown, who I hadn't met yet. Lunch would be supervised by Ma Brown when the girls returned as a group from wherever they had been. And in the evening, one girl would be selected to ring the outdoor metal bell on the lawn, to let the entire campus know it was dinnertime. Ma Brown did emphasize that if you were late, you did not eat. Period.

Upstairs on the main floor, Ma Brown pointed out the office area at the end of the living room. It had two oversized desks and several chairs. If I received any phone calls from my social worker, family, or friends, I would be using one of the black rotary phones here. All the rooms on the first floor had large, curtain-clad windows for light to flow in. It gave the place a sunny, welcoming feel.

On the other side of the front foyer was another room of considerable size that served as the study hall, TV, and game room. It had couches, square and rectangular tables with chairs, and a Ping-Pong table. Along the side walls were cubbyhole-type shelving filled with games, magazines, and books.

Ma Brown pointed to a door in the corner of this room and said,

"My private residence is back there. That's where my family and I live. If you ever need anything, just knock on the door, but no one ever comes inside there. Okay?"

I immediately nodded and said, "Yes."

Following simple, straightforward directions was easy for me. Mrs. Thompson had made sure of that years earlier in Greenburgh.

We then climbed up two sets of stairs to the bedrooms, which were all located on the outskirts of a long hallway that took you around in a large square. In the middle area was a small apartment that Ma Brown said the part-time cottage parent stayed in, whenever she and her husband were off duty. The bathroom was old, but spotless and painted all white. It had two walk-in showers, about four porcelain sinks with a trash can under each, and several toilet stalls.

Ma Brown continued down the hall, past every bedroom door, and opened it if it was closed. The thing I noticed immediately was that all the twin-size beds with their orange corduroy-looking covers were made, and the rooms were tidy. Every room had a window with mini-blinds and sheer curtains. Most of the windows were opened to let the fresh air in through the screens. When we got to the door of the last bedroom, Ma Brown said,

"This is your room. You'll be sharing it with Nancy. We only have four single rooms, for our girls who are responsible leaders. They've shown us that they deserve to be in a room by themselves."

I glanced at my half of the small room. On top of the same, orange-covered bed was a new set of sheets, towels, and washcloths folded inside clear plastic wrap. There was a small wooden desk with a single drawer and a beige plastic chair underneath it. The side of the desk was attached to the open closet to hang my clothes, and four drawers, on top of which to place my toiletries and knick-knacks. Behind the top-drawer area, attached to the back wall, was a large, recessed mirror.

Nancy's half of the room had the same amenities but was outfitted in every spot with personal pictures, drawings, books, bobble-head dolls, and stuffed animals. Her closet, I noticed, was jam-packed with clothes, boxes, and shoes.

We went back downstairs, where Mrs. Wesson was still lounging in the same upholstered chair where we had left her.

"So, what do you think?" she asked, standing up as we approached.

"It's nice," I said. "Different."

"Don't worry, you'll get used to it. Mrs. Brown and the other girls will help you," she said to reassure me.

Turning to Ma Brown, she said, "Let her come by my office tomorrow around two." With that, Mrs. Wesson put her hand on my shoulder.

"It's going to be fine." And then she headed out to her black sedan parked out front, just beyond the front lawn, with the iron bell.

I spent the rest of the afternoon trying to organize my belongings in this new living space. Time was moving right along, but I was so absorbed in my task, I hadn't noticed just how late it was getting. From downstairs, I could hear loud talking and peals of laughter as my new cottage mates made their way in from the day's activities. They were racing up the steps, bounding down the halls to the bathroom or their respective bedrooms. I decided to stay put, being too shy to step outside the confines of my room, to face a group of girls I didn't know.

Bending over, I was squeezing the last few items into the bottom drawer when I heard sneaker-clad feet screeching on the floor by my open door. I looked up into the face of my new roommate, Nancy.

Nancy was light-skinned with a head full of jet-black, unruly long hair. She had a huge smile that amplified her rosy cheeks.

A wide smile lit up her face as she plopped down on the bed and adjusted the cat-rimmed glasses on her nose.

"Hey, you must be my new roommate. I'm Nancy," she said in a thick Spanish accent, which surprised me. I had assumed that Nancy was going to be a white girl, since the few Nancys I had ever met in my life were white.

"I-I'm Carolyn," I said, trying hard not to stutter. "You speak Spanish?"

"I understand more than I speak. My parents are from Puerto Rico," she offered.

"I know a little bit of Spanish. I tried to teach myself some words from a library book. My junior high didn't offer different languages to us."

"Wow, that's neat. What words do you know?"

And that's how I bonded with my new roommate, who became a good friend during my next few years at Leake and Watts. A few more minutes of light chitchat followed, until we heard the loud, deep bonging sound of the metal bell outside on the lawn.

A man's deep voice from the bottom foyer area yelled out,

"Dinnertime, dinnertime." I could hear girls running around the halls and down the flights of stairs toward the basement. Nancy jumped up.

"Come on, that's Pa Brown. It's dinnertime. I'll introduce you to him and the other girls." With that, I followed Nancy out of our bedroom to meet the rest of my new extended family.

Pa Brown was short, shorter than his wife, and half her size. He was very thin, skinny in fact. He was about the same complexion as Ma Brown. His hair was shaved so close, he was almost bald. When I first saw him in the kitchen, taking the huge lids off the large containers, I thought maybe he was the man who delivered the food. Then Nancy introduced us. He acknowledged me but never stopped moving.

"Hello, young lady," he said in a businesslike manner.

Before we could serve ourselves, we assembled in the dining room and stood behind a chair. One girl led us, reciting a quick grace, as Pa

Brown observed quietly from the kitchen. Then we lined up inside the kitchen to serve ourselves food from the huge, circular, metal containers that were delivered for each meal.

After having my first dinner with eleven loud, lively, animated girls my age, Nancy and Pa Brown took me upstairs to our cottage living room, where a cork board of announcements was posted. One page was a list of weekly chores, with the name of the girl who was responsible for each and how often it should be done. The space for dusting, sweeping, and mopping the rec room was empty. Pa Brown penciled my name in that slot. Other jobs included washing dishes after meals. Those slots had different girls' names for each meal. Mopping, sweeping, and cleaning the dining room after meals also had three slots. Cleaning the bathroom had its own space, along with the upstairs hall, steps, and foyer. There were two slots for taking out the trash daily. And there were the names of two captains who had the job of overseeing five girls each, to make sure their chores were done properly and on time according to the posted schedule.

Each girl was also responsible for washing, drying, and ironing her own clothes. The washer, dryer and laundry soap were located in the basement, next to the dining room. The cottage had one iron and ironing board in a closet in the rec room. Irons were not allowed upstairs, for safety reasons. This closet was also where extra brooms, dustpans, and rags were kept.

Good manners, no profanity, no fighting or stealing were always supposed to be observed. Bedtime, mealtimes, and church service times were to be strictly followed.

My last pieces of instruction were that I would be responsible for leaving the bathroom clean, just like I found it, along with keeping my side of the room tidy and my trash can emptied daily.

I was to get a weekly allowance for doing my chores and following the rules. Pa Brown said without smiling,

"If you break the rules or don't follow your daily schedule, you won't get your allowance, won't be able to go on any of the special campus field trips or have off-campus home visitations. Do you understand?"

Pa Brown looked like he was finished with his speech and was ready to move on to something else.

"I-I think so," I said in a hesitant voice.

"Don't worry, if you have any questions, Nancy, the other girls, and Ma Brown will be around to help you out."

He gave me a stiff, businesslike smile before turning and heading across the foyer to his private residence.

"It'll be all right. I'll help you," Nancy said in a jovial, big-hearted way.

"Okay, I can do this." With that, I gave my new roommate a high-five.

Plain, simple, and direct. Just the way I liked it. After what I had been subjected to for years at the Thompsons' house, this was going to be a piece of cake. I wasn't lazy, and I was used to hard work. Plus, for the first time in my life, I'd be getting a weekly allowance to spend on whatever I wanted.

The two hours after dinner were considered free time for the older girls who lived in Gould Cottage. We could hang out down at the recreation center, which had a gym; take part in one of the short, off-campus field trips if we earned it; go swimming in the outdoor pool; lounge around the swing area and huge expanse of grassy areas; or stay in the cottage to play games, watch TV, read, or do nothing at all. I absolutely loved the idea of having some time for myself, where I could pick and choose what I wanted to do.

That night, I lay in my new bed, reflecting on these different surroundings that were going to shape my life for the next four years. I wasn't on the loud, crowded, litter-scattered Harlem city streets. But I wasn't out somewhere in the middle of the suburbs, with roads without sidewalks and no way to get around but long, solitary walks. I wasn't sleeping in a dark, ominous emergency shelter in a large gym-type auditorium, with dozens of unruly girls. Nor was I in an outwardly happy, pretentious home, alone in the basement, answering to a mentally and physically abusive foster mother.

Here I wouldn't be living in a world of loneliness, isolation, and relentless punishments, but I wouldn't be recklessly free either. There would be lots of new rules and routines to get used to and follow. I wasn't with my whole family, but somewhere nearby was my baby brother Gardiner, and that made me smile. Breathing in slow and deep, I was nervous, but made a promise to myself to embrace the challenges and experiences my new life was sure to bring.

I saw my brother the next day from a distance. He was racing with some of his little cottage mates, across the rolling hill of grass that led to their house called Hayden North. I yelled out his name. He stopped horse-playing with his friends, long enough to turn around and paused, wide-eyed, before giving me a surprised, big smile and enthusiastic wave.

"Pippa, hi Pippa!" he shrieked, once he realized it was me.

I heard one of the rowdy boys say, "Who's that?"

To which Gardiner announced as he shoved the boy further down the grassy hill, "That's my sister."

That was all I needed to see and hear. My little brother was happy and free. He had friends his own age to laugh and play with, without fear. As long as I knew he was safe and all right, I could relax a little and try to settle into my own new normal.

That afternoon, around two, I went to see Mrs. Wesson in her small, cramped office, which had a strong cigarette smell hanging in the air. In the middle of her paper- and folder-strewn desk was a round ashtray, overflowing with half-smoked, lipstick-smeared cigarettes. She greeted me with a warm smile as she pushed a pile of clipped papers to the side and asked me,

"Hey there, how was your first day here on campus? How are you adjusting?"

"I think I'm going to like it here, plus I get to see my little brother Gardiner." I settled back into the deep-brown leather-cushioned seat.

"Yes, that's good. Your brother has been here for almost two years now, ever since he left the foster home in Greenburgh. He's made a lot of friends, I think." She smashed her current cigarette out in the mound of ashes. "Mr. Burton has told me that Gardiner is making a lot of progress in the cottage and in school," she continued.

Mrs. Wesson was not my brother's social worker. His social worker was a man named Mr. Burton; whose office was somewhere else in the building.

"I think I'm going to like my roommate, Nancy. She's Puerto Rican and is gonna help me learn some new Spanish words. The Browns seem nice too, strict but not too strict," I said, gazing around at the floor-to-ceiling bookcase, crowded with thick binders and the nearby wall full of letters, memos, schedules, and Leake and Watts announcements.

We talked a little more about my first impressions of cottage life. Then Mrs. Wesson stood up and said,

"I have to take you upstairs to the clothing room to pick out a few new items for yourself."

This surprised me, but I jumped up from the chair and followed her down the hall and up a wide staircase that was just inside the main entrance of the building.

The clothing room was massive. It was on the top floor, on the back side of the building. It looked like it stretched from one end all the way to the other. The entire area was filled with dozens of metal racks, with a wide array of clothes hanging on them. There were rows of open wooden shelves along the walls and in the middle of the room. These contained articles of clothing, some in clear plastic bags, others neatly folded in piles. One side of the clothing room was for boys and the opposite side for girls. There was a makeshift fitting room with hanging curtains for privacy, and a long, leaning mirror right outside it, to view whatever you were trying on. A table had an old-looking black Singer sewing machine set up.

A short, matronly woman, with eyeglasses hanging on a beaded chain around her neck, greeted us.

"Well, hello there. I haven't seen you in a while." She smiled at Mrs. Wesson.

"I know, but I've still been busy. This is Carolyn. She just arrived yesterday and will be staying in Gould Cottage with the older girls. Carolyn, this is Miss Dee. She's going to take good care of you."

The woman looked me up and down as she approached me.

"Okay, turn around. Let's look at you, so we can pick out some new clothes." She made a circular motion with her finger, as I slowly turned.

We spent the next forty minutes with me picking out and trying on jeans, shorts, summer tops, bras, underwear, sneakers, and bathing suits. Miss Dee explained to me that I would come to the clothing room to see her about four times a year, at the beginning of each season, to pick out clothes to add to my wardrobe. I was picking out my summer stuff now and would return in early September to get more things for school. This was very exciting, but I tried not to show it, concentrating on the different directions Miss Dee was giving me.

"Stand up on this stool so I can take your measurements. Do you like these? Try these on. No, those are too big. Get seven of these, two of those, one pair of these."

It was a whirlwind shopping spree. We packed my new items in several brown bags and headed back downstairs. When we got to the open foyer, by the receptionist who was stationed just inside the front door, Mrs. Wesson said,

"Do you think you can make it back to your cottage by yourself, or do you need help?"

"I can make it," I said, rearranging some of the overflowing bags I held in each hand.

"Okay, I'm going to call Mrs. Brown and let her know I'm scheduling you to come see me every week. She'll let you know what day and time. But if something comes up in between and you can't wait that long, just let her or your camp counselor know, and they can reach me." She gave me a warm, reassuring smile.

"Thank you." I said with a big, gap-tooth grin.

Mrs. Wesson turned and headed down the hall toward her office, and I stepped out into the heat of the glaring sun, to make my way past the kids splashing in the pool, and back to Gould Cottage. I had some more organizing and rearranging to do, to accommodate my new acquisitions.

24

My first few weeks of summer at Leake and Watts were flying by. I was meeting new kids and staff members every day. In the cottage, I was adjusting to the new routines, as well as the hierarchy of cliques the girls divided themselves into. Gloria and Nita were the two cottage captains who assisted the Browns in keeping the rest of us on track. They, of course, had their own, private bedrooms. Ampara was the other Spanish girl in the house. She had been there for a couple of years, stayed out of trouble, kept mostly to herself, and had earned the right to have her own room.

In the back of my mind, I had already decided to do whatever it took to move into my own room too. After all, that was what I had grown accustomed to in all my foster homes. I had never shared a bedroom with anyone but my brothers. And I wasn't invested in the notion of sharing one with another girl. So, in the secret compartments of my mind, my first goal was set.

Each weekday after breakfast, the girls and I would make our way to the recreation building, which everyone called the rec. We met our two camp counselors upstairs in the gym, on a specific area of the bleachers. There, the counselors would tell us what the activities for the day would be. We had certain times allocated for enrichment activities that were rotated among the other male and female age groups on campus. Each of these activities had an adult who specialized in that class. Sometimes it was art, wood shop, or photography. Other times it was steel band, swimming lessons, or gym.

Built into the last hour of every afternoon, the older kids were assigned to the game room, which was less structured. There we could relax a little as we listened to music or played board games, cards, or Ping-Pong. The girls really liked this time because it was co-ed. They could mingle and flirt a little with their boyfriends if they had one.

During this time, I pretty much kept to myself or followed Nancy's lead to get a taste of all that Leake and Watts had to offer. I found that I enjoyed art and fashioned several items out of clay. I learned how to swim and dive. It didn't take me long to notice that Gardiner had already learned how to swim and loved showing off in the deep water.

My other absolute favorite activity was learning to play the steel drums, with Mr. Benjamin our teacher, who was originally from the island of Antigua. In his class he had enough drums set up for each girl to play by herself. Mr. Benjamin never had a sheet of music to guide him; he played by ear. He was serious but patient as he taught each of us our parts to the latest songs that were out at that time.

There were some other experiences I didn't enjoy as much, but like the other girls, I was expected to participate. One was softball, which we played outside in the heat of the day, during our allotted gym time. Our counselors, two cute college girls, didn't spend more than fifteen minutes out there with us. Once they got our teams organized, positions assigned, and equipment passed out, they usually left Gloria and Nita in charge.

Standing out there in the dusty field, covering third base, it didn't take me long to start sweating. This was a boring game that moved too slow and didn't capture my interest at all. The softball mitt I was holding was old, cracked, and nasty looking. I really didn't want to put my fingers inside, for fear of ants or spiders that might be lurking there.

Anyway, one of my cottage mates from the opposing team came up to bat, swung at the ball, and hit it high in the air, directly above my head. I raised my mitt-covered hand halfheartedly and should have caught it. But the ball sailed on by, past my outstretched mitt. The girl started running to first base. As I turned to chase the ball, still rolling way behind me, I thought it would be cool to yell,

"Oh shit, I should've had that!"

Wrong. Several of the girls from both teams started screaming at me as I attempted to retrieve the wayward ball and throw it back to the pitcher.

"Watch your mouth," Gloria hollered.

"We don't use profanity on the playing field," Nita, who was my team captain, screamed.

"You got poor sportsmanship," some other girl shrilled from behind the catcher.

Well, I was embarrassed and humiliated. Not only had I missed catching the ball, allowing the opposing team to have a home run, but my feeble attempt at impressing my new cottage mates with my street language had failed miserably.

Okay, lesson learned. The girls felt it was acceptable to curse around each other, out of earshot of cottage parents and counselors, but not while playing team sports. I stashed that lesson away in my mind, knowing it was a mistake that I would not be repeating.

I had my second mishap on a Friday evening, during free movie time. All the older kids were in the auditorium, where a film was being flashed on a white screen, from a reel-to-reel movie projector. The large room was dim as the long, thick, dusty drapes had been pulled together. Couples were huddled together in chairs along the side walls and way in the back, as far away from the counselors' eyes as possible. Other residents were sitting in the rows of hard, black, plastic and metal chairs that had been set up. About a dozen kids were sprawled out on the floor, pretending they were watching the movie or trying to catch a quick nap, from the day's packed activities.

My seat was in a small cluster of chairs occupied by Nancy and several other cottage mates who didn't have boyfriends. We were talking in low whispers, only showing a lukewarm interest in the movie. The counselors were scattered about the room, not interested in the movie or us. Several had slipped out once the opening credits had started; the few who remained were chatting among themselves. This was a much-needed break for them too.

A boy I didn't know but had seen around the grounds made his way over to our group and stood next to me. We all stopped talking and looked up at him.

"Skip wants you to meet him by the swings," he said, looking at me.

"What?" Nancy and I both said at the same time.

"Who is Skip?" I asked Nancy in a puzzled voice.

"One of the older guys from Shrady Cottage."

I turned back to the lanky boy standing in front of us and asked in a loud whisper,

"Why, what does he want?"

"He just wants to ask you something," the messenger boy said, tilting his head toward the door, where this so-called Skip was standing.

I looked in that direction and standing in the doorway was one of the guys I'd seen several times in the gym, playing basketball with the oldest teenage boys on campus. He was looking directly at me and motioning with his head for me to come on.

Turning to Nancy and the other girls, who by this time had stopped talking to see how this was going to play out, I said,

"I don't know that dude. What do you think?"

"Well, just see what he wants and come straight back," Nancy whispered.

I hesitated, not sure what to do, when the flunky repeated, "Come on, see what he wants. He just wants to ask you something."

I stood up and said to Nancy, "Save my seat. I'll be right back." I made my way past the masses of bodies, to the hallway and out the front door. The counselors didn't stop me. They weren't even paying attention to us.

I crossed the parking lot and headed the short way across the grass to the swing area. The boy named Skip was already there, leaning against one of the metal poles on the swing set. I approached, taking slow strides, and stopped a few yards in front of him.

"What's up," he said, looking at me from head to toe.

"Not much," was my reply.

"I seen you around here. You new."

"Yeah, that's right." I nodded, not sure what this guy wanted with me. I looked around; there was no one in sight, and it was just starting to get dark.

"What do you want? Your friend said you wanted to ask me something." I got right to it because I was starting to feel a bit uneasy. This guy was quite a few years older than me, stronger, much taller, more streetwise, and I didn't know what the heck he wanted. He looked creepy, like a stalker.

"I been watching you. I think you're kinda cute," he said folding his arms across his chest, still leaning against the pole.

"Okay," I answered in a questioning tone, looking him straight in the face.

"So, I called you out here to kiss. Do you wanna kiss me?" he asked in what was supposed to be his smooth, come-and-get-it tone, I guess.

"What? For real? You called me all the way out here, thinking I'm gonna kiss you? Boy, I don't even know you." I was disgusted and started to take a couple of steps backward.

"Come on, girl, don't be like that. Just one small kiss. Who knows, you might even like it."

"I might like to kiss, but it sure as hell won't be with you." I turned and started marching back to the main building, indignant.

"I wish my brothers were here to kick your ass," I said in a low voice that I knew he didn't hear.

"You'll pay for that," he yelled as I stomped off. "Wait and see."

By the end of the movie, many of the couples were looking at me and smiling but not saying a word. Several of the older boys were outright laughing as I walked by.

"Hey girl, we heard you can't kiss," one called out.

"Yeah, Skip said you kiss like a fish," the messenger boy hollered, causing several others to join in, snickering and laughing.

Standing right by the open door, leaning back with one foot up against the wall was lying Skip, with a nasty smirk on his face. Yes, he thought he was a hot shot, ladies' man, king of the night.

When I passed him, he started laughing.

"Say what you want, you lying dog, but we both know you didn't touch me." I glared at him. This one sentence came out of me straight and clear, without a single stutter.

As the summer progressed, I became more comfortable with my new routines at the house and how campus life operated throughout the week. The boys and girls weren't allowed in each other's cottage, so I didn't visit Gardiner, but I saw him around the grounds, in the pool, and in church on Sundays. Many times, we had a chance to catch up with each other and say a few words. That was good enough for both of us.

My days were full, from the time I got up for breakfast until I fell in bed exhausted at ten o'clock, when Pa Brown yelled,

"Lights out, everybody."

Besides our daily camp schedule, which stayed the same each week, we were sometimes treated to off-campus field trips. The counselors would load us on a yellow school bus and take us to Rye Playland, Cross-Country Shopping Center, or Van Cortland Park. These were fun-filled all-day excursions.

I got on almost every ride at Playland except the roller coaster, which I was still deathly afraid of. When we went to the shopping center, I spent most of my time wistfully looking at all the things my little $2.50 weekly allowance couldn't afford. At Van Cortland Park, we spent the day strolling along the vast trails, or playing kickball or dodgeball in the open fields. I felt free and alive for the first time since I was taken from Ma, so many years earlier.

During one of my weekly meetings with Mrs. Wesson, I asked her when I could go home to visit my mother. She informed me that only older high school-age residents could travel off campus by themselves for home visits. She did say that parents could make arrangements to come on campus to see their kids, but that had to be prearranged through the social worker and campus administrators.

The conversation then shifted to us talking about school, since the summer was almost over, and classes started right after Labor Day. Mrs. Wesson pulled out and opened a manila folder, which I assumed was information about me. She put out her cigarette, adjusted her glasses, and studied the papers in front of her.

"Carolyn, most of the residents who come to Leake and Watts have to start out in one of our schools on campus. Then we evaluate how they are doing and make a determination to keep them in campus school or let them attend school in the community."

I listened to this and nodded, to let her know I was paying attention, as she really hadn't asked me a question.

She continued, "I see you did really well in eighth grade. You made the honor roll. And you were a member of the band. What instrument did you play?"

"The flute," I answered.

"Did you like it?"

"I loved it; the music was starting to get hard. But I practiced every day." I moved around in my seat.

"That's really good. We don't get too many residents who show an interest in playing an instrument in school." Mrs. Wesson smiled as she looked at me over the rim of her glasses.

"I'm learning how to play the steel drums in Mr. Benjamin's class too. It's cool. I really like it."

"Well, looking at your school records, I'm going to recommend that you start ninth grade off campus at Yonkers High School. I think you will do well there."

"Okay," I responded, not knowing the seriousness of that decision. After all, I had been in public schools all my life, so this wasn't a big deal to me. I had no idea what an on-grounds campus school was like, or why some kids went there and others didn't.

My social worker got quiet and scribbled some notes on the paper in the folder. She then looked at me and asked,

"Would you be interested in playing the flute in your new school?"

"Wow, I'd love that." Now she had my full attention. I sat up straight on the edge of the seat. "But I don't have a flute. The Parkers were renting the one I had. When I left, I guess they returned it to the music store."

"You let me worry about that part, young lady. I'll speak to my boss, Mr. Hammond, and see if I can work some magic. Next week, I'm going to take you to the school and get you registered."

I was very excited, thrilled in fact. The thought never crossed my mind that I could play in my high school band. Well, if Mrs. Wesson could get me my own flute, that's exactly what I was going to do. I added that to my mental list of goals, things I was going to strive to do in this new setting called Leake and Watts.

Later that evening, while we were getting ready for bed, I shared with Nancy that my social worker was going to take me to Yonkers High to get registered. Nancy was elated, because that was the school she and Ampara were going to attend also. The three of us would be walking together, a few blocks up the street to Valentine Lane, to catch the public bus to school. Once a month, our social workers would give us a bus pass to ride free.

I asked Nancy and Ampara about Mr. Hammond.

Nancy said, "He's the tall, skinny Black man who wears a suit and walks around all day with a pipe in his mouth."

Ampara added, "He's in charge of the whole campus and lives in a house up on the hill, just beyond the tennis courts. Everybody answers to him."

That was interesting to me, that a Black man was in charge of this entire setup. He was the boss and ran things.

"Well, if Mr. Hammond is in charge, who are those other two white men who are always walking around outside with him?" I pressed for more information.

Ampara continued to fill me in.

"Oh them, they wanna be important, but they're not. Mr. Blotcher is the tall one with the big belly and the fat dog who looks just like him. He's in charge of security. But he doesn't do nothing. He can't even run; neither can his dog."

They both started laughing.

"And who is the other guy?" I asked.

Nancy answered, "The short one is Mr. Knee. He's just in charge of maintenance around here, you know like the buildings, grounds, and the kitchen."

"That's a lot of stuff," I said.

"Yeah, I think he really wants Mr. Hammond's job. And there's another guy you'll see with them sometimes. His name is Mr. Willshire. His daughter goes to school with us, but he drives her every day," Nancy finished as she put her hair up in a ponytail.

This was a lot of information for me to absorb. But at least I knew who the three important-looking men were, as I often saw them strolling leisurely about the campus right before or after dinner. I didn't know it then, but I would have a couple of run-ins of my own with at least two of them.

Mrs. Wesson did as she promised, taking me to my new school for registration. She and the counselor went over my previous school records and decided on my schedule. I got the feeling that Mrs. Wesson had been through this process many times before with other Leake and Watts residents. Together, she and the counselor decided that I would be placed on an academic track and have a band class. While they were doing this, a teacher came in and asked me to fill out a sheet that had lots of beginning Spanish words and phrases on it. When I completed it, the teacher said a few words to the counselor, who turned to me and said,

"Carolyn, since you already know quite a bit of Spanish, we are going to enroll you in Spanish Two, instead of Spanish One."

I looked at her and nodded, thinking to myself, *learning Spanish from that book I got from the library really paid off.* And of course, at that moment, I had no idea what an academic track was, as I had never heard that term before. All I knew was that I was taking physical education, English, algebra, history/geography, biology, band, and Spanish Two. When the necessary paperwork was complete, a high school-age female office helper took us on a quick tour of the school. While we walked and talked, I learned that she was going into twelfth grade, and working in the school office was her summer job. I tucked that tidbit of information away for future reference, thinking I wouldn't mind working in the school office one day.

Two weeks later, I was busy getting ready for my first day as a freshman in my new high school. I had spent the previous night laboring over my outfit, finally deciding on a pair of beige bell-bottom pants, short floral blouse, and thick wedge sandals. Bangle hoop earrings, and beige and brown plastic bracelets completed my fresh look.

My hair was natural and cut short, as I had started wearing it in an afro almost as soon as I arrived on campus. It was easier to maintain after all my trips to the swimming pool. Plus, most of the older, cool girls who didn't have hair like Nancy or Ampara were sporting afros. I had spent my whole $2.50 allowance on new afro pics and Afro Sheen hairspray.

The next morning, after breakfast, the three of us walked up to the corner of Valentine Lane and Riverdale Avenue to catch the public bus. We were so excited about starting the new semester out together. There were just a handful of other kids from Leake and Watts who rode with us, but most of them changed buses in Getty Square to ride to Gorton High, which I soon learned was our number-one rival school.

The halls were jam-packed with new and returning students. My mission was to find my classes, arrive on time to each one, and pick out a good seat if possible. I was so glad that Mrs. Wesson had brought me to the school building and the office helper had given us a tour. I was able to navigate the building without too many problems.

That is, except for one incident with Bland, a tall, lanky, older kid who also lived at Leake and Watts. I knew him from around the campus. He was always in the gym shooting hoops with the boys from Shrady and DePeyster cottages. He and I never had a reason to speak to each other, and that was fine with me. I didn't want to be the butt of another one of those stupid boys' jokes.

As the first day was coming to an end, I had one final class to make my way to. It was Spanish, located upstairs, all the way down the hall. The bell rang for us to change classes, and I was hustling along with the throng of students. I had come from the gym at the other end of the school, so by the time I made it to the stairwell, the masses of students had thinned out. I raced up the flight of stairs to the second floor. My arms were heavy with textbooks and binders.

Just as I got to the top of the stairs, still panting from the exertion, I realized someone was standing still, in my way, in the middle of the top step. It was Bland.

"Where you going, little girl?" he asked with a smirk.

I was irritated and didn't say a word but moved to the right to get around him. He moved to the right and started laughing. I moved to the other side, and so did he.

"Where you going? You look like you're in a rush." He was taunting me now.

"Move, Bland," I said in what I hoped was a demanding voice.

But he just smiled even wider and laughed. "I said where you going in such a hurry?" he repeated.

"Move, I said. You're gonna make me late." My voice rose.

Two other students came up the steps behind me. I figured I would squeeze past this aggravating, six-foot pain in my neck when they did. He let them go by but quickly jumped back in front of me as I stepped up. I tried to push past him, but he just wiggled back and forth. This pushing and jostling caused my books and belongings to fall out of my arms, and were strewn all over the steps.

"Move, boy!" I yelled. "You gonna make me late." I bent over, trying to gather my items that were scattered on the top landing and the steps.

"Oh, the little girl's afraid she's gonna be late to class." He mocked me, but he finally moved. Not to help me pick up my things, but to continue down the steps to wherever he was going. I could still hear him laughing as he disappeared at the bottom of the steps.

I was distraught and busted out crying. By the time I walked into the class, the late bell was ringing, and I had just wiped the tears off my face. My nerves were frazzled. I rushed to the first available seat and slid into it, hoping not to be noticed. The students were talking and laughing amongst themselves, and the teacher, with her back turned, was writing her name on the board. I was grateful that no one was paying any attention to me.

By the end of the first week, it was abundantly clear that I was the only Black student in all my classes except gym and band, which were considered electives. When I spoke to Mrs. Wesson about this, she explained that the school had three education tracks for students, academic, general, and vocational. Because of my good grades in middle school, she and the counselor thought I should be placed on the academic track, where most of the students went to college after they graduated. She explained that the vocational track was for students who were more interested in a specific trade or job like woodwork, electrical, plumbing, automotive, or secretarial. All other students were placed on the general track.

"But I still don't understand why there are no Black kids in my classes," I persisted. "There's only one Black girl who is in my English and algebra class. There's just one Black guy in the whole band," I lamented.

"I know, dear, but that's just how the school system is set up."

"There are Black, white, and Spanish kids all over the building, in the halls, cafeteria, library, and gym. But you're telling me that when the bell rings, they send us to classes that are either all white or all Black?" I didn't like this at all.

"No, what I am trying to say, Carolyn, is that students are placed based on their academic ability and interests."

"Okay, so—" I waited for her to continue.

"We feel you have the potential to do well academically and shouldn't waste your time on a general or vocational track."

I was trying to wrap my head around all this information and didn't like the way it sounded. Later, in the cottage, I found out that both Ampara and Nancy were on the general track, so we would never be in the same classes unless it was gym. This was a little unsettling, as I was sure the three of us would be together.

When I spoke to Ma Brown about this privately in the cottage office, she said,

"Carolyn, apparently Mrs. Wesson and the counselor believe you have what it takes to be on the academic track. But you have to believe that. Don't waste time worrying about what Ampara or Nancy got going on. You can have fun and still focus on your schoolwork."

"But I don't like being the only Black kid in my classes. I feel like I stand out."

"I understand," Ma Brown said softly. "And you will stand out; that's why you have to work hard and give it your best."

"What if I don't know as much as those white kids? They're gonna laugh at me and think I'm dumb."

I was still trying to rationalize why I thought this whole setup was unfair and ridiculous. But Ma Brown wasn't letting me off the hook.

"Look here," she said, folding her arms across her chest. "There's always gonna be somebody smarter and somebody not as smart. You can't spend your time worrying about them. All you need to worry about is Carolyn, and that's a full-time job." She poked me on my shoulder.

"I-I don't know if I can do it. I'm scared."

"There's nothing wrong with being scared, as long as you give it your best," she said.

I exhaled a little, still not convinced as I looked out the cottage office window.

"Stop worrying. As long as you try, Mrs. Wesson and I will support you 100 percent. Just tell us what you need." Ma Brown stood up and gave me a comforting hug.

I looked at her, still feeling anxious, but relieved that I had at least two people I could count on during this new and unnerving chapter in my life.

After a few weeks passed, I came to the realization that my life was going to be different, in fact, quite a bit different than the rest of my cottage mates. Most of the girls went to the junior high and high school located on campus. It was abundantly clear to me that either they didn't have any homework assignments or didn't care about doing them, because they didn't. And Ampara and Nancy, who went to school with me, never seemed to have work to do either. During the so-called study hour that we had to engage in Monday through Thursday, the rule of thumb seemed to be as long as you had a book or magazine open and were quiet, you met the requirements for study hall.

The girls who attended school on campus were not interested in school at all. Even the cottage captain leaders displayed an apathy and indifference toward education. I could tell from their comments that they thought it was absurd to be spending time on schoolwork, when their efforts needed to be focused on the latest hairstyles, fashion trends, and what the older boys were up to. Their attentiveness to anything related to school went right out the window, unless it could be correlated with something within their narrow realm of interest that related to the here and now.

My work expectations and requirements were such that I had little to converse with Nancy and Ampara about. Since they weren't in my classes or even on the same academic track, there was nothing to talk about or compare. I couldn't ask them their opinions on an assignment or thoughts about a teacher, because we traveled in different circles, once the bell rang in the morning for first-period class.

I was all alone and expected—or should I say, challenged—to do well. To do something that no other girl in my cottage, or for that matter, on the whole campus was aspiring to do.

The one hour of study hall, four days a week became a joke to me. I had to spend at least an hour every day just practicing my flute. Mrs. Wesson certainly worked her magic with Mr. Hammond. She called me into her office my second week of school and presented me with a brand-new alto flute. I was elated and emerged from her office thinking, *Maybe she is serious about helping me, so I better get serious too.*

My workload at school was going to require a minimum of two to three hours of homework time every night, including weekends. I had to ask for permission to skip the afterschool rec schedule, so I could stay in the cottage to practice my band music, then start on my assignments for my five core classes. After I practiced the sheet music upstairs in my room, I'd carry a load of textbooks and notebook binders downstairs to the playroom that also served as our study hall. Rarely was I even halfway finished with my litany of assignments, before the girls came bursting through the door from rec.

After dinner, if I wasn't assigned dishes or dining room cleanup, I'd squeeze in a few short conversations with Nancy or Ampara, before recommencing on my academic expectations. Because Ma Brown knew that I had already spent at least ninety minutes on schoolwork prior to the girls coming in, she didn't require me to stay downstairs with them for the study hall hour. I could retreat upstairs, in the quiet of my room, to pursue my struggle of becoming more proficient with Spanish vocabulary, the single-cell life forms in biology, or the numerous algebraic formulas.

In class, I was still very self-conscious about being the only person of color. My senses were on high alert for any look or comment from the other students or teachers that would let me know they thought less of me. I was keenly aware how often each teacher did or didn't call on me. I wasn't ignorant to the fact that my very color made me stand out, not in the school, but in every all-white class I was assigned to. My being in the room with them gave me the feeling, justifiable or not, that I had to earn the right to be there. I stepped into every class feeling self-conscious and ready to gauge the tension barometer when I entered. Was I supposed to act invisible and stay in my place? Or could I actively participate and engage freely like my counterparts? Would they invite me to be on class teams and projects? Or would I be the last one chosen, added to a group by default?

It was a fine line I was trying to navigate, compounded by the fact that I still stuttered profusely when nervous and was wary of what people would think if they found out I lived in a home for children. Maybe some or most of these feelings were my own psychotic fears, but they were real to me, nonetheless.

Thank goodness I had Ma Brown and Mrs. Wesson to vent to, as on many days my resolve was tested. I wasn't sure if I had the necessary spunk and staying power to hang with these white kids, who maybe overtly or secretly didn't want me around. I wasn't sure if I possessed the stamina and persistence that it was going to take for me to be successful academically with these classmates.

25

Late one fall afternoon I saw Mr. Hammond, puffing on his trusty mahogany pipe, standing on the sidewalk right outside the main building. He was with Mr. Willshire, who was another campus administrator, and Mr. Blotcher. The overweight French bulldog was lying on the pavement, with ribbons of saliva dripping from his mouth. I had tried to see if Mrs. Wesson was in her office but was told by the on-duty receptionist that she was gone for the day.

I had an urgent request and if Mrs. Wesson wasn't there, I might as well try the man in charge.

"Excuse me, Mr. Hammond," I said, not wanting to appear rude by barging in on their conversation.

The three men turned and looked at me, as though seeing me for the first time.

"Yes, what can I do for you, young lady?" he said, one arm folded across his chest and the other falling and rising as he took intermittent puffs on his pipe. The three waited for me to speak. The dog even raised his massive head from the puddle of slimy water that had accumulated under his mouth. I guess it wasn't often that one of the residents approached them to interrupt their important conversations.

"I-I just wanted to say thank you first of all, for letting me have a new flute." The words were coming out, but so was the stuttering. Heck, it wasn't often that I had to address three men in authority at one time.

"Oh yeah, you're the one that Mrs. Wesson made us spend that extra money on." He smiled ever so slightly. "How's it working out, your flute playing?" He took another puff and blew out a ring of smoke.

"Really good, I think. I-I practice every day for about an hour, and I'm in the band at school."

"You don't say."

The three men turned to look as a car drove by. I felt like a mosquito who they probably wanted to swat and get rid of.

"Yes, that's what I wanted to talk to you about."

He turned to look at me, as though he was surprised I was still standing there. If I was going to say something, I had to make it fast.

"Mr. Hammond, I need money for my band uniform." There, I got it out. The three of them looked flabbergasted.

"You don't say," was his only response. The other two men didn't take their eyes off me.

"Yes, sir. I just went in to see Mrs. Wesson about it, but she's gone for the day. So, I thought I'd ask you. I have a paper from the band director with all the details and prices."

Whew, I was nervous, but it was out. The answer was either going to be yes or no. But at least I asked.

"Give the paper to the receptionist and ask her to put it in my mail-box. I'll discuss it with Mrs. Wesson on Monday."

"Thank you. Thank you, Mr. Hammond." I had a silly grin on my face, which is probably why he smiled a little more.

"I'm not making any promises. See your social worker. She'll let you know what we decide."

With that, I could tell the conversation was over and I was being dismissed. Half skipping, half running, I made it back to the cottage in record time. I went straight to the Browns' residence door and knocked several times. When Ma Brown opened it, I spilled out my conversation with Mr. Hammond.

She was so happy for me and said with a wink,

"Don't worry, you just keep doing your part. Good things are gonna happen, you'll see."

I increased the amount of time I practiced on my flute. It was apparent to anyone who knew me that I enjoyed it and took it seriously. No one had to make me practice. In fact, sometimes kids passing in front of the cottage would yell up to the open window,

"We hear you. You think you can play that thing? Keep on practicing, girl."

Other times, the weekend cottage parent would come to my door, stick her head in, and say,

"All right my darling, that's enough for tonight." Which I guess it was, since her resident apartment was on the floor with our bedrooms.

I had a driving need to practice my instrument. Not just because I liked it or because the agency spent money getting me a new flute. I saw how seriously the other kids in the band and orchestra took their music playing. When they entered the band room, I noticed there was very little horsing around and even less chit-chat if it wasn't about the piece of music in front of them.

After the second full week of band class, the director, Mr. Federico, organized us in chairs according to our level of proficiency in playing our instrument. Needless to say, I was in the third row of flute players. I wanted to know what made that one girl, Lynn, who sat in the first row, first chair of flute players so special. But I didn't dare ask her. She never looked around or even spoke to anybody in the band. When she came in, she sat down, got out her instrument and music sheets, and immediately started warming up.

The girls next to me shared that the first chair was reserved for the person who was the absolute best player in your instrument group. Apparently, that girl Lynn had been playing since early elementary school, had private lessons, and was quite accomplished. The skill and accuracy with which her fingers flew across the slender instrument was unmatched by any of the other twenty or so flute players. So, without knowing it, she was my motivation, my role model for wanting to work harder and practice longer. I wanted to strive to be better than what I was, and that would require me to be even more focused.

And I was focused—that is, at least until Chip strutted into the band room. How could I not notice him? We were the only two Black students in that huge room. He was one grade ahead of me, so this was his second year in the band, playing the bass drum. Everyone seemed to know and like him.

He had a huge mouth, thick lips that always looked a little moist, like he never needed Vaseline. His teeth were white and straight, which made me that much more self-conscious of the gap in my teeth. Chip had the smoothest, clear, soft brown skin I had seen on a guy in a long time. The kind that made you want to reach out and touch, ever so lightly. He wore his ebony-black, glistening hair in a perfectly cut two-inch-high afro. How could a girl not notice him, prancing in, all bowlegged, with arms swinging like he was on a mission? I wore glasses, but I wasn't blind. Like I said, I just had to focus on my music sheets on the stand in front of me and pretend I hadn't noticed him.

Mr. Hammond and Mrs. Wesson came through for me again. I was able to pay the necessary band fees to rent my complete uniform, which we needed to perform during the football games and march in parades. As the year progressed, so did the expectations for band. We started to practice before and after school. We needed to be on the field outside to practice our marching routines for the football game halftime shows. I did get to peek at Chip a little more often, but we basically ignored each other.

I found myself thanking Mr. Hammond again, this time for the Yonkers High blue-and-gold band uniform, complete with boots and tassels. I made it a point to invite him to the football games to see me play. He did give me that small, barely visible smile, but I don't think he attended any of our games.

The Friday before Thanksgiving, I played with the marching band during our annual football game against Gorton High School. This was a huge game in the Yonkers community. Current and former members from each school packed the stadium. You could feel the electricity and excitement in the air. But I had to devote all my nervous energy to the music and steps that we had practiced and memorized. I couldn't tell you where the football was, what the umpire calls meant, the difference between offense and defense, nor was I even remotely interested. My concentration was 100 percent on making sure that I didn't mess up. Many of the cottage parents from the campus were bringing their kids to the game as an off-campus field trip. I was representing not just my school but also Leake and Watts. So, I felt the added pressure to do well, and I did.

Some of my cottage mates had attended the high school rival football game, thinking it would be a great opportunity to scout for guys. And it was, since most of the kids who went to Gorton were predominantly Black and Hispanic. This would be the one game that guaranteed swarms of good-looking, eligible hot guys. By the time I made it back home, they had already beaten me there and were excitedly telling Ma and Pa Brown all the juicy details. What groups of boys they had seen, how many, what they were wearing, and if they exchanged any phone numbers. When I joined the raucous group in our study room, Nancy said,

"Girl, y'all did your thing out there."

Nita said, "I never seen so many good-looking brothers in one place. I got me a few numbers for sure."

"These boys on campus need to step their game up. Did you see all those fine guys on Gorton's football team?" Ampara said in her thick Spanish accent.

The Browns turned their attention to me.

"So, how did you like it?" Pa Brown asked.

"It was the absolute best, but I was so nervous."

"Don't worry, the more games you play in, the more you'll get used to it." Pa Brown gave me a high-five and said as he walked away,

"Good job, proud of you."

The other girls started upstairs toward their rooms, leaving Ma Brown and me behind.

"It was awesome, Ma Brown, and I didn't even mess up. I was sweating bullets, hoping not to trip up out there and look stupid."

"Girl, you did great. Never worry about messing up, and if you do, just get back in there and do your best. Mr. Hammond is proud of you. He may not say it or show it, but he is."

"How do you know?" I asked, my curiosity getting the better of me. "He acts like he doesn't even know I exist."

"Oh, believe me, he knows who you are. Mrs. Wesson makes sure of that. We've never had a resident play in the band at any of the off-campus community schools. Carolyn, you're the first."

"Sheetz, I hadn't thought of that." I said, letting this bit of information sink in. After a moment, I fingered the flute case that was still in my hand.

"You know what I noticed, Ma Brown? Gorton's band is almost all Black, but our band is mostly white."

She looked at me, nodding slowly, as if encouraging me to keep talking.

"And their band plays the latest songs by Stevie Wonder and Gladys Knight. But not us. We were good, but their band had the crowd really pumped up."

She nodded again, smiled, and said,

"Well, if you want to play in a predominantly all-Black marching band, you can."

"How? Do I have to switch schools and go to Gorton?" I was puzzled.

"Nope, but you can play in the band at a HBCU."

"What is that?" I was even more confused by Ma Brown throwing some letters out at me.

"A historically Black college or university." She leaned back in her chair, eyeing me.

"Like where, like what?" I wasn't even sure of what to ask, as no one in my life had ever spoken about college. In fact, I was sure that no one in my family had ever attended one. I wasn't even certain that Ma had completed high school.

"Well, there's so many. Morgan State, Alabama A and M, Clark Atlanta, Spellman, Bennett College, Fisk, North Carolina Central." Ma Brown started rattling them off, as if she had them memorized.

"Wow, I didn't know that." I was intrigued; she had piqued my interest.

"There are dozens of them all around the country. Their schools are fabulous, and their marching bands are amazing. They even have battle of the bands, where the colleges compete against each other during homecoming activities."

"I never knew that," I remarked, slowly letting the thought of not just a predominantly Black band, but an entire college composed of Black students, sink in.

"Think about it. You can make it happen if you want." With that, Ma Brown stood up to head across the floor to her apartment door.

I rose from the table, stiff and tired from the physical and mental stress of the day. Carrying my instrument case and band uniform hat, I made my way upstairs, thankful that my roommate was not there. I needed some time to process the information Ma Brown had just shared. She always gave me something to think about, to muse over. I smiled to myself. But this was different. This was a huge stretch, a mental paradigm shift, slowly and stealthily taking shape in my mind.

Many residents went home for the holidays to visit their families. They had to be old enough to travel by themselves, or family members had to come to the campus to get them. Their home had to be deemed safe, with a place for the kid to sleep, as well as always have a responsible adult family member around.

I had been in contact with Ma by letters since my stay with the Parkers, so I knew where she was living. By the time Thanksgiving rolled around, I was settled in high school, had already turned fifteen, and was old enough to travel off campus by myself. So, weeks in advance, I started bugging Mrs. Wesson about letting me go home for the four-day Thanksgiving break.

Ma used a payphone to call the agency to speak to my social worker. It was decided that I could go home to my Aunt Stella's house for the visit, but not my brother Gardiner. As it turned out, Gardiner was quite happy staying on campus, in familiar surroundings with his playmates. He had been taken from Ma at such an early age that he really didn't remember her or our brothers. Unlike me, he didn't have a need or yearning to go home.

My Aunt Stella and her husband, Cherry, lived in the Bronx, in a three-story apartment building that they owned. Ma, my brothers, and I were going to celebrate the Thanksgiving holiday at their house. They had enough room for all of us. I hadn't seen my cousins in the eight years I had been in foster care. It was going to be great, just like old times. I packed my smallest piece of luggage, carefully folding and smoothing each piece of clothing so that I didn't have to iron once I got to Aunt Stella's.

Ma had given me explicit directions after I got to the Number One subway line, on 242nd Street and Van Cortland Park. I was to take the subway and get off at the Yankee Stadium stop.

When I arrived at their brownstone apartment building, I gave Ma the tightest hug I could. She didn't let me go for a couple of minutes, touching me all over, making me turn around and fingering my freshly shaped afro.

"Pippa, I can't believe how much you've grown, and cute too. Ain't that right, Stella?" she said to her sister, not taking her eyes off me.

I met my two youngest female cousins, Michelle and Elaine. They hadn't been born when I left. I hugged their brothers Tyrone and Lionel, who were a few years younger than me. And of course, I was ecstatic to see Kevin and Ronald. They couldn't get over how big I had gotten, and I couldn't believe how good looking they were. Between Aunt Stella's four kids and Ma's three, it was like one big family reunion. Momma Louise and Uncle Steve were supposed to bring Googie over later. We were told that Michael and Anthony were going to show up for dinner tomorrow.

Aunt Stella and Ma stayed up all night getting the twenty-five-pound turkey ready, then started on the trimmings. We were going to have stuffing, collard greens, potato salad, sweet potatoes with marshmallows, cornbread, and a lot of other stuff that Uncle Cherry, who was from the islands, wanted on the menu.

We spent the night laughing and talking about old times. I tried to tell my brothers a little about life at Leake and Watts but totally omitted the years that Gardiner and I spent together in that horrible house in Greenburgh. They told me some of what they had been up to, mostly playing basketball at Taft High School where they attended or at the community center with Mr. Boyd. I was a little surprised that this man was still in the picture, but then they shared that he had been taking care of them since the state came and took all of us away.

That first night back with my family was wonderful. Ma in the kitchen smoking her cigarettes, while she and Aunt Stella caught up on all the family gossip as they prepared the big feast. Music blaring from

Uncle Cherry's record player, with a mixture of island reggae and the latest Motown sounds. I stayed out on the front steps with my brothers and older cousins, keeping an eye on their little sisters, who were running up and down, back and forth, like we used to do at that age.

Somewhere around midnight, I carried Michelle to the bedroom with Elaine close behind. Kevin and Ronald slept on the living room couches. Aunt Stella and Ma were still back in the kitchen, trying to make a dent in their long list of holiday food side items. Eventually the music ceased playing, the house got quiet, and we kids went to sleep for the night.

I was startled out of my early morning sleep by a loud pounding sound and the constant ringing of the front doorbell.

"All right, all right I'm coming," I heard an annoyed voice yell out. It was Aunt Stella shuffling down the hall in her slippers toward the front door. About a minute later, I heard Aunt Stella scream for Ma,

"Ruth, Ruth! Wake up. Come to the front door. Ruth, Ruth, get up!"

With all this noise, I sat up in a foggy haze and decided to make my way toward the living room. Ma, hair standing up all over her head and trying to secure her housecoat around her waist, walked past me, to see what her sister wanted so early in the morning. Even I thought *If it was a visitor, why didn't Aunt Stella just open the door? Why was she yelling and making such a racket?*

My brothers, wearing nothing but their Fruit of the Loom underwear, were sprawled out on the two living room couches. I plopped down on one of the fancy matching chairs and was just about to curl my legs underneath me to get comfortable when I heard a loud, anguished,

"No, no Lord, no!" coming from Ma. It was gut wrenching. "No, Stella, no, this can't be true."

I got up from the seat and started toward the hall and front door. Kevin and Ronald stirred and sat up. Even they were confused as to what could be going on so early on Thanksgiving morning.

When I got to the hallway, I peeked around toward the door. Ma was in a heap on the floor; Aunt Stella was bending over, rubbing her shoulders. And just beyond her, on the other side of the open front door, were two New York City cops.

Ma was bawling, crying, and screaming uncontrollably. The cops were trying to tell Aunt Stella something, but it was impossible to make out what they were saying over Ma's increasing sobs and cries of

"No, not my baby," over and over.

By this time, Uncle Cherry had come to the door, and Ronald and Kevin were pushing me out of the way so they could see what was going on.

"I'm sorry, ma'am. You can call the station for more details. Here's the number." The policeman reached out his hand with a card in it that Aunt Stella took.

"Thank you," she said, as she and Uncle Cherry lifted Ma off the floor. And then I heard, "Once again, ma'am, we are so sorry for your loss."

What, what loss? I started questioning in my head, as Ma was helped to the couch where my brothers had been sleeping.

"What happened, Ma?" Ronald asked in his concerned, take-charge manner that I used to remember.

"Kevin, get your mother some water from the kitchen," Aunt Stella said in a low but stern voice. "Take it easy, Ruth. We are going to find out what happened. We are going to get through this."

By this time, I was beside myself and ready to bust out in tears. Ma was bent over, head in her hands, rocking and crying. Aunt Stella looked like she was on the verge of a breakdown too, and I was one step away from a hysterical fit if someone didn't tell me something.

I bent down in front of Ma, hoping she could see my face through her tears.

"Ma, Ma, what happened? What did the police want? What did they say, Ma?" There was a sense of urgency in my voice.

She lifted her head, to look at her sister first, then me.

"Your brother Anthony is dead. He was stabbed this morning." Her voice was halting between words. She was barely able to catch her breath. That was all she could get out before burying her head, her body racked with heaving sobs.

"Anthony? Anthony is dead?" I said in disbelief, and with that I collapsed at her feet.

26

Over the next few days, I moved as if in a heavy fog, feeling like a zombie just aimlessly wandering the earth with no purpose. What was supposed to be one of the happiest holidays of my life turned out to be anything but. I sat sad and depressed in a corner of the living room, as I watched people coming in and out of Aunt Stella's house all day. Not to eat and take part in the festivities, but to offer condolences, prayers, and baskets of food to the family.

Through bits and pieces of conversation that I heard from the adults, I learned that my brother Anthony had been stabbed in the heart early Thanksgiving morning. He was with some girl outside her apartment door; it wasn't clear if he was going in or had just come out. Other people said it was neither and that he was just escorting her home. Needless to say, her boyfriend showed up, there was an argument, then a scuffle, and Anthony was stabbed and died right there in the girl's hallway. My brother was dead at eighteen.

I remember my oldest brother Michael and I rode in the cab with Ma to identify the body. Once we got to the hospital and made our way down to the morgue, they didn't let me go in the room where Anthony was. Ma and Michael were noticeably quiet and subdued when they came out. In my mind, I pictured my brother Anthony lying there, lifeless on the metal table, with a white sheet covering him.

The rest of my time was spent trying to remember and recreate every memory I had of Anthony. Even though I hadn't seen or spoken to him in years, he was still my big brother, one of the Paige boys.

When I returned to Leake and Watts, I told the Browns and Mrs. Wesson the tragic news about my brother. Everyone felt bad for me, even my cottage mates. The very thought of going home to see my family for the first time in years, and to have something so horrific and heartbreaking happen was unimaginable, painful, and traumatic for me.

Later the next week, I was excused from school to travel back to Aunt Stella's house. Gardiner said he did not want to go and stayed behind on the campus. The family was going to meet at my aunt's house and ride together in limousines to the church for Anthony's funeral. Ma told me that Mike had made the arrangements and paid for everything.

That was the first funeral I had ever been to. It was held in a big Catholic church somewhere in the city. The whole morning, everyone was quiet, speaking in hushed tones that matched the sadness of the occasion. Even my little cousins from the city and those who traveled from Beacon and Newburgh were on their best behavior.

The church was packed when we slowly marched in, led by the preacher, as he read his words from the Bible. Neighborhood people, close and distant friends of the family, and a multitude of high school kids, who I guess where classmates of Anthony's, filled the opposite side of the church.

There were so many family members ahead of me that my brothers and I sat packed together in the third row. We were well into the service before I realized that Mike was sitting on the first pew. When I had asked Ma earlier if he was coming to the funeral, she simply said, "I don't know," and turned her attention to whatever she was doing to get ready to bury her son.

Visitors and friends were occupying all her time, and I didn't want to be a pain in the neck. She was doing everything she could to get through this unimaginable painful day of burying one of her children.

I could not concentrate on the speakers or singers during the service. My mind was on Mike. I wanted to see him; I wanted him to see me. Years had passed, and I wondered if he even knew where I was. Did he even care? Did he miss me? Would he even recognize me? So many questions were swirling around in my head.

Then somebody up front gave a signal, and we all stood. The pall-bearers pushed the casket down the center aisle, with the preacher and family members following. I strained to see Mike over the shoulders of the mourners in front of me and on my row. I finally caught a glimpse of him as he slowly made his way past, still using his cane. He didn't look left or right, but straight ahead, I guess at the back of the casket that carried his son.

By the time I got to the entrance of the church, Mike was already in a limousine with dark-tinted windows, so I couldn't see him. I wanted desperately to ask Ma if I could go over to say something to him, but she had broken down again, as the hearse door was being closed on my brother's casket. Our aunts - Lillian, Stella and Lizzie, were on both sides, trying to console her. I thought for sure I would get a chance to say something to Mike at the burial site, until one of the adults yelled out,

"All you kids come this way. Y'all not going to the cemetery. Y'all going back to the house."

And with that, it was over, my last chance to see and speak to Mike. I never saw him again after that.

The sudden death of a loved one hits you in different ways. For me, I buried my pain inside. I felt there was no one my age to talk to who could possibly understand what I was feeling. Not the girls in my cottage, the kids in school, and my brother Gardiner was so young, he didn't even remember Anthony. Ma Brown and Mrs. Wesson kept a close eye on me in the weeks right after Anthony's murder. Ma Brown let me talk in private with her for as long as I wanted. Mrs. Wesson allowed me to come to her office more frequently during the week.

I found myself sharing with them the two other incidences of death that I had witnessed at an early age, the man lying in the wet gutter and the smell of the decomposing corpse that was brought out of the apartment building. As I talked, I thought it was interesting that Mike was present at all three of these occurrences.

To help me get through this traumatic event in my life, I needed an outlet. So many thoughts of Anthony were flooding and taking over my mind. I kept making up scenarios in my head about what happened, how it happened, and how things would have been different if he wasn't with that girl. None of these emotional tapes served any purpose, except to further my sadness and depression.

One Sunday afternoon, as I completed a solitary walk around the outskirts of the entire campus, I decided to focus on something else. I needed to rededicate myself to my studies and flute practice, which had suffered for about three weeks. Just because my brother passed, my assignments at school didn't diminish. In fact, midterms were coming up, and I wasn't as prepared as I should have been.

Remembering what Ma Brown told me earlier about asking her if I needed anything, I decided to test that theory out. The home had already purchased me my own flute and paid for my entire band uniform. I was getting ready to stretch things a bit further.

"Ma Brown." I stopped her as she was heading toward the cottage office area. "Can I ask you something?"

"Of course, what's up?" She had that nice, mischievous smile on her face, like she knew a secret but wasn't going to tell it.

"You told me to ask you if I needed anything to help me in school."

"Yes, I did say that." She paused in her walking and looked at me.

"Well, I don't think I'm doing as good as I should be in my classes."

"Oh no?" She raised her eyebrows slightly in surprise. "What seems to be the problem? You study more than anybody else in this whole cottage."

"It's not that. I'm having trouble concentrating and remembering things. There's nobody here for me to ask for help or to explain stuff that I don't understand."

Ma Brown listened, with an intent look on her face.

"Okay, so what can we do to help you?"

I took in a deep breath and said to myself, *Here goes.*

"I was wondering if y'all could get me a tutor for algebra and biology? Those are the two subjects I'm having the most trouble with, and I don't want to fail them." *There, I got it out.*

She nodded, and I saw that little smile again.

"Let me see what we can do. It's never been done before, but there's a first time for everything."

My hopes picked up a little.

"Have you spoken to Mrs. Wesson about this?"

"No, not yet. I wanted to run it by you first." We were standing inside the office door.

"I'll call your social worker today. Let's see what can be worked out."

I don't know what Ma Brown said to Mrs. Wesson, and I don't know what strings the two of them had to pull. But what I do know is, one week later, I was introduced to my two new tutors from Mount Saint Vincent College, which was located less than a mile from the campus. Mrs. Wesson appeared at the cottage door with the two hippie-looking young adults who were going to help me study.

The tutors were friendly and eager to get to work; the male majored in biology, the female in mathematics. I was to meet with each twice a week for an hour, in the cottage study room. My cottage mates were told by the Browns that when they saw me in the study room with the tutors, they were not to come through there to knock on their residence door, unless it was a life-or-death situation. I laughed when Nancy told me this.

Both tutors came on Tuesdays and Thursdays, starting at four o'clock. I finished up just in time to join my cottage mates for dinner as the metal bell gonged at six o'clock. The tutors answered questions that I was too embarrassed to ask in class. They explained things in easy, clear terms. We prepped for quizzes, reviewed vocabulary, worked out mathematical formulas, drew science projects, and studied for tests. Even though they smiled, laughed, and joked, their aim was always to make sure I thoroughly understood the material in front of me.

My interest and efforts in school were rejuvenated after being slug-gish and almost abandoned for a month. I looked forward to meeting with the tutors and picking their brains. There didn't seem to be a question or concept that they couldn't answer or explain.

Ma Brown and Mrs. Wesson were proud and kept checking on my progress and encouraging me every time we talked. Mr. Hammond would nod and smile more often when he saw me around the campus. He still was a man of few words, but that was okay with me. I found out that Mrs. Wesson shared with him that I wanted tutors to help me with my schoolwork. I guess he didn't argue with her about it, seeing that I was serious about my grades.

At the end of the school year, those of us who were enrolled in certain courses in the academic track had to take statewide tests called Regents Exams. This meant I was slated to take major tests in algebra, biology, and US History. History and geography had always been my favorite subjects since middle school, so I didn't have a problem in that area. But I was so glad that I asked for extra help early on, because at the end of the year, I not only passed my classes with top grades, I got A's on all my Regents Exams.

The following school year, I had another request for my social worker and Mr. Hammond. Once again, I thought to myself, *If I ask, they can only tell me yes or no. But if I don't ask, I will never know the answer.* I needed a job and needed permission to get one.

Fashions were changing much faster than the clothing closet was able or willing to keep up with. And the pitiful $2.50 allowance I was getting didn't begin to buy the cute outfits I saw other girls my age wearing. A few of my cottage mates had parents who were supplying them with new, up-to-date clothes every time they went on a home visit. I didn't have that luxury because Ma didn't have money like that. Most of the girls around school had chic, contemporary clothes that they wore every day of the week.

I needed to step my game up, especially if I wanted to attract the eye of that cute guy in the band. He was still prancing around like he hadn't noticed me, as if I blended in with all the white girls in the band. He knew I was the only other speck of pepper in that saltshaker besides him.

I had heard he was smart academically, so that didn't bother me. I knew my class grades and grade point average were probably just as good or better than his, even though he was a year ahead of me. This year in band, I was going to make sure he noticed me.

Seeing Mr. Hammond out by the main building one day with his three talking buddies, I decided to go for it. As I approached, their conversation stopped, as usual. I was used to that by now, so it didn't bother me. I was on another mission, a mission to update my school wardrobe.

"Yes, young lady, what can we do for you?"

Mr. Hammond was taking his customary short puffs on the ever-present trusty pipe hanging from the corner of his mouth. He probably knew I wanted to talk to him and not the other three. I never had cause to address them. In my mind, they didn't have anything I needed. They gave me the feeling that I was just as annoying to them as the fly that was circling the huge head of Mr. Blotcher's dog.

"I don't mean to keep bothering you, Mr. Hammond, but I wanted to ask you about the possibility of me getting a job to earn some extra money." I kept my eyes on him, because I didn't want the other three to think I came to see them.

"A job?" Mr. Hammond was puzzled. "What for. Don't you get an allowance from your cottage parents?"

One of the three men chuckled. I didn't think it was funny, but I kept my eyes peeled on the one who had the most decision-making power.

"Yes, I do get an allowance, but it's not enough for me to buy the extra things and clothes I want."

"I see," Mr. Hammond said. "What do you have in mind?"

"I don't know, maybe something around the campus like helping out in somebody's office or tutoring some of the younger kids."

I was grasping for straws, but almost anything was better than not having enough money to get the things I wanted.

"I see," Mr. Hammond said again, this time like he was mulling it over in his head.

One of the three other men spoke.

"You don't have time for a job with all your schoolwork. Your grades will start dropping." This came from Mr. Willshire, who had never spoken to me once since I arrived on campus.

I whipped my head around to face him and said,

"Mr. Willshire, I'm in the marching and concert bands, and I take a more advanced Spanish class than most of the other ninth graders. Besides, your daughter is in some of my classes, and I know for a fact that my grades are better than hers." Mr. Willshire's face turned bright red, and I think Mr. Knee snickered.

With that, I turned my attention back to Mr. Hammond.

Mr. Hammond, still formal as ever, said, "We'll talk about it." He looked at the other men. "And I'll get with Mrs. Wesson."

"Thank you," I muttered to Mr. Hammond, but not before rolling my eyes at Mr. Willshire. With that, I turned and sauntered off in the direction of Gould Cottage for my afternoon flute practice.

A couple of days later, Mrs. Wesson called me into her office.

"Hi, Carolyn. I heard you want a job to make some extra money." She had her elbow on the desk, arm up, with a lit cigarette in her hand. Fumbling through the ever-present pile of papers on her desk, she continued without looking up. "And I also heard you had a little run-in with Mr. Willshire."

I started apologizing.

"I'm sorry, Mrs. Wesson, but I wasn't even talking to him. And what does he know about my grades? My grades are better than his daughter's."

"Yes, I heard you made that point quite clear." She finally looked up at me and smiled a little. "We found something that you can do to make a few extra dollars each week."

"Okay, great, what is it?" My feelings of hope and anticipation jumped a notch.

"Mr. Knee's wife would like some help with light house cleaning."

I cocked my head to the side as I took this in.

"Mrs. Knee? Don't they live in that little house on the corner next to my cottage?"

"Yes, that's the one. She wants some help twice a week and will pay you cash. Do you think you might be interested in helping her out?"

"Sure, I can do that." I knew I could. After all the grueling, free labor Mrs. Thompson had squeezed out of me, whatever Mrs. Knee wanted me to do would be a breeze.

"There's just one condition, Carolyn."

I braced myself.

"If your grades start to drop, the job is over. Do you understand?" Mrs. Wesson said in a serious tone.

"Yes, yes I understand." And I did.

Somewhere in the recesses of my mind, I knew that Mr. Willshire probably wanted me to fail, because of the crack I made about his daughter. But I was going to prove him wrong, make my money, and up my wardrobe.

I liked Mrs. Knee. She was always kind, pleasant, and had a smile whenever I came to their house. Her hair was kept short, and every curl was held in place with stiff hairspray. She definitely did not want to be bothered washing dishes or polishing silverware, as she got her nails manicured and painted bright red every week. I spent that fall helping with light cleaning projects around her house. Sometimes I dusted the dozens of knickknacks that she had all over the living and dining rooms. Other times I got on my hands and knees to wipe down her wooden stairs.

At the end of each visit, she put a crisp ten-dollar bill in my hand. My weekly clothing budget jumped from two dollars to twenty-two dollars. I was a happy camper. Now when I went off campus on a shopping trip, I could do more than just look, I could buy. And that's exactly what I did. Cute tops, the latest in pants and sweaters, fashionable eyeglasses, and let's not forget a little makeup for my lips and eyes.

People began to notice the change in my appearance. I started to get frequent compliments from the girls in the cottage and at school. Guys on campus stopped what they were doing to gawk. They weren't laughing at me anymore. Now they were looking and lusting. I was now that cute, smart, stuck-up girl on the grounds who didn't pay the campus fellows any attention.

The truth of the matter is, I didn't have time to pay them any attention. And besides, their menial aspirations weren't heading in the same direction as mine. I was serious about work and school. They were only serious about whose panties they could get into next.

So, it caught me off guard when one of my older cottage mates told me that her brother liked me. Her name was Trina. She dated and was supposedly engaged to a white guy name Melvin, who worked in the main kitchen, helping to prepare meals for the entire campus. Her brother Torrey was about a year younger, lived in the older boys' cottage, and attended school on grounds.

"He really likes you, Carolyn. Give him a chance. Please at least talk to him." She was almost begging.

I didn't want to hurt her feelings, because after all, we lived in the same house. But I knew for sure that I wasn't going to be bothered with her big, slew-foot, slow talking, awkward brother.

I met him one evening right after dinner. He was waiting for me in front of the cottage, across the road by a large tree. He didn't waste any time telling me that he had been watching me for a while, liked me, and really thought we would make a great couple. I said,

"Boy I don't even know you. I just found out your name from your sister."

"Yeah, I know. But you can get to know me. If you just give me a chance, I'll give you the sun, the moon, and the stars." He said this with all the sincerity that he could muster up.

When those words came out of his mouth, I thought, *This guy must have lost his damn mind.* But I was nice.

"I am so sorry. I don't think that's going to work. It's just not going to happen."

Giving him a half-hearted smile, I made an excuse about my homework and returned to the cottage.

Well, I don't know what he told his sister about our little encounter that obviously didn't go as they had hoped. But I was on her hit list after that. Tensions were high every time she passed me.

One evening, another younger cottage mate and I were in the kitchen cleaning up the dishes and wiping down the dining room tables, when Trina appeared at the back door. This was the door that the kitchen staff used to deliver our meals daily. Pa Brown had told us that we were to never open that door for anybody, period. If it was locked, the food-delivery people had master keys to get in.

Trina peered in through the glass and saw us and yelled out several times for us to open the door. The two of us looked at each other, but neither moved to open the door. I feared the wrath of Pa Brown much more than I did Trina. She pointed her finger at us and yelled,

"Imma get you, Imma kick your ass."

Well, I instinctively knew she meant me. She was still salty about me not giving her goofy, stars-and-moon-promising brother a chance. A minute later, we could hear Trina coming down the steps to the kitchen. She walked right up to me and started snarling,

"You saw me out there, you heard me. You should've opened the door."

The younger girl and I looked at each other. I took a deep breath. "Here we go, more drama," I said to the younger girl standing behind me.

"Take off your glasses. Take your damn glasses off. Imma whip your ass," Trina hissed, sprays of spit coming out of her mouth.

Our little cottage mate tried to intervene.

"Stop, Trina, this is not necessary. You know we're not supposed to open that door."

"Shut up. I'm not talking to you. I'm talking to her." With that, she poked me in my chest. "Take your glasses off," she demanded again.

I was never quite sure why she was so insistent about me taking off my glasses, but I did, knowing I wouldn't be able to see a thing at that point. I handed my glasses to the younger girl, and as soon as I did, Trina pounced on me, grabbing, punching, and swinging wildly as if she were in a boxing match. I tried to avoid her pummeling blows. She swung me around and knocked me to the ground. Then she jumped on my chest, straddling me, grabbing my hair with both of her hands, and smashed the back of my head into the concrete kitchen floor.

Our cottage mate was begging her to stop. But Trina was like a raving maniac, taking the pain of her jilted brother and the insult of me not opening the back door out on my head. One crash of my head, then another. I knew I wouldn't survive a third. With her fingers still entwined in my afro, she yanked my head up again, getting ready to knock me back into the unforgiving cold floor. And when she did, I surprised her by lunging forward as hard as I could, and bit her squarely in the middle of her forehead. My entire mouth chomped down on her face, and I squeezed my teeth together with the full force of my jaw.

She was stunned and let me go. She fell back and covered her face, as blood streamed down like tiny fire-red rivers, staining her clothes and the floor. I stood up, reached for my glasses, and put them on in time to see her running out the same door that I had refused to open. I guess she ran all the way to the nurse's office by the main building, for some much-needed first aid.

I was never reprimanded or punished for that incident. The way Pa Brown looked at it, I was following his directions, the witness supported my account, and, in the end, I was simply defending myself. Trina and her brother moved off campus right after that incident. I heard that she had to get numerous stitches and wear long bangs, to cover the large scar left by my teeth.

27

When I turned sixteen, I went on my first outing with a boy from Leake and Watts. His name was Herbie, and we had become good friends. He was kind, quiet, easy to talk to, and sort of cute. He had big eyes and a huge smile. We went to an evening basketball game together at Yonkers High. No one else on campus seemed to be interested, and since we both liked basketball, we just decided to go together as friends.

I know I was cute, dressed in one of my new outfits purchased with the money I made working at the Knees' house. My long-sleeve beige blouse was cut short, just below my ribcage, and I wore low-waisted, striped bell-bottomed pants with colorful wedge shoes. I had a gold-ring belt to highlight my little waist and wide hips. An ivory-colored flower was stuck in my hair right above my ear. My afro was freshly trimmed and glistening with hair sheen spray. Gold hoop earrings, black mascara, and a tint of red lipstick finished off my fresh look.

Feeling and looking good, I walked into the packed gym with my nice-looking friend trailing close behind. It was obvious we were together, giving the appearance that we were a couple. Herbie and I searched for seats, as the game had already started. Walking across the gym floor, we both scoured the crowd for empty spaces to sit. Up in the middle of the bleachers, I caught sight of Chip. He was clearly staring at me, not interacting with the rowdy guys on either side of him. We locked eyes for a long moment. I smiled, nodded, and kept walking, until Herbie grabbed my arm and led me up to some available seats.

Yes, Chip noticed me from that day forward. He found an excuse to make small talk every time I entered the band room. Our other bandmates started to notice and comment on what a nice pair we made. I played it cool and calm; after all, I had two boyfriends prior to him and four older brothers who were wonderful teachers. Talking and interacting with the opposite sex was easy for me, light stuff.

After about a month of light band room flirting, Chip asked me to go with him. That was the term back then for going steady. My heart jumped, and I wanted to say, "It took you long enough." But my mouth simply said, "Sure." And with that we became a constant, steady couple for the next three years.

My living at Leake and Watts didn't faze him. He seemed to like that I was a loner, not having a crowd of loud, obnoxious girlfriends hanging around. I had a part-time job, and so did he, driving cabs on the weekends. Playing an instrument in the band and a love of basketball were other big interests we had in common. And when he found out just how serious I was about my grades, he was hooked. I was cute, so he got the whole package, beauty and brains.

Mrs. Wesson knew about him because of my weekly visits to her office but never met him because he only came to the campus on the weekends. Ma Brown was impressed by his good manners and book smarts. She liked him right away, sensing that he wasn't going to distract me from my studies but would help encourage me to do my best. Apparently, Chip had three older brothers who were known to be highly intelligent, as well as good looking. So, getting a solid education was important to his family as well.

He started walking me to my classes when his schedule permitted and always waited for me after school. During band trips, it was expected that we would sit together on the bus. Mr. Federico, the band director, always smiled at us but never said a word. That was another reason for me to like him even more; he was such a cool teacher.

Chip and I didn't have a lot of free time, so we had to make the time we had count. According to the cottage rules, now that I was sixteen, I could officially date off campus. My curfew on Friday and Saturday nights was eleven o'clock. We went to the park, movies, bowling alley, roller-skating rink, zoo, basketball games, and all the things that young teenagers in love do.

Yes, all the things that teenagers in love take part in. Our flirting led to kissing, which advanced to heavy petting, which culminated in sex. Lots of it, some long marathons, other times a spontaneous quickie. He was my first, with all the bells, whistles, and fireworks that go along with it. Things got so good; it was like a drug. We were akin to junkies who needed a regular fix, a hit before each weekend ended.

Ma Brown finally moved me into my own bedroom. Now, if I wanted to sneak out at night, I didn't have a nosey roommate to snitch on me. Ampara had her own bedroom next to mine. We used to take turns jamming the upstairs emergency door with toilet paper, so it wouldn't lock. That way we both could sneak in and out, without going through the downstairs front door, which was locked promptly at eleven on the weekends.

Many weekends, Chip on his cab route would drop me off just before eleven. I'd come in, say good night to the Browns or the other weekend cottage parent, wait fifteen or twenty minutes, and sneak out the emergency door to meet Chip around the back, in the dark, where the delivery trucks dropped off our food. I would jump back in the front seat of his cab to accompany him on some more calls until his shift ended.

Most of the money he made from his job was spent on motels. We knew them all, up and down Getty Square and into the Bronx along Broadway. Whenever he had the money, we would get a room. If it was only for a few hours, that was good enough for us.

One Saturday night, after a long, steamy session, we both must have dozed off from sheer exhaustion. I awoke with a start, frantic to know what time it was. It was almost six thirty in the morning. I was in a panic, as we threw on our clothes and he called a cab to take me home. The driver weaved through the nearly deserted streets, as the early morning light was just beginning to filter out the darkness. We pulled into the back area of Gould Cottage, as Chip planted one last quick kiss on my lips.

I bounded up the emergency steps to the door, praying that Ampara had remembered to leave it ajar with a wad of toilet paper. Much to my relief, it was. I took off my shoes and scampered down the quiet hallway to my room and closed the door behind me. Everyone was still asleep.

I sat on the edge of the bed, trying to calm my frayed nerves. This was a dangerous close call. Less than a minute later, I heard Ma Brown coming up the flight of steps.

"Good morning, good morning, time to get up for church." I could hear her going from door to door, opening each and saying in a cheerful voice,

"Time to get up, everybody. Good morning, ladies. Time for church." She got to my door and opened it; lights on, me on the edge of the bed, and fully clothed.

"Good morning. You're up and ready early." She smiled at me and closed the door. I fell back on my pillow as I heard her open Ampara's door.

"That was too close," I whispered out loud to myself.

Life was good. I had the handsomest guy in the entire school as my boyfriend, an easy job, and extra money for clothes. The boys on campus were barely a blip on the radar screen of my mind. They no longer existed, as far as I was concerned.

During that time, I believed Chip was the missing piece in my life. He provided the comfort, security, and love that I didn't get from Ma and Mike. He was gentle, caring, and listened with genuine empathy, when I was finally able to share some of the horrors of my past. Talking to someone who cared about me filled a huge void that was exacerbated by my years of loneliness spent in the basement.

Chip came from an intact family, with his mom and dad who had been married for years and were still together. There was no physical violence in his home. He had no experiences with shelters, foster homes, or social workers. He had never been molested or sexually abused. We were able to talk for hours at a time, pouring out our life stories. Chip was just as intrigued with my life as I was with his. We were able to bridge the gaping differences in our lives and forge a tight bond built on love, trust, and respect.

The months flew by at a dizzying speed. The following spring, I took a chance on bringing Chip to Ma's small apartment in the Bronx. It was a warm, sunny Sunday afternoon. I felt we had dated long enough for me to introduce him to another member of my family. He had already seen Gardiner a few times on campus.

Nothing was eventful about this trip home, except that my steady boyfriend was accompanying me. I had been coming home about once a month for short day visits. When we finally arrived, Ma greeted us at the door, juggling a cigarette and can of beer in the same hand. After a quick hug for me and mumbled hello to Chip, she hastily retreated to her bedroom. We stood in the middle of the kitchen, puzzled.

"Pippa, I'll be right out," she yelled from the back. "I just gotta get something."

Chip stood at attention, taking in the surroundings of the sparsely furnished place. I started to sit down at the oval table, and then I saw what Ma was looking for. Her full set of pink-and-ivory-colored acrylic dentures were in plain sight on the bare table. Upper and lower choppers just lying there, as if that was their regular storage location. For a split second, I was mortified; this was not the way I wanted my boyfriend to meet Ma.

It was too late; Chip saw the false teeth and started to laugh. My feelings of embarrassment quickly dissipated, because he didn't recoil in disgust as he could have.

"Ma," I yelled, "If you're looking for your teeth, they're out here."

We didn't stay long, as there was really nothing to do but make small talk. After thirty minutes or so, we headed back up to Yonkers.

Later that evening when I made it to my room, I realized my glasses were at Ma's house. I probably left them on the kitchen counter. My eyesight was bad; I wouldn't be able to see a thing in my textbooks or on the chalkboards. In band, I wouldn't be able to see the notes on the sheets of music. I needed those glasses. In desperation I made a split-second decision to cut school the next day and head back to Ma's house to retrieve my priceless eyewear.

The following morning, after breakfast, I made my way across the six blocks to Broadway to catch the bus to the train station. I was hustling, taking long, fast strides. My goal was to be back in school before lunchtime and continue with my day as usual. The plan didn't go exactly that way.

I exited the subway and was marching up Third Avenue, with two short blocks to go when I froze in my tracks. Because of my poor sight, I didn't see Pa Brown until I almost bumped into him. He stopped in front of me and said in his deep, stern voice,

"What are you doing down here? Why aren't you in school?"

There was no point in me lying. I was already caught. *I'm just gonna tell him the truth and take whatever punishment he throws my way,* I thought to myself.

"I left my glasses at my ma's house yesterday when I went home for a visit. I can't see without them, so I came back to pick them up, then go to school."

I was scared as hell. Pa Brown looked me up and down before saying,

"I'll see you back at the house, young lady."

Without another word, he strode past me and kept marching to wherever he was going. It never occurred to me in a million years that I would see somebody I knew on Third Avenue on a Monday morning, least of all Pa Brown. It took me a few long seconds to compose myself before I was able to continue to Ma's.

Of course, Ma wasn't expecting me. Why would she? I only visited her on the weekends, and I was just there yesterday. I banged on her door with a sense of renewed urgency since my run-in with Pa Brown.

"Who is it?" She sounded highly agitated that someone was waking her up so early in the morning.

"It's me, Ma. It's Pippa," I yelled at the closed door in front of me.

"Wait a minute, I'm coming," she called back.

I thought I heard a door slamming, then a chair being shoved across the kitchen floor, as if she bumped into it.

She finally unlocked and opened the door, and I could tell she was not expecting visitors. Black mascara was smeared around her eyes, and the hair on her head was standing as if she had just pulled her finger out of an electrical socket.

"Pippa, what are you doing back here?" She sounded slightly annoyed.

"Ma, I left my glasses here. I need them for school." I was already inside and looking around the kitchen.

"I put them over there on the counter, by the fridge." She made a sweeping motion in that direction with her hand.

"I wish you had told me you was coming." She was still agitated, uneasy.

"Ma, how could I? You don't have a phone."

Now I was getting a little ruffled myself. Something was off, but I didn't know what. I just needed my glasses and be on my way to school. Just then, a man's high voice called out from the bedroom,

"Ruth, who's that?"

Ma didn't answer, instead grabbing her pack of Pall Malls and a book of matches off the table. I stopped moving. I recognized that distinctive voice.

"Ruth, I said who's that, who's out there?"

"It's Pippa," Ma finally answered. She sat down wearily in the chair.

I could hear some movement, and then the man who owned the high-pitched voice sauntered into the kitchen, barefoot and shirtless. He looked at me, and I stared back at him. He was the same short, dark-skinned man who used to come to all of Ma's card parties. The one I always thought dressed like a little flashy pimp. Then the stark awareness hit me—this was the same man who was in Ma's bed, the night I sneaked in there to sleep years ago.

"Hey, Pippa, how you doing? You sure got big, girl."

He was talking to me like we were old friends. Ma didn't look at either of us. She was taking long, slow drags on her cigarette.

I managed to get out a "Hey," to the little man.

The tension was palpable. Obviously I was interrupting something, and I was ready to get out of there.

He came over a little closer and stood between Ma and me. He looked at her, then at me.

"Ruth, what's the matter with you?" The man's squeaky voice matched his little stature.

Ma didn't budge. I turned to leave.

"Ruth, you didn't tell this girl?" he asked, incredulous.

That question caused me to stop and turn back around to face them.

"No, Jimmy," she finally said, looking at her lit cigarette as if she was having a conversation with it.

"Tell me what?" I eyeballed the two of them.

"Tell her, Ruth." He moved and leaned back against the stove.

"Ma, what is he talking about? Tell me what?" My voice was rising slightly because they were wasting my time, and I was already in a bad mood for getting caught by Pa Brown.

Ma sat there at the table, legs crossed under her robe, not saying a word, taking slow drags on her cigarette as if she was deep in thought. A few seconds of silence filled the kitchen; the tension was thick.

Exasperated, I shook my head and turned to leave again, when the little man with his high-pitched voice announced,

"Pippa, she didn't tell you that I'm your father."

Ma couldn't face me. She looked drained, like the last ounce of strength had been sucked out of her.

My mouth fell open, but nothing came out.

"She should've told you years ago, Pippa. I'm your father. You need to know. You need to know who your family is."

I was shell shocked, blown out of the water by this little man's unexpected, major declaration of paternity.

"Ma, Ma," I repeated in an insistent voice, but she wouldn't look at me.

I was incensed, throwing up my hand at the two of them.

"What the hell, Ma? Y'all waited till I was sixteen to drop this bomb on me? Why?" Infuriated, I stormed out and slammed the door behind me.

28

That evening, I barely heard Pa Brown as he reprimanded me in his stern, deep voice. My mind had been in a dense fog ever since the unexpected revelation of who my daddy was. That blow was much heavier than the three-week punishment I got for cutting school and going to the city without permission, even though I thought it was for a good cause. I wouldn't be able to go off campus for any reason, unless it was school related.

All day and night, during the next few weeks, I was consumed with the news of finding out that the man I thought was my father wasn't. Another man, who I had only seen at Ma's house parties and heard in her bed one night, was the real sperm donor.

Why hadn't Ma told me herself in all these years? Maybe because she was ashamed, since the brothers older and younger than me were obviously half-white, Italian in fact. Did this mean she was cheating on Mike? Or maybe she didn't say anything for fear of more physical violence from him. The horrendous abuse she suffered was enough to make her guard any indiscretions. Maybe she was worried that her primary source of income would be cut off.

And who the hell was Jimmy? What was his claim to fame? How did I get so damn lucky to have this little, short leprechaun as my daddy? Where had he been for the past sixteen years, and what was his excuse for not making his presence known in my life? Where was he when Child Protective Services ripped me from my family and sentenced me to almost six years of damnation, in the abyss of that Greenburgh foster home? He had to know I was a ward of the state, but apparently, he didn't care enough to contact me or come get me.

What about Mike? Did he really think I was his little chocolate baby, with my nappy hair and big nose? Did Ma run a con game on him that good? He cared about me, that I was sure of, taking me places, buying me things, and his constant show of affection told me he cared. At least until I was snatched away by the social workers; then he disappeared just like early morning fog.

I don't know what Ma was thinking or feeling during this time. She didn't have a phone, and I couldn't leave campus to visit her. I was so angry; I didn't want to see her anyway. There were so many questions, and in my mind, no excuse or justification for any of them was good enough. Ma, Mike, or that Jimmy fellow couldn't do or say anything that was going to appease me. The adults in my life who were supposed to protect me, abandoned me with little to no concern for my welfare. No one in the family bothered to check on me or Gardiner, to see how we were doing, not once in all those years.

This was so much for me to take in, it was starting to swallow me up in raw emotion. I was perplexed one minute, depressed and confused the next. But my anger at all of them was unbridled. I had to turn this emotional switch off before it destroyed me. I decided to obliterate them from my mind; they were my past, and there was nothing I could do about it.

My focus and energies had to be on the ever-present, unrelenting schoolwork and the constant push of learning new band music. I didn't share with Ma Brown or Mrs. Wesson my new daddy news. It was just too soon to talk about it without breaking down in tears. At school, Chip thought my quiet, sullen attitude was due to my extended punishment. I couldn't see him, other than brief encounters in the halls or band room, and I sure wasn't going to discuss these private, intimate problems there.

I turned my attention back to my schoolwork. My tutors from the local college were phenomenal in helping me not only to maintain good grades, but to excel at a much higher level. My lowest grade in any class was a B. But most of the grades in my core classes were solid A's. Every Regents Exam I had coming up, I'd ask well in advance for a tutor in that subject. I wasn't going to wait, fall behind, and then struggle to catch up. As time passed, Mrs. Wesson and Mr. Hammond got used to me asking for extra tutorial help, even before I needed it. They knew I wanted something whenever I appeared in their office doorway unannounced. I guess you could say I was being proactive. They never once told me no, especially after seeing that I was consistently making the honor roll every marking period.

If I didn't know any better, I think Mr. Willshire and definitely Mr. Knee looked at me through a more positive lens. Mrs. Knee was singing my praises at the fine job I was doing keeping her home spotless, thus allowing her to save those pretty, polished nails. The girls in the cottage left me alone, knowing I didn't have time to get involved in their day-to-day romantic antics at the rec.

I left the grounds to participate in evening band concerts, perform at games, or march in parades through downtown Yonkers. Mrs. Wesson also gave me permission to try out for the twirling squad, which I made. I added a nice touch of ebony to that ivory group. Chip and I, still going strong, as always met early before each event and hung out for about an hour when things wrapped up. And of course, we still sat together and chatted on any bus trips to the other schools we performed at.

The next school year, Mrs. Davis, another social worker, shared with Mrs. Wesson that she was looking for a responsible babysitter. Mrs. Wesson recommended me. So, I got another stream of income, by watching the Davises' two young daughters in their Bronx apartment, which was right off the Broadway bus line.

The Davises were wonderful examples for me of what a solid, functional family should look like. They were both college educated, with excellent jobs in their fields. Mr. Davis held a high administrative job at a huge telephone company that served the northeastern area of the country. Mrs. Davis was not only a social worker at Leake and Watts, but worked with and supervised students in the nursing program at Bronx Community College. Their home was a virtual museum of Black art, sculptures, books, magazines, and music. Mr. Davis took pride in the numerous important contributions Black people made to our culture and country and enjoyed sharing his vast collections of notable possessions with me.

I watched their kids at night during the week when both parents had late meetings and occasionally on the weekends so they could go on dates alone or with other couples. When I worked on the weekends, they let Chip come over, as long as I told them in advance. They liked that he escorted me home, thus not having to worry about my traveling alone back to Leake and Watts in the dark.

The Davises spent a lot of time talking to me about Black colleges and universities when I broached the subject. As it turned out, Mrs. Davis graduated from Bennett College, which is a HBCU girls' college in Greensboro, North Carolina. I was spellbound with stories they shared about the history of Black institutions of higher learning and all the famous people who graduated from them. They told me about the campus wide excitement generated by annual homecoming activities, and the prestige of belonging to a Greek sorority or fraternity. Both Davises encouraged me to go to the school library and do some research for myself, which I did.

I grew to love Mr. and Mrs. Davis for welcoming me into their home, the positive family life they modeled, and I respected them for igniting the flame of higher education that was first sparked by Ma Brown months earlier. Mr. Hammond, I heard, had also attended a HBCU. I admired the sophisticated, no-nonsense, take-charge way he carried himself. Now I had several prominent Black adults to look up to, to serve as positive role models. Without me consciously realizing it, they were instilling in me values, qualities, and traits that I would carry with me the rest of my life.

Back at school, as each semester passed and I completed more course requirements, I was having free blocks of time during the day. Mr. Sher, who was my history teacher, enlisted me one period each day to assist him in grading, recording, and filing the numerous student assignments he gave out and collected each week. I loved working for him. He was a young, white, blond-headed, beard-wearing motivator of all the high school students who were enrolled in his classes. He was jovial, laid back, easygoing, and made learning fun. All his students, including me, liked to spend any extra time we had in his class.

Mr. Sher also built on what the Davises and Ma Brown had started. He talked to me about my plans after graduation. When I told him I wanted to go to college, he championed the idea. He stressed that it was time for me to research colleges and possible scholarships, since my grade point average was so high.

I did such a great job working for Mr. Sher that in my senior year, he suggested I join the school's office helpers club. My duties, along with about six other club members, were to do clerical-type things that the paid secretaries didn't want to do. We had a lot of fun laughing and joking as we made copies for teachers, labeled and stuffed envelopes, distributed mail, passed out administrative notices, and ran countless errands between the classrooms and the office.

I was again the only student of color in the club, and thus the only Black student parents and visitors would see consistently hanging around the office, behind the counter. As time passed, this fact bothered me less, and I wasn't as self-conscious. What was bothering me was something else.

This was the late sixties, and the country was in the throes of conflict over our participation in the Vietnam War and ongoing racial unrest here at home. Huey Newton and Angela Davis of the Black Panther Party were prominent figures, leading the nationwide Civil Rights Movement. They helped organize the subsequent protests for equal rights in voting, housing, jobs, healthcare, education, and other social reforms. Malcolm X had been assassinated a few years earlier, and nationwide feelings were still boiling, over the killing of Dr. Martin Luther King Jr. The country's emotionally charged looting, riots, and unrest spilled over into the schools. There was a resurgence in self-pride resulting in the Black Is Beautiful culture.

Citywide high school student protests led to walkouts and marches through downtown Yonkers to the courthouse by hundreds of young people, followed by the news media. I, along with the throngs of other students from local schools, objected to the lack of culturally diverse course offerings in the curriculum. The board of education and school administrators finally agreed to offer one course in African American studies. I guess they thought they had to do something to get us off the city streets and back into the classrooms.

That was okay, a starting point, but the course was only offered to students on the academic track. Once again, I was the only Black kid sitting in my class. The teacher's class roster was diverse, and full of students from Spanish, Irish, Greek, and Italian backgrounds. I wondered if they were just as tired of the same old one-sided, skewed American history as I was. Or maybe they thought this was going to be an easy elective to fill up one of their empty time blocks. Either way, two things were abundantly clear to me. One was my absolute lack of knowledge about my own heritage. The other was, every time a question was asked, if no one raised their hands, the students looked at me as if I was supposed to know the answer, by virtue of my skin color.

I struggled through the class, ingesting all the newly acquired education on the history of my people. This experience highlighted for me the glaring omissions of African Americans and their contributions to our country and the world, in all social studies and history classes I had ever taken throughout my twelve years of schooling. This further solidified my resolve to attend a Black college or university upon graduation. I was thirsty and ready to be totally immersed in an environment of higher education, which offered a Black campus experience.

One early fall afternoon, when all my lightweight duties were completed for Mr. Sher, I asked to go to the counselor's office to talk about college options and scholarships. This was my first and last visit to see my senior counselor.

After introducing myself and stating the purpose of my visit, she thumbed through her metal file cabinet and pulled out what I guess was the official history of my time at Yonkers High. She studied it in silence for a couple of minutes, then looked up at me across her catalog-and-paper-strewn desk.

"Well, Carolyn, your grades and test scores are certainly impressive," she started.

"There are many great colleges and universities in New York that you can definitely apply to. We can probably find you some scholarships and grants, but you will have to attend school in state."

I cocked my head and looked at the middle-aged lady in front of me. Maybe she didn't understand me.

"I'm looking to apply to historically Black colleges and universities," I repeated.

"Yes, I heard you. But there is no way you will be able to attend college out of state. The tuition, fees, room, and board are astronomical for out-of-state students. You will have to make your selections from one of the many fine colleges and universities here in New York."

I am not sure what else she said. I completely tuned her out after that. She must have thought I was just another little Black girl sitting in her office, spouting off lofty ideas. But I wasn't just another nobody. I had worked my ass off to get to that point, and I wasn't going to let her simply look through a folder and tell me what I couldn't do. For three years I had been the token Black in just about all my academic classes, the band, twirling squad, and office helpers club. It was time for a major change in my educational landscape. My grades, class tests, Regents Exams, and report cards reflected that I had the ability to compete with anybody. This lady who knew me all of fifteen minutes was not about to dictate my future.

When I told Ma Brown and later the Davises of my singular encounter with the counselor, they were incensed.

"What did she mean, you can't go to a school out of state?" Ma Brown was pissed off.

"She was just probably ticked off because you said you wanted to go to an all-Black school. I bet she was a white woman, wasn't she?"

"Yeah, she was," I acknowledged. "But Ma Brown, she didn't even try to work with me or give me any real suggestions on how to attend an out-of-state school. She totally shut down that option for me."

"Well, she knew she couldn't help you with any in-state Black colleges, because there aren't any. So, she was simply doing what was easiest for her, not what was best for you. Don't worry, you are going to a HBCU, that's for sure. You need to go see Mrs. Wesson right now. I'm calling her."

I knew when Ma Brown meant business. She turned and marched across the room to the cottage office, where the phones were located. I headed to the main building, not feeling as distraught as I had earlier. At least I knew that Ma Brown was in my corner. She grew up in the Deep South and knew of the great pride the Black communities, professors, and students took in their colleges and universities. She was going to do whatever she could to make sure I didn't miss out on this opportunity because of one school counselor's narrow frame of mind.

When I arrived at my social worker's office, she took me straight to Mr. Hammond, who was standing outside his door with Mrs. Davis.

Okay, this must be serious. They mean business, I thought to myself as I gave a feeble smile to the other adults.

The last time I got to sit in Mr. Hammond's office was the day I informed him the area high school students were planning a massive walkout and that I was going to take part. He had listened intently, puffing as usual on his pipe, and told me not to get into trouble. That was it, short and to the point.

"Come in, everybody, take a seat." Mr. Hammond stood back so we could all enter first.

Once we were all seated in the cushioned leather chairs in front of his huge, dark wooden desk, he turned his attention to me.

"All right, young lady, what's going on now? I see you've gotten the attention of your cottage parent and two of my best social workers again."

Mrs. Wesson nodded for me to start, and Mrs. Davis gave me a reassuring smile. I sat on the edge of my seat, leaned forward, and talked for at least fifteen minutes, telling Mr. Hammond everything he probably already knew. I shared about me being the only Black female in most of my classes, my job in the school office, playing in the band, making the twirling squad, and how much I enjoyed all those experiences and tried to do my best. I talked about my grades, report cards, and making A's on every Regents Test that I ever took. I thanked him again for making it possible for me to get my own flute, uniform for the band, providing the college tutors to help me, and letting me earn extra money working for the Knees and Davises.

He continued to listen as he filled his curved, mahogany pipe with tobacco, lit it, and took some short puffs. I talked about my participation in the protest for a change in the school curriculum, to finally get a Black history course added in, only to be the single Black student in that class as well.

Mrs. Wesson and Mrs. Davis hung on every word I was saying. Neither had ever heard me speak that long or passionately before. I shared some of my early school failures and lack of help from my Ma and the first two foster parents. I shared with them that my fifth-grade teacher was the first person to spark my interest in school, how I was challenged by an eighth-grade teacher to strive for the honor roll, and when I did, how I broke down and cried in the girls' bathroom.

The three adults sat quietly as I gave credit to every adult who inspired, motivated, and believed in me, even when I didn't believe in myself. I spoke of the major impact that all of them, Ma Brown, Mrs. Wesson, Mr. and Mrs. Davis, and even Mr. Hammond himself, had on my life. How the five of them in their own ways gave me something to believe in, hold on to, until I could envision it for myself. The corners of Mr. Hammond's mouth curled up ever so slightly when I included him in my litany of life-changing motivators and people I looked up to.

When I finally paused, he asked, "So, what is it that you want, young lady?"

"Mr. Hammond, I want to go to an all-Black college or university, and there aren't any here in New York. I need, and feel I deserve an education at the school of my choosing. I don't want to be told where I can and can't go. And I don't understand why I should have to listen to that school counselor. She doesn't know me. All she probably sees is a poor Black girl, who lives at Leake and Watts, is a ward of the state, trying to do something she's not supposed to do." My voice started to crack, and I began to get emotional and choke up.

"Nobody in my family has finished four years of college. If I do, I'll be the first." I was exhausted and had pleaded my case to the best of my ability. My fate was in their hands. I exhaled and slumped back in my chair.

"I'll tell you what." Mr. Hammond spoke slowly, methodically drawing in and blowing out smoke from his pipe.

"Let's see what we can work out. Mrs. Wesson and Mrs. Davis, can you two make arrangements for Carolyn to visit some colleges in and out of state? Then, young lady, you go through the application process, with Mrs. Wesson helping you. We'll see what happens."

The ladies looked at me and smiled. Mr. Hammond took another puff and blew out a small ring of smoke, then pushed back in his leather chair. The meeting was over.

L ater, after dinner, I told Ma and Pa Brown about my big meeting in the main building. Pa Brown chuckled and said,

"Don't worry, Mr. Hammond really likes you. You probably remind him a little of himself, back in his younger, militant heydays."

Ma Brown put her hand on my shoulder.

"Yeah, don't worry about nothin', Carolyn. Just keep doing what you're doing. Some people didn't expect you to get this far, but you did. You're gonna make it, just wait and see."

That winter was a flurry of activities for me. Mrs. Wesson made the necessary arrangements for us to tour the campuses of Hofstra University on Long Island and the State University of New York at Albany. Both campuses were beautiful and offered the degrees in speech pathology and elementary education that I was interested in. During each visit, I insisted on visiting the student unions, main libraries, and cafeterias. That told me everything I suspected and needed to know. There were very few students of color anywhere, a few token Black kids sprinkled here and there. These institutions, although well-known and prestigious, could not offer me what I was looking for. I was determined to get a top-notch education and a Black campus experience. Period.

Then Mr. and Mrs. Davis worked their magic. Mr. Davis had a close friend who not only graduated from Howard University in Washington, DC, but still lived in the area and maintained close connections to people who worked in the administrative offices on campus. I would stay with his friend Burt and their family during my visit. Burt made arrangements for members of the university's student government to give me a tour. The Davises paid for my round-trip Amtrak train ticket to Union Station, and Mrs. Wesson made sure I had some extra spending money.

It was around January, my last year in high school, when I walked across the huge open courtyard in the middle of the Howard University campus with my two senior guides. There were students of color everywhere. Many were making their way in and out of the various buildings that surrounded the courtyard, where the classrooms and labs were located. We stopped by the outside lawn area, still covered with melting snow, that was reserved for the various sororities and fraternities, where several benches and huge boulders were decorated with their unique colors and symbols.

Since I was interested in the Howard University marching band, my escorts took me to the fine arts building and the football field where the band practiced. We toured the Quad, a group of four residential buildings where all freshmen girls lived. The stone-and-brick wall outside the Quad was lined with groups of young people interacting. The massive campus library was full of students studying individually and in small groups. The two cafeterias were packed with young adults eating, socializing, and having a good time.

Each area or building we visited, my guides made sure they talked about the impressive number of famous, influential African Americans who graduated from Howard. My female escort was an English literature major and was proud to share that Paul Laurence Dunbar, Toni Morrison, and Zora Neale Hurston were graduates. As we passed the law building, they talked about the contributions of Thurgood Marshall, Andrew Young, Ralph Bunch, and Stokely Carmichael to the civil rights and black power movement. The male guide was into theater, and as we toured the fine arts building, he pointed out such notables as Ossie Davis, Debbie Allen and Donny Hathaway. I was enthralled by Howard's rich history of producing so many influential people. The new African American history course I was enrolled in had at least introduced me to many of these powerful and distinguished figures.

By the end of my daylong tour, I had made up my mind that Howard University was where I wanted to be. Being able to interact and rub elbows with students who not only looked like me, but were highly motivated in pursuing their educational dreams was exactly what I was craving. Yonkers High did an excellent job of preparing me academically to compete on a college level, but they could not offer me the social experiences and cultural benefits that I was going to get here on a HBCU campus.

No one was surprised when I told them I didn't need to look any further, that there was no reason for me to visit any other colleges or universities. I was hooked. I thanked Burt and his wife for the invitation to their home and for providing such amazing hospitality. I was deeply appreciative of them utilizing their Howard connections and showing me around the Washington, DC area.

I returned to New York filled with excitement and anticipation for my future. Mr. and Mrs. Davis said it was going to be a marvelous opportunity for me. Mr. Hammond smiled and nodded his approval of my university choice.

My social worker, Mrs. Wesson, was happy that I found exactly what I was looking for in a college institution. She said it was time to start filling out the necessary forms and applications and applying for scholarships. I spent several afternoons in her office as she guided me in completing the proper university paperwork. We talked about the yearly cost of attending Howard and tried to project about how much extra money I would need for clothes, laundry, travel back home to New York, and other miscellaneous things. We researched scholarships and grants, double checked that the appropriate ones were completed correctly and mailed out on time.

By early spring, not only had I received my acceptance letter to attend Howard University, but they had awarded me a full academic scholarship that covered room, board, and tuition. The only stipulation to keep it was that I had to maintain a 3.0 or B grade point average. In addition, Mrs. Wesson found other sources of money that supplemented my budget. By the time we finished with this process, I had more than enough money to cover all my expenses, plus give myself a weekly allowance.

This accomplishment was a major feat for me, a cause for celebration. It was the direct result of all the hard work and long hours I had invested in my academic work since the first day I enrolled in Yonkers High. In fact, it really began back in junior high, when my teacher first challenged me to strive to make the honor roll. I was bubbling inside with pride.

Right before dinner, the Browns and my cottage mates put together a surprise, congratulatory party for me, complete with pizza, cookies, chips, soda, and a cake. They also had the table decorated with big blue and white balloons, representing Howard's colors. Even Mrs. Davis and Mrs. Wesson stopped by. I remember getting hugs and high-fives from everyone, but I couldn't stay downstairs long to enjoy it.

The monster, my monthly cycle, had visited me again with a vengeance. My stomach was churning and cramping with pain. I went straight to my room, lay back on the bed, and put my feet up on the wall, praying and waiting for the pain to subside.

Later that evening, Ma Brown came upstairs to check on me. She told me that Mr. Hammond had stopped by for the celebration. While he was waiting in the foyer, he heard the loud sounds of me vomiting my insides out, echoing down from the bathroom. She told him it was me, and said he was genuinely concerned to know that I experienced that level of agony every month. That did make me smile a little, just knowing that stiff, quiet Mr. Hammond had a soft spot for me.

During the spring, the yearbook staff asked me to pose for an individual shot on the steps in front of the school. I was thrilled to be singled out for that, as very few Black female students appeared solo in Yonkers High yearbook candid shots. In addition to my formal graduation picture, I was also in group shots with the twirling squad and office helpers club. My name was listed with the rest of the band members. Yes, my involvement in school activities certainly paid off, and I was proud of that.

I visited Mr. Hammond again, this time carrying a list and small stack of brochures from the school. It was time to order specialty items to close out my final year, and I didn't want to forget anything.

"Mr. Hammond, can I come in?" I asked in a hesitant voice, as I stood outside the open door to his office. He was standing behind his desk, deep in thought, looking out the huge, heavily draped window.

He turned to face me, his trusty pipe in hand.

"Yes, young lady, what can I do for you today?"

Mr. Hammond knew I wanted something, because quite frankly those were the only times I came to his office. I was still a little intimidated by his presence. After all, he was the man in charge of everything and everybody, and I respected that. He motioned for me to take a seat.

"I wanted to invite you to my graduation in June. I know how busy you are, so I wanted to tell you about it early."

Mr. Hammond penciled in the date and time that I gave him on a large desk calendar.

"I can't make you any promises, but I certainly appreciate the invitation." He pursed his lips and took several short puffs on the mahogany pipe before letting the smoke drift out of his mouth. He waited for me to continue.

"All right, Mr. Hammond." I took in a deep breath, determined to speak slow and not to stutter. Opening the brochures and pushing them toward him, I said, "The end of the school year is coming fast, and there's a few extra things I need help with."

He looked and nodded.

"Well, there's the school ring I would like to get if possible, and my yearbook. Then there's the cost of my graduation cap and gown."

He had his head down, looking at the pictures and prices I had circled in red in the opened brochures. I was prepared and didn't want to waste his time. When I got quiet, he looked up, with an expressionless face and said,

"Is there anything else, young lady?"

"As a matter of fact, there is, Mr. Hammond, just one more thing." I needed to get this last request out.

"My prom is coming up, and I'd like to buy a dress, a long one, and some new shoes to go with it." There, I got it out. For some reason, this made him smile.

"Ah yes, I remember when my daughter went to her prom." He seemed to be going way back in his mind, reminiscing. He held up one of the brochures.

"I see you made a list of what you want and the prices. That's good."

"Yes, but I couldn't quite figure out how much to ask for the dress, because I never had one before." I could feel myself getting nervous. I didn't want Mr. Hammond to think I was being greedy.

He closed the brochures and pushed them together in a neat stack.

"That's okay. Get with Mrs. Wesson. I'm sure she'll be able to help you figure it out. You've worked hard, and we're all proud of you."

He stood up, and so did I. That was my usual signal that the meeting was over. I felt relieved, like a weight had been lifted. Then with a steady, serious gaze, he said,

"Carolyn, I'm proud of you," as he nodded and took another puff of his pipe.

Coming from Mr. Hammond, those words meant the world to me. Ma Brown had told me he felt that way, but to hear him actually verbalize it was totally different. I had the stamp of approval, the vote of confidence coming from this man who I looked up to and admired for the past four years. This was further validation for me that I was headed in the right direction with my life.

Knowing that in a few short months I would be leaving the state to attend college, I made up my mind to visit Ma. I hadn't seen her in almost two years. We had been in brief contact by way of holiday and birthday cards, but nothing else. She never came to the campus to visit Gardiner or me. I wanted to reconnect with her and find out what was going on with the rest of my brothers.

The weekend that I arrived at her apartment, I had already planned to make my visit a short one. I didn't want to have to deal with any boyfriends who might be visiting or living with her. And I knew for sure, if Jimmy, my supposed daddy was there, I wasn't even going to sit down. The only thing I knew was that I didn't need any unnecessary family drama. I had isolated myself for so long from all those negative feelings, and I didn't want them to resurface and take control of my life again. Not now, when everything was coming together, and I was about to start a new journey.

When I saw Ma and entered her apartment, it was as if time had stood still. She looked the same as when I last saw her, wearing an old bathrobe, with a lit cigarette and can of beer close by. The house was unkempt, with dirty dishes in the sink and an overflowing trash can. But she was alone, and that was good enough for me.

She was glad to see me, and her face beamed when she let me in. We sat down at the little table, where Chip and I had found her false teeth so many months ago. Ma brought me up to date about my brothers. Googie was doing great and still living with his godparents, Momma Louise and Uncle Steve. My oldest brothers Michael and Ronald had enlisted in the army.

When she talked about Kevin, her voice trembled a little. Kevin graduated the year before from Taft High School in the Bronx and had attended North Carolina Central University on a track scholarship. But this was tragically cut short when he was trying to break up a fight his best friend was involved in. Kevin was stabbed by a guy they didn't even know. This ended his track and college dreams. He survived this senseless attack and was living with the cop named Mr. Boyd.

I thought it was interesting that Ma only briefly asked about Gardiner and what he was up to at Leake and Watts. She really didn't have much contact with him at all since the state took him away years earlier. I assured her that he was doing fine, looking good, attending junior high school off campus in Yonkers, and playing lots of basketball.

She never said why she didn't come to the campus to visit or check on us. She never bought up Jimmy, my fake daddy, and when I asked her about Mike, she simply said she hadn't seen him and didn't know where he was. It was evident to me by her short responses that she didn't want to talk about any subject that would open old wounds, so I didn't press her.

Ma asked me about Chip, and I told her we were still together and that he was taking me to my prom. She smiled and thought that was nice. I shared with her that I had gotten a full four-year scholarship to Howard University and would be leaving for Washington, DC in August. She perked up.

"Pippa, that is so good. I'm proud of you."

That was the first time in my life that Ma had ever said those words to me. I believe they were genuine and heartfelt. It may have taken her eighteen years to get it out, but it was still good to hear. It's one thing to hear that validation from my teachers, cottage parents, or social workers. But it takes on a deeper, more meaningful affirmation when it comes from your biological parent. I had to smile when Ma had one request for me upon learning my good news.

"Pippa, just do me one favor," Ma said with all seriousness.

"What's that?" I asked.

"Just don't get pregnant before you finish your first year of college."

I wasn't prepared for that request.

"Ma, I don't plan on getting pregnant at all. What I plan to do is finish all four years of college, graduate, and get a job," I said with all the conviction I could muster.

Ma hadn't finished high school when she dropped out pregnant with my oldest brother. So, I guess it was important to her that I graduate from high school and get at least one year of college under my belt before I followed in her footsteps. I was going to not only honor but surpass that special request.

As we walked together outside, me heading to the train station and Ma to the deli to get some cigarettes, a couple of her neighbors called out to her,

"Hey, Ruth, how you doing?"

"Who's that with you?"

"That's Pippa, my daughter. She's going to college." Ma yelled back, quite pleased.

I felt a sense of relief and closure. Relief that I had reached out and mended the long rift that existed between us. I didn't want to leave the state without at least communicating with Ma and knowing that she was okay. Closure over unanswered questions about why she hadn't tried to rescue me and Gardiner from the foster care system or if she even cared about what happened to us. It finally became crystal clear to me that Ma was just surviving, living her life day to day, doing the best she could. She was uneducated, unskilled, unmarried, unemployed, and the mother of seven children by the time she was twenty-eight years old.

Even with all these negative cards that were dealt her, my Ma's life still served as a barometer for what I wanted mine to be like. I knew before I took another step in my life's journey that I would not let a man physically or verbally abuse me. I knew that I would get the type of education that would afford me a good job, to provide for my basic needs without having to depend on someone else. I knew I wanted to be married before I started having kids. And I also knew that under no circumstances was I going to be in a situation where the state came in and took my kids from me. Yes Ma, without knowing it, provided me with a lot of valuable life lessons that I took with me that day.

In late March, Ampara, Nancy, and I posed outside Gould Cottage for pictures before heading off to our school prom. I wore a soft pink, scooped neck, flowing chiffon dress, with a dainty satin sash underneath my bosom. Chip was breathtaking in his tux and presented me with a white corsage wrapped with pink ribbon. He had borrowed his parents' car for this special occasion.

Ma and Pa Brown did not give us a curfew that night. I guess they wanted us to have a taste of complete freedom before we left Leake and Watts and entered the real world.

Like most of my high school friends, we spent all of ninety minutes at our lavishly decorated prom, held in a local hotel event center. We hugged and complimented each other on our outfits, picked over the fancy food that no one ate, and posed for the formal pictures to prove that we had really attended the prom that everyone's parents paid for. Then we made our way to the famous Hawaii Kai Polynesian Restaurant in New York City. We did order a scrumptious dinner, along with some delicious pina coladas that the young waiter was happy to serve us, when Chip kept giving him big tips.

Many of my more well-to-do classmates had older siblings or even parents who rented out hotel suites for them to spend the night. Chip and I didn't have that luxury, so we opted to stay at an apartment that belonged to a friend of his older brother. It was dark, musty smelling, and had a dingy blanket on the bed. But it offered the quiet privacy and alone time that we were looking for. We took full advantage of me not having to be home at a certain time or sneak in the fire escape door in the back of the cottage. With the sun shining brightly the next morning, I made my way, smiling but exhausted, up the walkway, past the metal bell to the front door. My prom night was all I hoped it would be and more.

On the third Friday in June, I walked across the Yonkers High School stage one final time, as a graduate of the class of 1970. No one in my family came, not Ma, Gardiner, or any of my other brothers. That didn't dampen my spirits. Mr. Hammond didn't make it either, but Leake and Watts was well represented. Ma and Pa Brown came with several of my cottage mates, along with Mrs. Wesson and Mrs. Davis. The auditorium was jam packed, as I looked out on the sea of loud, proud, and happy faces. Everyone was there to celebrate the accomplishments and achievements of my fellow 250 classmates.

When my name was called out, each step I took was with confidence and pride. Once on the stage, Principal Guzzo and Assistant Principal Manello both gave me an extended handshake, along with their big smiles and my hard-earned academic diploma. They both knew me personally from helping in the office every day. Once the ceremony was over, I found Mr. Sher in the huge crowd of students and parents. I wanted to thank him personally for all his help and encouragement.

Much later, in the peace and quiet of my room, I looked through my yearbook, fingered my diploma, and reflected on my life. Looking back over the years from my earliest memories right up to that moment, I felt grateful and blessed.

There were so many awful things that I could have spent my days lamenting about, wallowing in self-pity and misery. But I always felt, that somehow even in the worst situations, somewhere there was a lesson to be learned. The lessons were not always crystal clear and evident, but they always came through eventually.

It was Ma whipping my butt for going to the park alone, which taught me to respect my elders and their rules. My brothers always challenging me to do something different and daring taught me to step out of my comfort zone and try things, even if I wasn't successful at it. Or learning how to forgive myself after dealing with extreme bouts of guilt for stealing from Dot, my classmate, and Alexander's Department Store. The lessons learned from being sexually molested, that it was not my fault, and vowing to do everything in my power to not let that happen to me again, or my child if I was ever blessed to have one. After many years of being bullied, learning the importance of accepting people for who they are, and not judging them for how they look, where they live, how they speak, what they wear, or who they love.

I even learned some lifelong lessons from my abusive foster mother in Greenburgh. How to entertain and be comfortable with myself, when left alone in the basement year after year. How to remember and follow explicit directions the first time they are given. How to wash, dry, iron, and fold clothes for an entire household, and certainly how to clean and disinfect anyone's kitchen and bathroom to the highest expectations. I am certain she thought she was punishing me by making me walk miles each week to get a pair of stockings, but what she was teaching me was building endurance and stamina for a lifelong love of exercise. Not allowing me to have female company at the house but giving me implicit permission to hang out all night with a boy, taught me that young people need direction and clear expectations for acceptable behavior.

God. Yes, the abusive foster mother was the first to introduce me to God by attending and participating in church, learning about a holy, spiritual being, and ultimately believing in and relying on a higher power that even she couldn't destroy. In some of my darkest moments, I thought I was having one-sided conversations with God. I didn't know if He heard me, but I knew I felt a sense of comfort just verbalizing my most secret, inner thoughts. It was years later that I realized not only was He listening, but He would be answering me in his own way and on his timeline, not mine.

What I thought about too, were the people who were placed in my life at pivotal moments to guide, push, and encourage me. I knew without a doubt that certain individuals came into my life at my lowest or most confusing times to lift me up. Mr. Chesden, my fifth-grade teacher, who first discovered and nourished my love for writing. My junior high school science teacher, who saw academic potential in me and challenged me to strive to make the honor roll. Mr. Sher, who encouraged me to branch out and join the office helpers club, which taught me how to interact with a diverse group of staff, parents, and community members.

Mrs. Parker, who gave me reasonable parameters for my preteen years, even though I was too young and angry to appreciate it then. She showed her love and concern by constantly asking me what I needed for school and then making sure I had all those items. Most of all, she pushed me to learn how to play the flute, which I did all the way through high school and planned to do once I entered college.

All these people collectively prepped and molded me, laying the foundations for many of my core values and beliefs. However, it was my extended family at Leake and Watts who shaped me into the young adult who walked across that graduation stage. They took a young, angry, insecure girl and helped to transform her into a self-assured, laser-focused, confident, respectful young woman ready to enter the real world.

There is absolutely no way I could have made it without leaning and relying on the strength and wisdom of the Browns, Mrs. Wesson, the Davises, and Mr. Hammond. They opened their arms of encouragement, and support, allowing me to achieve higher, guiding and prodding me for as long as I needed. These six adults saw something in me that I didn't see in myself. They envisioned a bigger dream for me than I could have possibly dared to dream for myself, given my background and circumstances.

Pa Brown gave me discipline, order, and routines to follow. Ma Brown provided reassurance when I wavered in my resolve to stand up and speak out for what I wanted. Mrs. Wesson demonstrated patience, kindness, and the importance of listening to understand me, then worked to find ways to secure the resources I needed to be successful. The Davises provided a blueprint for what a Black, educated, intact family could and should look like. They extended their wings to further cover me with their resources, both within their home and contacts out of state. Mr. Hammond showed me what quiet, competent leadership looked like. He didn't like fanfare or drama, but he respected hard work, persistence, and diligence. I might have been a little militant pain in the butt, but Mr. Hammond gave me everything I asked for, if it was to benefit and enhance my educational endeavors. In my heart and in my mind, I thank them every day for showing up, stepping in, and embracing me.

Sitting there in my room, and reflecting on my life journey to this point, I have so many things to be grateful for. Overcoming trials and tribulations that individually and collectively helped push me to the next level. The struggles and hardships that I endured only served to prepare me for my future. So many gratifying and rewarding experiences that I know I will cherish and carry with me the rest of my life.

I know I made it this far not by my wings alone, but with the support of so many inspiring and motivating people who came, lifted and carried me, until I could soar on my own, toward the next chapter of my life. For them, I am now and will always be eternally grateful.

The End

If you enjoyed my story, PLEASE go to the site where the
book was purchased and post a REVIEW.
Thank you!

Please go to the website below to get your
FREE Digital Bookmark and Discussion/Bonus Questions
for reading clubs and/or students:
www.subscribepage.com/carolynphenry

Epilogue

I had a wonderful four years at Howard University, participating in the marching band and drill team and being crowned Miss Congeniality. I received my BA degree in elementary education and graduated cum laude in 1974.

Leake and Watts Home for Children served as my summer anchor, where I would return each year and work as a camp counselor for preteens and later as a cottage parent. My first teaching job was at Greenburg-Graham Home for Children, which was another nearby residential children's facility. I taught elementary and middle-school-age students there for ten years, during which time I earned a MS degree in special education from Lehman College.

My rough start in life and my own experiences with Child Protective Services, foster homes, and residential treatment facilities enabled me to intimately relate to the students I served and taught. My life lessons paved the way for me to see the troubled lives they lived through very real and personal lenses. I was and have always been able to recognize a child who is suffering in silence and listen with empathy when they trusted me enough to share their own life stories.

For thirty-seven years, during my career as a schoolteacher and building-level administrator, I dedicated my life to helping and mentoring young people. During my six-year tenure as principal of Bragg Street Academy, an alternative school in North Carolina, which serves students experiencing severe academic, behavior, and/or attendance issues, I was able to effect significant positive changes and was named

Principal of the Year. The students there were mirror images of me at that age.

I believe it is often easier to recognize someone's pain when you have walked in that person's shoes yourself. Lending a listening ear, giving my last dollar bill, sharing my lunch, buying a coat or pair of sneakers, providing a ride home, I would do whatever a child needed most at that moment. Words of support and encouragement, trips to see their teenage peers in other schools doing positive things, planning college tours, initiating school clubs and awards programs, implementing before- and after-school tutorial programs, and providing access to outstanding community leaders—whatever it took to give a child that one little spark of hope that maybe he or she needed. That warm feeling of inspiration and motivation by a few key people, who aren't even related to the child, is sometimes all that's needed. Someone who believes in them and their potential, someone who can see the good inside and nurture that budding seed, until the child can see it for himself, is often all that is required to set them on a path in the right direction.

Over the years I stayed in contact with the Parkers, Ma Brown and the Davises. I had the opportunity to visit with Mr. Hammond years after he retired from Leake and Watts and moved to North Carolina.

I spend my retirement years continuing to serve, assist, and mentor young people, whether it's in the neighborhood, the local gym, my church, or the schools where I substitute teach. There is always a child out there who needs and can benefit from the wisdom, empathy, inspiration, care, and concern that we all have within us and makes us that much richer by giving it away.

About the Author

C arolyn P. Henry is a graduate of Howard University (Washington, DC) with a Bachelor of Arts in elementary education. She earned a Master of Science degree from Lehman College (Bronx, NY) in special education/learning disabilities and received certification in education administration/supervision from North Carolina Central University (Durham, NC).

She has a passion for serving and mentoring young people and is a retired educator with thirty-seven years of experience as a special education teacher, assistant principal, and principal. Ms. Henry also served as a state assistance team leader for the North Carolina Department of Public Instruction.

She is a member of Delta Sigma Theta Sorority Incorporated. Her hobbies include reading, traveling, exercising, and listening to music. She lives in a suburb of Atlanta, Georgia, with her husband, Andre'.

Made in the USA
Middletown, DE
17 June 2021